THE
National ⚾ Pastime
A REVIEW OF BASEBALL HISTORY

CONTENTS

Editor: James Charlton   Copy Editor: John Paine Designer: Glenn LeDoux
Designated readers and peer reviewers: Phil Birnbaum, Tom Simon, Lyle Spatz, John Zajc,
Jules Tygiel, Bob Schaefer, Norman Macht, Charlie Bevis, Bill Nowlin, John Pastier, Merritt
Clifton, Dixie Tourangeau, Bill Mead, Keith Carlson, Steve Gietschier, Dick Thompson.

A Note from the Editor

If there is a theme in this issue of *The National Pastime* it is about baseball in the 1940s. Seven articles discuss some aspect of baseball during WW2 or immediately following the war. Jim Smith's wonderful homage to Chicago photographer George Brace, written and edited with the cooperation of George's daughter Mary Brace, is the cover article. Her recollections form the captions for her father's wonderful images. Brace's career photographing ballplayers began in the late 1920s and covered eight decades. Not even Minnie Minoso can match that! For forty years Brace shot in black & white, but finally switched to color in 1959. His cover image of the great Stan Musial at Wrigley Field was shot that season, while the back cover photo of Billy Williams and Curt Flood was made ten years later.

Tom Barthel writes a lively account of Joe Medwick and Leo Durocher's little-known USO trip to Italy at the height of WW2, while Steve Bullock's analysis on the war's impact on hitters is an intriguing one. Eric Moskowitz recounts how *The Sporting News* was on the forefront of the effort to support the war—and baseball.

Going back a few decades, Bill Nowlin makes a persuasive case that the Pilgrims—Boston, that is—never existed. Steve Steinberg's account of spitballers before and after 1920 is admirably researched, while Sam Bernstein looks at the same era, discussing George Sisler and the National Commission. A quartet of profiles of little known major leaguers—one of which is from SABR's noteworthy Bioproject—are fine reading.

Jim Charlton
August 2003

The Old Brawl Game

Cubs vs. Dodgers in the '40s

by Art Ahrens

During the 1940s National League baseball was largely dominated by the Cardinals and the Dodgers. St. Louis won four pennants in the decade while finishing second five times. Brooklyn took three flags and were runner-ups three as well. Besides a horrendous 1944 season, "dem Bums" were third the rest of the time. It was the era of Stan Musial against Dixie Walker.

But if the Dodgers played their money games against the Redbirds, they had their blood matches with the Cubs. Between 1940 and '49, Brooklyn took Chicago on 119 occasions while the Cubs were victorious 101 times. Considering that the Dodgers nearly always had a far superior team, it was a fine showing for the Cubs.

In 1940, the Dodgers had become a force to be reckoned with after years of general dormancy, thanks mainly to the often controversial leadership of fiery manager Leo Durocher. The Cubs, on the other hand, were a franchise on the decline. After 14 straight years as contenders with four pennants—yes, that actually happened—the Chicago Nationals would drop to fifth place that season. While the Dodgers and Cardinals had built massive farm chains, the Cubs waited for apples to fall in their direction.

Such was the scene when the Lords of Flatbush locked horns with Chicago's North Side gang on July

Art Ahrens lives within walking distance of Wrigley Field. He attended his first game there on September 26, 1959, when Chicago beat Brooklyn, 12–2. He is the author of many articles on the Cubs.

19, 1940, at Wrigley Field. In the bottom of the eighth inning, one-time Cub Hugh Casey on the mound for the visiting team. The Cubs had already scored two runs on Bill Nicholson's 14th home run of the year, and Hank Leiber was on third base when Cub ace Claude Passeau came to bat. According to *Chicago Tribune* sportswriter Ed Burns, "Hughie wasn't feeling especially chummy."

Casey's first offering to his mound rival was a wild pitch, Leiber scored easily. Now a bit incensed, Casey plunked Passeau between the shoulder blades. Not known as a pacifist, Claude hurled his bat at the offending Brooklynite as the dugouts emptied. After ducking the missile, Casey charged on Passeau with help from teammate Joe "Muscles" Gallagher, who attacked the Cub pitcher. As Cub manager Gabby Hartnett pulled him off Passeau's back, Chicago third baseman Stan Hack put Gallagher out of commission with a haymaker.

Eventually, the umpires, ushers, and Chicago police brought the brawl to an end as the Cubs went on to an 11-4 victory. It was Passeau's 11th win of the season and his fourth in a row.

The stage had been set. During the winter of 1940-41, Cub owner Phillip K. Wrigley hired former sportswriter Jim Gallagher (no relation to Joe) as general manager and Jimmy Wilson as field boss. Together, the "James boys" embarked on a series of trades that made the Cubs look like a farm team for the Dodgers.

Jealous of the popularity of Cub second baseman

Billy Herman, Wilson and Gallagher swapped him to the Dodgers for $40,000, infielder Johnny Hudson, and a player to be named later. Not long thereafter, pitcher Larry French and outfielder Augie Galan were handed to Brooklyn on silver platters as well. Thought to be over the hill, all of these players soon found the fountain of youth in Brooklyn uniforms. The blood rivalry was heating up!

The Dodgers were back in Chicago on May 19, 1941. In the bottom of the second inning, the Cubs were already ahead 3-0 when Hugh Casey walked Bill Nicholson to start the inning. Usually a fireman, Casey appeared uneasy in a starting assignment. Nicholson easily stole second behind his back, after which "the Mad Russian," Lou Novikoff, drew a free pass to first.

Up to the plate came the bulky rookie Cub catcher, Clyde McCullough. Although slower than a rock moving uphill, McCullough beat out a drag bunt to load the bases. Chicago second baseman Lou Stringer then coaxed Casey's third walk of the inning to force Nicholson home. Seconds later, Dodger third baseman Cookie Lavagetto muffed Bobby Sturgeon's grounder, allowing Novikoff to score. As if this were not humiliating enough, pitcher Claude Passeau smashed a grand-slam homer to make the score 9-0 with still nobody out.

At that point, Casey went to the showers and Mace Brown took the mound. It looked like a forerunner of instant replay as Stan Hack drew a walk and went to third on Phil Cavarretta's double. Dom Dallessandro then flied to Pete Reiser for the first Cub out, with Hack scoring on the sacrifice. Up for the second time in the frame, Bill Nicholson swished a home run for the eighth and ninth Cub runs of the inning. Novikoff singled and went to second on McCullough's sacrifice. Stringer walked, but Sturgeon flied to Joe Medwick to end the inning. The score was Cubs 12, Dodgers zip.

That was the way it stood in the top of the fifth inning when Leo Durocher announced to plate umpire Lee Ballafant that his team was playing the game under protest on grounds that the Cubs were allegedly over the player limit. Interestingly, the Cub of controversy was the "player to be named later" in the Billy Herman trade, Charlie Gilbert. In reality, Gilbert had indeed reported to Chicago on May 6 but was still on the disabled list due to an ankle injury.

Ballafant requested that Cub field announcer Pat Pieper relay Durocher's message to the audience, but Pieper's translation to the partisan crowd was that Leo was complaining "because the Cubs have too many runs."

Chicago went on to a 14-1 victory as Leo the Lion's grievances were dismissed by league officials.

As that fateful season neared its end, the rivalry was already entering its "believe it or not" stage. In the first game of a September 10 doubleheader in Chicago, Brooklyn held a 4-2 lead. With one out in the top of the ninth, Cub pitcher Johnny Schmitz—in his major league debut—replaced Bill Lee, who had earlier relieved Claude Passeau. On Schmitz's first offering, Cookie Lavagetto grounded into a double play to end the inning. In the bottom of the frame, Chicago bailed it out to win, 5-4. In hurling but a single pitch, Schmitz had gained his first victory!

To add icing on the cake, the Cubs won the second game by the same score. Despite the victories Brooklyn would win its first flag in 21 years while the Cubs dropped in the standings to sixth place.

By 1942, the Cubs had acquired the services of a temperamental rookie pitcher named Hiram Bithorn. Brooklyn was in town on July 15 and Bithorn was on the mound. Durocher began needling the young hurler from the visitors' dugout. Getting a bit fed up, Bithorn whirled and fired a fastball at Leo's skull in the top of the fifth inning. Players emptied onto the field from both benches, but the umpires managed to restore order before a full-scale rumble erupted. Hardly intimidated, the Dodgers bumped off their hosts, 10-5. Ex-Cub Billy Herman knocked a home run as ex-Cub Kirby Higbe took the win with relief help from ex-Cub Hugh Casey. As the Cubs ended up sixth again, the only consolation they could take was that the Cardinals surpassed the Dodgers at the end of the season to win the pennant by two games.

Wartime shortages were soon hitting home in baseball. The Brooklynites were back in Chicago on July 30, 1943, for an apparently unique event in history. With Johnny Allen on the hill for the Dodgers in the third inning, Phil Cavarretta cracked a home run off the left-field foul pole. In pre-war times, the baseball would have been discarded. But this time the umps gave it back to the Brooklyn pitcher. On the next pitch, Bill Nicholson slapped the pellet onto Sheffield Avenue for his 15th round-tripper of the year. To this writer's knowledge, it was the only time that two homers were hit off successive pitches *and* with the same baseball. The Cubs sailed away to an easy 12-3 victory, a sweet taste of revenge for pitcher Hiram Bithorn. But Brooklyn enjoyed the last laugh, finishing third to Chicago's fifth.

As the Chicago-Brooklyn antagonism continued, strange happenings resumed along with it. On May

18, 1945, Dodger outfielder Luis Olmo made history by hitting a grand slam home run *plus* a bases-loaded triple (along with a double for good measure), as the Dodgers outslugged the Cubs, 15-12, at Ebbets Field. It was Chicago's sixth straight loss. Earlier, Bill Nicholson's three-run homer with two out in the sixth had temporarily knotted the score at 9-9.

But in '45 the Chicagoans were not to be stopped. They won their "most recent" pennant, leaving Brooklyn 11 games behind in third place. Included in the championship drive was a 20-6 mauling of the Dodgers at Brooklyn on August 15. Cub catcher Paul Gillespie, chiefly remembered (if at all) as their first player to wear a crew cut, drove in six runs with two homers and a single. Andy Pafko and Heinz Becker also homered for Chicago, while Hank Borowy went the distance for the victory.

But the Cubs had won the 1945 flag largely because they had more 4-F's than any team in the league and because the Cardinals (who finished a close second) lost Stan Musial to the Navy. By 1946, that temporary advantage had gone up in smoke. While the Dodgers and Cardinals had superstars coming back from the service, the Cubs had a few good journeymen at best.

The defending league champs were once again in Flatbush on May 22, 1946. With the score tied at one apiece in the top of the 10th, Cub shortstop Lennie Merullo slid into Dodger second baseman Eddie Stanky spikes high to break up a double play. Merullo and Stanky, who had not gotten along when they were Cub teammates in 1943-44, were wrestling it out in the dust before umpire Lynn Boggess and Brooklyn shortstop Pee Wee Reese broke it up. The two fighters were ejected from the game, which Brooklyn finally won, 2-1, as Dixie Walker's double off Johnny Schmitz drove in Dick Whitman with the winning run in the bottom of the 13th.

The bad blood was far from over. During a pregame practice the following day, Merullo walked into the batting cage to show Reese his black eye, reportedly telling him that if he wanted to hit him again to do it while he was looking so that he could break Reese's neck. Sneaking up from behind, Dixie Walker slugged Merullo on the back of the head, and then headed for the home dugout. Lennie grabbed Walker, tripped him to the ground, and knocked out one tooth while breaking another in half. By now everybody on either side of the fence had become involved in the melee. Phil Cavarretta was pushed back by the police, "who apparently thought the Dodgers needed

protection," according to writer Irving Vaughan of the *Chicago Tribune*. Cavarretta later denied taking part in the brawl but was conspicuously silent when asked if he had punched Leo Durocher in the nose.

From that point on, five policemen were stationed in each dugout. Again, the Dodgers pulled off a 2-1 victory, this time in only 11 innings. Walker, Reese, Merullo, Cavarretta, and Cub coach Red Smith were all slapped with fines. Jim Gallagher protested those of the Cub players, but his face-saving gesture went nowhere.

The Cubs were going nowhere either, finishing a distant third as the Cardinals and the Dodgers duked it out for the pennant. St. Louis eventually won it, along with the World Series. In their last gasp of winning ways for another two decades, the Cubs squared off with the Dodgers in Brooklyn on September 15, 1946, winning the first game of a twin bill, 4-3, in 10 innings. But in the sixth inning of the nightcap, a swarm of gnats descended upon Ebbets Field like an Old Testament plague. The obnoxious insects refused to depart, causing the contest to be called as a 2-0 Dodger win. Perhaps that was Brooklyn's way of saying to Chicago, "Gnats to you!"

Claude Passeau

Pitcher Hugh Casey and third baseman Stan Hack. Casey pitched briefly for the Cubs in 1934, before being traded to Brooklyn. Hack spent 16 seasons on the Windy City's north side, finishing with a .301 average.

Cub fans gloated over the winter as commissioner Happy Chandler suspended Durocher for alleged associations with gamblers and other unsavory characters. But with Leo gone and Burt Shotton as their "temporary" manager, the Dodgers changed baseball forever by hiring Jackie Robinson, the first African American player in the majors since 1884 as well as the first to make racial integration permanent. On May 18, 1947, a crowd of 46,572 shoehorned its way into Wrigley Field to see Robinson's Chicago debut. Although Jackie went hitless in his first Chicago appearance, the Dodgers won the game, 4-2, en route to another pennant while the Cubs sank to sixth.

By the end of the '40s, Leo Durocher deserted Brooklyn permanently to become field boss of the New York Giants, while the Cubs had become the doormat of the National League. But the smoldering Chicago embers could occasionally still turn into a blazing fire when Brooklyn was around. On June 19, 1949, another overflow Wrigley Field assemblage (42,089) saw Cub manager Frankie Frisch, catcher Bob Scheffing, and bench warmer Al Walker get tossed from the game over umpiring calls which they thought were a bit too much in favor of the Dodgers. Momentarily inspired, the Cubs snapped a seven-game losing streak with an 8-2 triumph, helped by the long ball hitting of Andy Pafko and Hank Sauer. Far from demoralized, Brooklyn went on to win 17 games from Chicago that year. Ironically, the Cubs even helped the hated Dodgers win the pennant by thumping the Cardinals two out of three during the final weekend of the season.

As the '40s evolved into the '50s, the Cub–Dodger hatred still simmered, even if the open belligerency declined. In July 1950, Hank Sauer, Ralph Kiner of the Pirates, and Enos Slaughter of the Cardinals were voted as the starting outfielders for the National League All-Star team. But team manager Burt Shotton decided to replace Sauer with his own Duke Snider of Brooklyn. Up went a roar of protests from Chicago as Shotton was besieged with derisive mail. Frankie Frisch said (publicly, at least) that he would not swap Sauer for five Sniders. Yielding to pressure, league president Ford Frick ruled that Sauer would indeed start the game and play at least three innings. The Dodger manager obeyed but yanked Sauer after the third inning. Diplomatically, he replaced him with Cub teammate Andy Pafko.

For good measure, the Cubs acted as spoilers in the pennant race again. This time, they spanked the Dodgers 12 times out of 22 to help the Phillies win their first flag since 1915.

It would be the Cubs' last major hurrah against their despised enemy for years to come. Throughout the 1950s, the Dodgers went on gathering pennants while the Cubs languished in or near the cellar. Not until 1964 would the Cubs again edge the Dodgers—by then relocated to the world's largest suburb—in a season's series. By 1966, the once loathed Leo Durocher had become the Cubs manager. That, however, is a story in itself.

We must look for some legislation before long in regard to the pitcher. We are all willing to concede that he is a plucky, determined Base Ball character, and the very fact that he is so persistent and combative makes it necessary now and then to subordinate him a little to the other men who are part of the game.
—*Spalding's Official Baseball Guide*, 1909

The fight against the predominance of the pitcher is almost as ancient as baseball itself.
—Irving Sanborn, "Consider the Pitcher," *Baseball Magazine*, September 1920

The Spitball and the End of the Deadball Era

by Steve L. Steinberg

1920 was a seminal year for baseball. Events had conspired to bring the Deadball Era to an end, and make way for the Lively Ball Era. This was no gradual transition: the rise in offense in 1919 (mainly in the AL) intensified and spread to the NL in 1920 and was confirmed as more than a fluke in 1921. The curtain went up on the new as quickly as it came down on the old.

On center stage was the *ball*. Yet the driving force was not so much what the owners ordered done to the ball by its makers as what they ordered not done to the ball by its hurlers and done with the ball by the umpires. What were commonly called "freak" pitches were the focus, and the spitball was lumped together with them in the eye of the storm. Just what impact did rule changes with these pitches have on the end of the Deadball Era? What other factors were involved?

The spitball had an enormous impact on the game since its origin in the early 1900s. One of its biggest foes, *Baseball Magazine* editor F. C. Lane, acknowledged its power:

It is a tricky and dangerous ball to control. But once mastered, as only a few have been able to master it, it is all but unhittable.
—"Should the Spitball Be Abolished?" June, 1919

Steve L. Steinberg has recently completed a book on Miller Huggins, The Genius of Hug. *He is finishing a book on spitball pitcher Urban Shocker,* Shocker! Discovering a Silent Hero of Baseball's Golden Age. *He lives in Seattle with his wife and three children.*

Statistics from the last 3 years of the Deadball Era and the first 3 years of the Lively Ball Era

	R	HR	K	BA	H/Game	ERA
1917 AL	4540	133	4192	.248	8.0	2.66
1917 NL	4408	202	4488	.249	8.2	2.70
1918 AL	3703	96	3004	.254	8.3	2.77
1918 NL	3682	139	2921	.254	8.4	2.76
1919 AL	4586	241	3561	.268	9.0	3.22
1919 NL	4071	207	3288	.258	8.6	2.91
1920 AL	5869	369	3653	.284	9.7	3.79
1920 NL	4893	261	3632	.270	9.1	3.13
1921 AL	6303	477	3583	.292	10.2	4.28
1921 NL	5632	460	3380	.289	10.0	3.78
1922 AL	5865	525	3573	.285	9.8	4.03
1922 NL	6194	530	3380	.292	10.2	4.10

* The 1918 season, shortened because of World War I, ended on September 2. Teams played an average of 127 games, as opposed to 154 games.

** The 1919 season was shortened to 140 games, in anticipation of weak attendance. 1919 attendance ended up exceeding 6.5 million, more than doubling the 1918 numbers and almost equaling the decade's high mark of 1911.

In *Babe Ruth's Own Book of Baseball*, he (or his ghost-writer) explained:

> The theory of the spitter is simple enough. The ball is wet on one side. Naturally that makes a slippery spot which reduces friction and gives added speed to the opposite side where friction is applied. All spitballs break down, but by turning the wet spot one way or the other, the pitcher can make the ball break in or out as he desires.

The spitter was also a psychological weapon, a powerful decoy. Spitball pitchers went through the motions of "loading up" (putting saliva on the ball) before almost every pitch by bringing the ball and glove to the mouth. They went through this ritual even when they were not "loading up," to sow confusion in the minds of batters. Some spitballers, like Urban Shocker, threw the pitch only a few times a game, yet the batter never knew when it was coming.

> Shocker is a great pitcher. But honestly I don't know whether he is a great spitball pitcher. In nine innings today he threw exactly four spitballs. I was surprised. I expected a flock of them. But he came up with everything a good pitcher should have.
> —Ed Walsh, 1924 *Reach Guide*

The two greatest purveyors of the pitch were Jack Chesbro and Ed Walsh. In 1904, Chesbro won 41 games for the New York Highlanders (forerunners to the Yankees). Sadly, he is most remembered for one spitter he lost control of on the final day of the season, in the ninth inning of a tie game with a runner on third base. With that wild pitch, the game and the pennant belonged to the Boston Americans, in one of Boston's biggest wins over New York in the 20th century. Walsh led the Hitless Wonders, the Chicago White Sox, to victory in the 1906 World Series and won 40 games for them in 1908.

Discussion on whether the pitch should be outlawed goes back almost as far as the pitch itself. In 1907, Chicago White Sox manager Fielder Jones spoke out strongly against it, even though he had a star in spitballer Ed Walsh (*Sporting Life*, August 8, 1907). In 1909, a debate on the spitter was the feature in the *Reach Guide*. Baseball writers were split on whether the pitch should be banned, and some were prescient in their remarks:

> While the spit ball is sloppy, dirty, and disgusting, it is, I fear, impossible to get rid of.
> —W. A. Phelon, *Chicago Journal*

More than a decade would go by before the pitch's foes were able to legislate its ban. Many arguments were used against it. Its unsanitary nature at the time of the deadly flu epidemic of 1918-19 certainly didn't help its cause. Already in 1907 a Cleveland public health doctor spoke of the connection between the pitch and tuberculosis:

> What would a man's feelings be with a batted ball covered with microbes coming at him like a shot out of a gun?
> —Dr. Martin Friedrich, *Sporting Life*, May 18, 1907

There were the fielding and throwing problems the slick ball created. There were the delays it caused, as the pitcher brought both ball and glove to his mouth before each pitch, whether he planned to throw the "wet one" or not. In an age when two-hour games are so rare, we can only chuckle at the humorous argument.

> These two-hour games wore on the nerves. They made the Boss Bug [fan] late for supper and when this happened the real Boss Bug grew peeved and knocked the game for making him late for meals.
> —"Scribbled by Scribes,"
> *The Sporting News,* May 20, 1920

Then there was the argument about the spitter's impact on the arm. Such a concern was not even mentioned in the 1909 *Reach* debate. Chesbro and Walsh had meteoric yet tragically short careers, but in 1908 both men were still pitching effectively. Respected umpire and columnist Billy Evans spoke out passionately against the pitch in *Harper's Weekly*.

> I have seen a score of pitchers drop out of the majors, because of the strain placed upon their arm through using the spitball.
> —May 2, 1914

> The history of the spitball is that it has ruined many an arm of steel.
> —June 13, 1914

At the same time, in the mid-teens there was a lull in great spitball pitching. It is interesting to note that there were more outstanding spitball pitchers in the 1920s than there were in the entire Deadball Era. Some observers even felt that the spitter was no longer a dominant pitch in the teens, that with the passing of Ed Walsh, it was practically eliminated.

Burleigh Grimes was the last legal spitballer, finishing his career in 1934.

New Ed Walshes may arise, but we much doubt . . .
Big Ed was almost in a class by himself, and the
moulder [sic] of men seldom duplicates such a feat.
    —*The Sporting News*, March 15, 1917

At least as old as the spitball were "freak" pitches that involved "doctoring" the ball to change its aerodynamics. Back in the 1890s Clark Griffith created the scuff ball by using his spikes to roughen its surface. As the decade of the teens moved forward, pitchers began to develop more trick pitches: the shine ball, emery ball, paraffin ball, licorice ball, mud ball, and more. All these pitches gave the ball added and unusual movement as it approached the plate. They were all (including the spitter) based on the concept that contrasting surfaces (of rough and smooth) affected the ball's flight and revolution and gave it a peculiar hop, usually dropping down. These pitches brought success to their hurlers and frustration to hitters, since they were so difficult to make contact with. Once they added such a pitch to their repertoire, pitchers like Russ Ford (emery ball), Eddie Cicotte (shine ball), and Hod Eller (shine ball) became much more successful. While there were rules against some

of these pitches, like the emery ball, they were not easy to enforce.

As with the spitter, artifice and deception were part of the weaponry. There was ongoing discussion whether Cicotte's shine ball was real or simply imagined. A 1917 article called the pitch a "mythical flicker" and "mental hazard" for superstitious players (*New York Times*, September 26, 1917). Sportswriter Tom Meany expressed the "mind game" that pitchers used:

Batters who are always seeking to detect some sign of
chicanery on a pitcher's part sometimes become so
engrossed in looking for illegal pitches that they forget to hit the legal ones.
    —*Baseball's Greatest Teams*, Barnes, 1949

All these pitches had an enormous effect on the confidence and thus the hitting of batters—because of what the ball did, what it might do (sail and hit the batter), and what it was reputed to do.

There were so many "doctored" pitches, surreptitiously prepared, that sentiment was building that the pitchers had gone too far. Among the owners the position was emerging that all trick pitches should be swept away. In February 1920, the Joint Rules Committee enacted laws that banned all "freak" pitches, including the spitter.

A couple of years earlier, National League President John Tener had explained his opposition to the "wet one."

I dislike the spitball because it affords an opening to
so many other illegal deliveries. An umpire must con-
tinually watch a spitball pitcher so that he does not use
his spitter as a subterfuge to cover up something else.
    —*New York World*, February 10, 1918

The Sporting News argued it would be too difficult for umpires to control "freak" pitches if the spitter were legal (September 11, 1919). Years later, shortstop Roger Peckinpaugh, whose long career spanned both the Deadball and Lively Ball Eras almost equally, explained it best:

*It wasn't the spitball exactly they wanted to ban. They
wanted to get rid of all those phony pitches. All of those
pitches were in the disguise of the spitter. You see, the
pitchers went to their mouths, but then they might throw
you a shine ball or a mud ball or an emery ball. . . . So
as I understand it, the only way they could stop them
fooling with that baseball was to bar the spitter, not let*

the pitcher go to his mouth.

If a pitcher didn't go to his mouth and still threw one of those freak pitches, the umpire would know damn well the guy was doctoring the ball. That's how they stopped it.
> —Donald Honig's *The Man in the Dugout*

Pitchers of the "freaks" could masquerade as spitball pitchers too easily. Every pitcher has been obliged to suffer for the sins of the freak delivery artists.
> —F. C. Lane, "Has the Lively Ball
> Revolutionized the Game?"
> *Baseball Magazine*, September 1921

Umpire Billy Evans agreed that pitchers had only themselves to blame, with all the ways they had "doctored" the ball (*St. Louis Post-Dispatch*, March 27, 1921). Perhaps Cincinnati pitcher Hod Eller was right when he wrote in an article entitled "Why the New Pitching Rules are Unjust,"

The world has gone mad over freak deliveries.
> —*Baseball Magazine*, August 1920

The rule changes took place against the backdrop of rumors of a "fix" in the 1919 World Series, even though the Black Sox scandal had not yet broken wide open. The owners had looked the other way far too often, whether the issue was gambling or emery balls. It was time for a bold and dramatic move, and they made one.

Ultimately, the rule changes were instituted to help the hitters and bring more fans into the ballparks. Washington owner-manager Clark Griffith may have turned on his former profession, but he was forthright.

Why encourage the stranglehold which the pitcher has on batting? . . . Batting is the most interesting part of the game. It ought to be encouraged.
> —"Ban the Spitter," *Baseball Magazine*, July 1917

His star pitcher Walter Johnson made a remarkable admission to a New York paper just a few months after the new rule was instituted.

Hitting plays the most important role in a ball game. There is no getting away from the fact that the baseball public likes to see the ball walloped hard. The home runs are meat for the fans. 'Babe' Ruth draws more people than a great pitcher does. It simply illustrates the theory that hitting is the

paramount issue of baseball.
> —*Evening Telegram*, August 22, 1920

In his landmark diatribe against the spitter, F. C. Lane expressed his opposition to it:

Last, and most important of all, the spit ball hurts batting and therefore strikes straight at the heart of the game's popularity. . . . The game has become one-sided; too much of a mere pitchers' duel. Something should be done for the downtrodden batter...One of the simplest and easiest ways to lighten the batter's load is to throw out the spitball.
> —"Should the Spitball be Abolished?"
> *Baseball Magazine*, June 1919

Simply put, it was time to swing the pendulum back toward the batter. Ironically, as hitting dominated the 1920s, Lane would become one

Eddie Cicotte

of the most outspoken foes of what he called the "home run epidemic," the "fever of batting which has run riot," and the "orgy at bat" (*Baseball Magazine*, July 1921, August 1925, and June 1927, respectively).

It is hard to understand nowadays just how rare and special a home run was before 1920. After an eighth-inning three-run blast beat the Yankees in a 1917 game, New York writer Walter Trumbull described it this way:

> There is nothing more extraordinary than a home run. No scene in melodrama can so grip the chords that thrill. . . . A circuit clout is the greatest transmitter of emotions. It makes smiles grow where none grew before, or smothers laughter beneath a pall of gloom.
> —*New York World*, April 26, 1917

And in 1919, Boston's Babe Ruth electrified the baseball world, and drew large crowds wherever he played, when he hit an almost unthinkable 29 home runs. The entire American League had hit only 96 circuit clouts the year before.

Where did the existing spitball pitchers stand? Before the winter meetings, there was still some support to protect them. Even AL president Ban Johnson, in a letter to *St. Louis Post-Dispatch* editor John Wray, wrote,

> No great restrictions will be placed upon the spitball pitchers of the present day.
> —August 31, 1919

But the sentiment had shifted by the time of the February 1920 meetings in Chicago (after the 1919 World Series). Echoing the sentiment of W. H. Lanigan a decade earlier ("Into the cuspidor with the spit ball," *Reach Guide*, 1909), existing spitballers were given one more year to throw that pitch and learn a replacement. By 1921, the spitter would be gone from major league baseball.

This was ominous news indeed for baseball's spitballers. They had gotten a reprieve, but only for a year. They banded together and organized a lobbying effort. Appropriately, Spittin' Bill Doak of the St. Louis Cardinals was one of the leaders of the group. They began to appeal to the sympathy of the writers and the fans. At the same time, their argument gave a strong hint of legal action based on an unfair labor practice by baseball's owners. Spitballer Jack Quinn of the Yankees framed the issue:

> Cutting out the spit ball after permitting me to pitch it all my life is like reaching into my pocket and taking money from me.
> —*New York Evening Telegram*, May 20, 1920

The spitballers had a remarkable stroke of good fortune. Four members of their exclusive fraternity were in the 1920 World Series between Cleveland and Brooklyn. The Dodgers' Burleigh Grimes was impressive with a shutout win in Game Two and a tough loss in Game Seven. The Indians' Stan Coveleski was spectacular: three complete-game wins and only two earned runs and two walks in 27 innings. How could baseball possibly pull the rug out from two of its biggest stars? (The other two spitballers were Cleveland's Ray Caldwell and Brooklyn's Clarence Mitchell.)

	H/9	ERA
Deadball Era, 1901-1919	8.5	2.88
Deadball Era of Grandfathered Pitchers, 1909-1919*	8.4	2.94
17 Grandfathered Spitballers, before 1920	8.2	2.67
Post-Deadball Era, 1920-1939	9.9	4.16
Post-Deadball Era of Grandfathered Spitballers, 1920-1934†	9.9	4.13
17 Grandfathered Spitballers, after 1919	9.8	3.63

*(Quinn started in 1909) less Spitballers (adj. league average)
†(Grimes ended in 1934) less Spitballers (adj. league average)
Figures assembled from *Total Baseball*, courtesy of SABR member Eric Sallee.

Protected Spitballers, NL: Bill Doak, Phil Douglas, Dana Fillingim, Ray Fisher, Marvin Goodwin, Burleigh Grimes, Clarence Mitchell, Dick Rudolph. AL: Doc Ayers, Ray Caldwell, Stan Coveleski, Red Faber, Dutch Leonard, Jack Quinn, Allan Russell, Urban Shocker, Allen Sothoron

While sentiment shifted toward these pitchers, *The Sporting News* remained firm in its support of the ban and accused the owners of waffling for selfish reasons.

They [owners] are unalterably opposed to doing anything for baseball or for anything or anybody else, when the act involves the loss of a dollar's worth of baseball property to themselves.

—February 3, 1921

In the end, the owners did back down and permitted the existing spitballers to continue using the pitch. Still, the owners got what they wanted: a ban on trick pitching, no new spitballers, and protection for the familiar faces and arms that threw the "wet one." These men were permitted to throw the pitch for the rest of their careers. Hurlers of other trick pitches faced no similar protection. In 1924, the *Reach Guide* tried to explain the distinction in "Passing of the Spitball Pitcher."

Not everyone could throw a spitball. It required years of painstaking effort to master. A pitcher who had reached the major leagues with it had accomplished something. It would be unfair to throw him out with the others who tampered unfairly with the ball. So baseball held one brief for the spitter, it voted to allow him to live out his career.

How much impact did the ban on the spitter have on the end of the Deadball Era? After all, 17 spitballers were protected, and offense still rose significantly. It is true that future spitballers were banned and, as the 1920s progressed, the spitball fraternity continued to shrink. But earned run averages and batting averages rose right away, at the start of the 1920s, not the end of the decade.

After 1919 the spitballers maintained their advantage of about 10% fewer earned runs than all major league pitchers. Yet their numbers were impacted negatively along with pitching as a whole, and the Lively Ball Era took off in 1920 in spite of these hurlers. It was simply tougher to pitch after 1919.

Clearly, factors other than the banning of the spitter (beyond the "club" of 17) drove the new age of hit-

Stan Coveleski spits into Muddy Ruel's glove.

ting. In 1920, batting averages and home runs began to climb dramatically in both leagues. The 1920s saw "The Reign of the Wallop:"

Batting is king. All other departments of the game are now subordinate subjects. The increased crowds at the present games strongly indicate that the public likes the present era of free and fancy swatting. . . . And if the public prefers the new game, the magnates prefer it.
—W. R. Hoefer, *Baseball Magazine*, July 1923

First, the ban on freak pitches other than the spitter (as well as a ban on new spitballers) had an enormous impact on the game. Hitters faced less effective pitchers, with fewer weapons at their disposal. Moreover, for years pitchers had ignored mastering the curveball, instead depending on "trick" pitches. Youngsters took the popular and easier route of learning the "latest" new pitch. They had "discarded the twirler's best weapon, a fast-breaking curve" (umpire and syndicated columnist Billy Evans, *The Times*, St. Louis, May 20, 1924). Pitchers were now in desperate straits- they had no pitch to fall back on.

In the 1920s there was much discussion about the absence of the curveball and its slow return to the game. NL president John Heydler spoke of the time lag that would be needed after the rule changes, for semi-pro and minor league pitchers to develop "legitimate pitching devices" like the curve and change of pace (*Evening Telegram*, New York, July 8, 1920). Just before former Yankee manager Wild Bill Donovan was killed in a train wreck in December 1923, his last conversation with baseball colleagues was widely publicized: he was lamenting the dearth of good curve ball pitchers in the game. A few months later, *Baseball Magazine* discussed this issue in a lengthy article by Irving Sanborn entitled "The Decline of Curve Ball Pitching" (April 1924).

In case the new rules were not clear enough for future major league pitchers, emphasis was added. Immediately after Rule 30, Section 2, Spalding's Official Guide (1921) noted:

Young pitchers should take special cognizance of this section. From now on, it will be foolish for pitchers to experiment with freak deliveries . . . absurd for a beginner to waste his time on anything except straight baseball . . .

Ty Cobb gave his perspective on the history of pitching in 1925:

Pitching has gone through three periods. First came the pitchers who developed the fastball and curve. Then came along the spit-ballers [sic]. Finally there were the trick pitchers such as Russell Ford with his emery ball. They have barred all that and we are back at the beginning again. It is going to take the pitchers of today some time to develop the curve to its full efficiency again.
—*New York Evening Post*, August 11, 1925

Furthermore, the increased confidence of hitters should not be overlooked. Because many of the trick pitches were hard to control, there was an intimidation factor at play: batters had been afraid of being hit. Now most of the tosses that used to worry batters and make them look foolish were part of the past. Also, is it possible that the disruption of World War I, with the dramatic cutback in the number of minor league teams, may have hurt pitchers more than it impacted hitters?

The Lively Ball Era is somewhat of a misnomer. Despite all the rumors and anecdotal evidence about a "juiced" or "rabbit" ball, it is generally accepted that the owners did not order a livelier ball and that the ball itself was not altered. The words of NL President John Heydler, a man of impeccable integrity, that there was no change in the ball's construction, were confirmed by numerous independent tests. (One of the most widely publicized was that done by Columbia University chemistry professor Harold Fales and announced at the NL summer meetings in mid-July 1925.) Besides, as Bill Curran notes in *Big Sticks* (William Morrow, 1990), if the owners had wanted to enliven the ball, they would have had no reason to hide this change. Why risk a conspiracy when the public's faith in the game was already shaken by the Black Sox scandal?

Baseball researcher Bob Schaefer recently uncovered a fascinating interview with George Reach of A. J. Reach and Company, manufacturer of AL baseballs (*Baseball Digest*, July 1949). He admits that his company did tinker with the liveliness of the ball from time to time. He credits the tighter tension of the wool yarn more than the makeup of the ball's core (rubber vs. cork) with the changes. He suggests that the Lively Ball Era could have been helped along by his company's shifting standards. Yet in September 1921, this very same George Reach was quoted in *Baseball Magazine*:

We try to manufacture the best baseball that money

can buy. There has been no change whatever in our methods of manufacture since 1910. . . . We have never been requested by the league officials to make any change whatever nor have we made any changes of our own volition [other than the introduction of the cork-centered ball in 1910-11].

This article went on to say that Reach's words must be accepted "on faith" because of the reputation of "a man whose word would not be lightly questioned by anyone who has ever seen him."

There was also a lengthy article in *The Sporting News* (March 12, 1936) by columnist and cartoonist Edgar F. Wolfe (under his pseudonym of Jim Nasium), written shortly after the death of Tom Shibe. Shibe was the President of the Philadelphia Athletics and part owner of the Reach Company. He had insisted that the ball had not been changed in the late teens or 1920s, "barring improvements in the method of manufacture."

It is possible to reconcile the denials of the owners, even those of ball manufacturers like Tom Shibe, with the fact that the ball may indeed have become livelier. It is time to consider this as *one* of the factors that affected play, without making it the key factor. Ball manufacturers were always trying to make a better and longer-lasting ball. (This was the impetus for the introduction of the cork-centered ball in 1910.) The use of better raw material—namely, Australian wool—after World War I deserves more attention than it has received. (It may have contributed to the rise of offense in 1919.) AL President Ban Johnson wrote to *Baseball Magazine*,

> It [Australian wool] permits of a firmer winding, a harder ball, and naturally one that is more elastic.
> —September 1921

This higher grade of yarn, which had more spring and could be wound tighter, coupled with mechanical improvements in the winding and sewing machines, did result in some change.

> The funny thing about it was that Tom Shibe, working only to improve the quality of the ball and make it more durable, never realized the effect that this would have on the playing of the game.
> —Jim Nasium, *The Sporting News*, March 12, 1936

SPITBALLER'S RANKINGS IN THE 1920s

Pitchers	League	1920	1921	1922	1923	1924	1925
Stan Coveleski	AL	ERA(2) W(3) SO(1)	—	—	ERA(1)	—	ERA(1) PCT(1) W(3)
Bill Doak	NL	—	ERA(1) PCT(1)	—	—	—	—
Phil Douglas	NL	—	—	ERA(1)	—	—	—
Urban Faber	AL	—	ERA(1) W(3)	ERA(1) SO(2)	—	—	—
Burleigh Grimes	NL	PCT(1) ERA(3) W(3) SO(3)	W(1) SO(1) PCT(3)	—	SO(3)	W(2) SO(2)	—
Allan Russell		—	—	—	ERA(3)	—	—
Urban Shocker	AL	ERA(3)	W(1), PCT(2) SO(2)	SO(1) W(3)	—	—	—

All statistics from *Total Baseball*.

Urban Shocker "loading up" with his spitball, early 1920s.

The Sporting News technically could state "the 1914 and the 1925 ball are twins, so far as their component parts are concerned" (editorial, July 23, 1925). It moved to shakier ground when it wrote (in the same editorial) that "not one iota, molecule or microbe of difference exists today in the manufacture and material of the ball from the original contract."

Even the Fales study noted that the seams of the 1920s ball seemed to be more countersunk and flush with the leather than the ball of the Deadball Era. The almost seamless ball (better sewing machines?) would have been harder to grip, with less "break" than its predecessor, thus making it easier to hit.

It is also possible to reconcile the explosion of hitting that started in 1920 with changes in the liveliness of the ball that may have occurred earlier (per Mr. Reach). Until Babe Ruth came along and showed the way, hitters did not try or know how to take advantage of a livelier ball, if there was one.

Perhaps the era was ushered in more by "lively bats" than by lively balls. Babe Ruth revolutionized the game by swinging for the fences from the end of the bat. Managers began designing their offense around the big blast, rather than "small ball." The "Inside Game" of bunt, steal, and sacrifice was quickly disappearing. This new hitting style meant that balls went farther and hit the gaps quicker than before.

A number of issues remain to be explored: Are the test studies, like that of Professor Fales, still available for review? After all, he concluded that the 1920s balls did *not* change in elasticity from those of the Deadball Era. It also should be noted note that strikeouts per game dropped significantly in the 1920s. This seems counter intuitive, with hitters free-swinging from the end of the bat. Perhaps the elimination of trick pitches may have set this off.

The tragic death of Cleveland's Ray Chapman, hit by a pitch thrown by Yankee submarine pitcher Carl Mays, resulted in a change that benefited hitters tremendously. Until that time the same ball stayed in play for long periods of time, even after it became grimy and dirty and thus a poor target for a hitter to see. Chapman might have had a difficult time picking up the darkened ball. Henceforth, the umpires were instructed to replace scuffed and soiled balls.

Mike Sowell, in his classic book *The Pitch That Killed*, notes that umpires were directed to introduce clean balls at the start of the 1920 season. But owners complained of needless increased costs, and the umpires backed off somewhat, at least until the Chapman tragedy. Not surprisingly, the lowest earned-run averages of the Lively Ball Era came in its first year. This could also be explained by the early stages of the new hitting styles and the relearning of the curve ball.

	NL	AL
1920 ERA	3.13	3.79
2nd Lowest ERA (1920-39)	3.34 ('33)	3.98 ('23)
3rd Lowest ERA (1920-39)	3.78 ('21, '38)	4.02 ('26)

Hitters now had a bright white ball to target throughout the game. The change was huge. There were 43,224 balls used in the National League in 1924, a dramatic increase from a total of 14,772 used in 1916 (*Baseball Magazine*, September 1925). Even more impressive is that 32,400 more balls were used in 1925 than in 1915 (*New York Sun*, January 4, 1926).

Finally, the introduction of better hitting backgrounds in many ballparks gave the hitter an even clearer view of the ball. Taken together, these changes had a profound impact on improving hitting, both for average and for power.

The fans loved the new style of play. Attendance climbed dramatically, clearly driven by more than the end of the war. The 1920s saw an average of well over nine million fans a year, as compared to less than six million in the teens (*Total Baseball*).

> There is very positive evidence in the jammed ball-yards that the multitude finds the cruder, more robust, freer walloping game of the present more attractive. And in baseball, more perhaps than any other sphere, the majority rules.
> —*Baseball Magazine*, July 1923

New York Giants pitcher Hugh McQuillan might have complained that the lively ball was making "bums out of pitchers" (*New York Herald Tribune*, June 21, 1925), but talented pitchers with great control like Grover Cleveland Alexander and Walter Johnson continued to excel. And the dearth of great spitballers had ended. In the 1920s, a number of great and near-great spitballers dominated the game: Coveleski, Faber, Grimes, Quinn, and Shocker.

Once the spitter was banned, there was no more discussion of its danger to the arms of the protected hurlers. No wonder. The dominant spitball pitchers had incredibly long and productive careers. Coveleski pitched until he was 39 years old; Faber until he was 45; Grimes until he was 41; and Methuselah Jack Quinn until he was 49. Urban Shocker pitched until he was 37 and was stopped only by heart disease that claimed his life less than a year after he went 18-6 for the 1927 Yankees.

> It's because I'm a spitball pitcher that I am able to keep on going. The spitter is the easiest delivery there is upon the arm. If it were not so, how do you account for the success of Jack Quinn . . . Ed Walsh did not have to quit because of the spitter. It was overwork that turned the trick.
> —Urban Faber, *New York World*, December 15, 1929

ADDENDUM

Ironically, the very baseball establishment that banned the spitter later voted five of its fraternity into the Hall of Fame: Chesbro and Walsh (elected by the Hall's Old Timers' Committee in 1946), and Coveleski, Faber, and Grimes (later elected by the Hall's Veterans' Committee). None won 300 games, and Chesbro and Walsh won less than 200 games. While they continued to be about 10% more effective than pitchers as a whole, all pitchers gave up about one more full run a game than they had before 1920.

A number of factors shut down the Deadball Era: the ban on "freaks" other than the spitter, no new spitballers, the new hitting style and improved hitting backgrounds, as well as the constant flow of fresh, bright, and better quality balls. Taken together, they provided the impetus for a stunning and sudden change, one of the biggest in baseball history.[1]

> "Bring back the spitball." It may be the wrong answer, it may be a romantic answer, but many old-timers share that dream. To them the spitball era does, truly and clearly, represent romance. It represents the time when the pitcher was king.
> —John L. Lardner, "Will They Bring Back the Spitter?" *Saturday Evening Post*, June 17, 1950

The rule changes that major league baseball instituted in February 1920 included two that affected the ball and pitching. Rule 14, Section 4, "Discolored or Damaged Balls," had previously read:

> In the event of a ball being intentionally discolored by rubbing it with the soil or otherwise by any player, or otherwise damaged by any player, the umpire shall forthwith demand the return of that ball and substitute for it another legal ball as hereinbefore described, and impose a fine of $5.00 on the offending player.
> —1918 *Reach Official Guide*

The new Rule 14 ("The Ball"), Section 4 was more expansive and punitive:

> In the event of the ball being intentionally discolored by any player, either by rubbing it with the soil, or by applying rosin, paraffin, licorice, or any other foreign substance to it, or otherwise intentionally damaging or roughening the same with sand or emery paper or other substance, the umpire shall forthwith demand the return of that the ball, and substitute for it another legal ball, and the offending player shall be disbarred from further participation in the game. If, how-

ever, the umpire cannot detect the violator of this rule, and the ball is delivered to the bat by the pitcher, then the latter shall be at once removed from the game, and as an additional penalty shall be automatically suspended for a period of ten days.

—1920 *Reach Official Guide*

Rule 30 ("The Pitching Rules") had previously discussed only "The Delivery of the Ball to the Bat." It now had a new Section 2 which stated:

At no time during the progress of the game shall the pitcher be allowed to (1) apply a foreign substance of any kind to the ball; (2) expectorate either on the ball or his glove; (3) to rub the ball on his glove, person, or clothing; (4) to deface the ball in any manner, or to deliver what is called the "shine" ball, "spit" ball, "mud" ball, or "emery" ball. For violation of any part of this rule the umpire shall at once order the pitcher from the game, and in addition he shall be automatically suspended for a period of ten days, on notice

from the President of the league.

Note: In adopting the foregoing rules against freak deliveries, it is understood and agreed that all bonafide spit ball pitchers shall be certified to their respective Presidents of the American and National League at least ten days prior to April 14th next, and that the pitchers so certified shall be exempt from the operation of the rule, so far as it relates to the spit ball only, during the playing season of 1920.

The language was the same in the Reach and Spalding Guides.

Notes:

1. In the 1950s and 1960s, there was a movement to legalize the spitter. Not only former hurlers Ed Walsh, Red Faber, and Burleigh Grimes supported the move; so did executive Branch Rickey and the Commissioner of Baseball, Ford Frick. Even Billy Evans, now a baseball executive, endorsed the move. The movement was not successful.

SOME OF THE FAVORITE WAYS OF HANDLING THE BALL (*From* The Sporting News *of January 21, 1893*)
"There are lots of things about baseball that very few people outside of professions know," said one of the local players, last evening. "In the first place whenever a new ball was thrown out last season and we were in the field it was tossed to the pitcher, who put his private mark on the same, so the visitors could not change the ball. With our pitchers it was the custom to put two marks with a long finger nail on the ball across one of the seams which would remain there as long as the ball was in play.

About a half dozen times last year the ball got pretty greased in the outfield, and it was pretty hard to hit. In using a greased ball our pitchers always had a lot of powdered rosin in their pockets, and it wasn't very hard to keep control of the ball. Now and then when the visitors were batting too hard we substituted brotherhood balls. The catcher usually made the change keeping the brotherhood ball under his chest protector, and when signaled making a lightning change. That old, innocent looking guy, Connie Mack, is full of such tricks. With that long arm of his I have seen him stand behind the batter, and with a ball coming down over the plate he would push his big gloved hand under the bat and lift the stick ever so slightly when the batter was trying to make a bunt or sacrifice hit. All of these tricks are played so nice and easy that it sometimes took the visitor some time to get on. The professionals never kick on these little pieces of play, but they make a mental memorandum of the same, and if the trick is useful, they do not hesitate to show them, as they are not patented."

— ROBERT H. SCHAEFER

August 10, 1883

Toledo, Ohio and Baseball's Color Line

by David L. Fleitz

Friday, August 10, 1883, promised excitement for baseball fans in Toledo. The Toledo Blue Stockings of the Northwest League played host to the three-time world champion Chicago White Stockings, and thousands jammed League Park at Monroe and 13th Streets to see the greatest team in baseball and its star player-manager, Cap Anson. What the crowd did not know was that this game would become one of the most critical in the history of the sport.

The White Stockings, following the custom of the day, played exhibition games against the better teams of the minor leagues on off days from National League play. The Blue Stockings, who would not be called Mud Hens for another decade, qualified as worthy opponents. After losing 11 of its first 17 games, the Toledo club pulled together under manager Charles Morton and won the pennant of the Northwest League that year.

The only storm cloud on the horizon settled over a member of the Toledo team. Toledo's catcher, Moses Walker, was a former Oberlin College student who played ball to earn money for law school at the University of Michigan. He also happened to be one of the few African American players in organized baseball at the time.

Anson, the playing manager of the Chicago team, had made it known to the Toledo management that he

David Fleitz is a SABR member and author of Shoeless: The Life and Times of Joe Jackson *and Seymour Medal finalist* Louis Sockalexis: The First Cleveland Indian, *both published by McFarland.*

objected to sharing the field with black players, and the locals planned to oblige him. Walker, suffering from a sore hand, had not been penciled into the line-up anyway. The Chicago team arrived at Union Station that Friday morning and was informed that Walker would be kept on the bench. However, according to the *Toledo Blade*, "not content with this, the visitors during their perambulations of the forenoon declared with the swagger for which they are noted" that they would not step onto the field "with no damned n——." Anson, further inflaming a situation that the Toledo management had thought resolved, loudly reiterated this demand upon arriving at League Park.

Charles Morton was not pleased with the demeanor of the visitors. "The order was given, then and there, to play Walker and the beefy bluffer [Anson] was informed that he could play his team or go, just as he blank pleased," reported the *Blade*.[1] When Anson saw Walker warming up before the contest, he exploded. "Get that n—— off the field!" he shrieked to manager Morton. He threatened to pull his team off the field without playing the game, but soon relented after a period of confusion and the threat of forfeiture of the gate receipts. The *Blade* quoted Anson as saying, "We'll play this here game, but we won't play never no more with the n—— in."[2]

The exhibition played in Toledo turned out to be one of the most important games in baseball history. From this game came the impetus for the systematic expulsion of blacks from the game, a ban that would last for 63 years.

During the early 1880s there was no official color line in professional baseball, although no African Americans had yet played in the National League. Eighteen years after the Civil War ended, America was still struggling with the placement of newly freed blacks in society. The cries grew louder that blacks did not belong on the same playing fields as whites. African Americans also began to find theaters, restaurants, transportation, union shops, and skilled vocations closed to them. Jim Crow laws and the Ku Klux Klan became more prominent in American political life.

Adrian Anson leaped into this controversy with both feet. Anson dominated baseball for three decades. He became one of the sport's earliest stars as a teenager in 1871 and moved to Chicago when the National League was formed in 1876. Anson became playing manager of the White Stockings in 1879, which gave him the nickname "Cap," and he held the post for 19 years before he retired as both player and manager in 1897. He was the first batter to reach 3,000 hits and win four batting championships, and the first manager to win five pennants. Loud, belligerent, and foul-mouthed, Anson also refined umpire intimidation to a science. He is usually considered the greatest player of the 19th century, and was inducted into the Baseball Hall of Fame in 1939.

Unfortunately, Cap Anson was also an outspoken bigot. His autobiography, written in 1900, made no mention of Moses Walker, but related in gleeful detail how the team treated its "mascot," a black man named Clarence Duval, who entertained the crowds before Chicago games. Anson described Duval as a "coon" and "a no-account n———." Historian Bill James wrote, "They treated Duval exactly as one would treat a dog." Anson made no secret of his contempt for African American ballplayers, repeating the statement "Gentlemen don't play baseball with n———s" to anyone who would listen. People listened to Cap Anson, the towering figure of baseball in the 1880s.

Though Anson's racial views were in no way unusual for the era, it appears that, even in the 1880s, he was considered an extremist. As the noted African American baseball historian and player Sol White wrote in 1907, "[Anson's] repugnant feeling, shown at every opportunity, toward colored ball players, was a source of comment throughout every league in the country."[3] What made Anson's apparent hatred of blacks unusual was the fact that he was not a Southerner, nor had he been a sympathizer of the Confederate cause during the recently completed Civil War. Anson was born and raised in Marshalltown, Iowa, where he played with Pottawatomie Indian children in his youth. Marshalltown was hardly a hotbed of racial strife.

On the other hand, Moses Walker earned respect for his play and his hard work on and off the field. Born in 1857, he was the son of Dr. Moses W. Walker, one of the first African American physicians in Ohio. The Walker family settled in Oberlin, where Moses spent two years at Oberlin Preparatory School before he was admitted to Oberlin College in 1879. Walker attended the college for three years and then enrolled in the law school at the University of Michigan in 1882, though he did not earn a diploma from either institution. The *Blade* story of August 11, 1883, praised Walker as "a gentleman and a scholar, in the literal sense," "entirely lacking in bummer instincts" and "the superior intellectually of any player on the Chicago club." The *Blade* also pointed out that Walker had already played for Toledo in exhibitions against teams from New York, St. Louis, and Columbus without incident or complaint.

The catching position was the most dangerous spot on the field in those days. Pitchers had been restricted to underhand throwing motions until the 1880s, but by 1883 the leagues allowed hurlers to throw faster pitches with sidearm and, soon after, overhand deliveries. Moses Walker wore a mask, but had only two thin, fingerless gloves to protect his hands. Broken fingers and sore hands were an occupational hazard for catchers in the 1880s, and Walker stood up to the pounding with the courage required of any catcher of that era. He played right field against the White Stockings because his hands were too sore to catch.

The game itself was, according to the *Blade*, "only a fair exhibition of ball playing," with the world champions winning 7-6 in ten innings. The Blue Stockings battered Fred Goldsmith, the champions' second-string pitcher, for sixteen hits and held Chicago to only ten. The score was tied three times before Toledo took the lead in the top of the tenth, only to see Chicago score twice in the bottom of the inning to win the game.[4] Anson hit a double and a single for Chicago, while Walker was the only Toledo batter without a hit. Walker reached base on an error and scored a run, and played errorless ball in right field. Chicago's home run champion, Ed Williamson, was held hitless. Billy Sunday, who later became America's leading evangelist, played right field and managed one hit for Chicago.

The *Blade* scorched Anson and his men the following day. "It is not putting it too strongly," said the paper, "to say they were the most untidy looking lot of ball players that have ever graced the City with their presence. Their baggy white uniforms, dirty white stockings, and variegated assortment of caps gave them a slouchy, uncouth appearance which, with their braggadocio manner, was in strange contrast to what most of the audience had expected to see." The *Blade* also stated, "It is likely to prove a very cold day when they again carry a substantial bundle of gate receipts out of Toledo."[5]

The game attracted national attention and crystallized the segregation forces already at work in professional baseball. The Peoria team of the Northwest League had petitioned the circuit to ban blacks, specifically Toledo's Moses Walker, before the 1883 season began, although Peoria withdrew its request after much "excited discussion." Cap Anson was not alone in his opposition to minorities in the professional ranks, and as the months passed, more high-level teams began to release black players and refuse to hire new ones. Historian Sol White placed the blame directly on the shoulders of Cap Anson. "[Anson's] opposition," wrote White some 25 years later, "with his great popularity and power in baseball circles, hastened the exclusion of the black man from white leagues."[6]

The American Association, then considered a major league, expanded to 12 teams after the 1883 season, and the Toledo Blue Stockings quit the Northwest League and joined the Association for the 1884 campaign. When Moses Walker caught for Toledo against the Louisville nine on May 1, 1884, he became the first African American to play in a major league game. The second black major leaguer made his debut for Toledo in July of that year when the injury-riddled ballclub hired Welday Walker, Moses's younger brother, to fill in as an outfielder for three weeks. Welday Walker played in five games and batted .222.

Anson did not enjoy his stay in Toledo, but the game was a profitable one, so the White Stockings scheduled another exhibition with Toledo for the 1884 campaign. However, Anson made certain to avoid a replay of the previous unpleasant controversy. In April 1884 the Chicago club sent a letter to Toledo manager Charles Morton which stated, "No colored man shall play in your nine and if your officers insist on playing him after we are there you forfeit the Guarantee and we refuse to play. Now I think this is fair as we refuse point blank to play colored men."[7] On July 25, 1884, Anson and the White Stockings returned to Toledo for another exhibition game, but this time controversy was avoided as Moses Walker remained on the bench. Anson belted a home run in the fourth inning of the contest, and the White Stockings defeated Toledo by a score of 10-8.

Fans around the circuit responded positively to Anson's campaign. Moses Walker was booed and

Chicago player-manager Cap Anson

hissed at a game in Louisville in early May, but matters took a more serious turn later in the season. Before a series against the Richmond Virginians, Charles Morton received a letter from four Richmond fans that threatened mob violence if Walker appeared on the field in uniform. *Sporting Life* magazine investigated and determined that the four names on the letter were bogus, but Walker did not play against the Virginians either in Toledo or in Richmond.

Walker also had trouble with teammate Tony Mullane, one of the great pitchers of the era, who joined the Toledo club for the 1884 season. Mullane was born in County Cork, Ireland, and, like Anson, freely expressed his low regard for players of African descent. Years later Mullane described his relationship with his catcher. "[Walker] was the best catcher I ever worked with," said Mullane in 1919, "but I disliked a Negro and whenever I had to pitch to him I used anything I wanted without looking at his signals." Mullane added, "One day he signaled me for a curve and I shot a fast ball at him. He caught it and walked down to me. He said, 'I'll catch you without signals, but I won't catch you if you are going to cross me when I give you signals.' And all the rest of the season he caught everything I pitched without knowing what was coming."[8]

Toledo employed eight catchers in 1884 (including a teenage "Deacon" Jim McGuire, whose major league career spanned 26 seasons), but Walker was the best of the lot, and he caught in most of Mullane's appearances that year until injuries drove him to the sidelines. Of course, Mullane's shenanigans added errors and passed balls to Walker's statistics and increased the possibility of injury. Walker batted .263 for the 1884 season, but he led the circuit in passed balls, and his sore hands caused his release on September 23, 1884. No African American would play in the major leagues again until Jackie Robinson joined the Brooklyn Dodgers in 1947.

Walker played for minor league teams in Cleveland, Newark, and other cities for several years thereafter, and he crossed paths with Cap Anson again. In 1887 Anson threatened to cancel an exhibition against the Newark club rather than face George Stovey, the black pitching star of the team. Stovey and his catcher, Walker, both remained on the bench for the duration of the game. After the season Newark released Stovey despite his 33 wins, and when the New York Giants tried to sign Stovey to a National League contract for 1888, Anson's ferocious objec-

tions forced the Giants to back off. By 1889 Walker was the only African American remaining in the high minor leagues, and within two years the color line was firmly in place throughout professional ball.

Moses Walker led a difficult life after baseball. He killed a man in a fight in 1891 and stood trial for murder, though he was eventually acquitted on a claim of self-defense. A few years later he was accused and convicted of stealing money from a mail sack, and served a year in prison. He turned to political pursuits upon his release, editing a newspaper with his brother Welday and advocating black resettlement in Africa. He died in Cleveland in 1924 and was buried in Steubenville. The grave remained unmarked until 1990, when a group of Oberlin graduates raised money for a proper headstone.

Anson also experienced his share of troubles. "Cap Anson was a blowhard," wrote Bill James, "and the older he got, the harder he blew." His obstinate nature caused his dismissal as Chicago manager in 1897 and kept him from returning to baseball. Bad investments soon forced him into bankruptcy. In 1920 Judge Kenesaw M. Landis was appointed the first commissioner of baseball; the 68-year-old Anson campaigned for the job, but was ignored by the press and the public. The National League paid Anson's funeral expenses when he died in 1922.

The Chicago White Stockings of the National League are now known as the Cubs, and Cap Anson is still the team's all-time leader in hits, runs batted in, and batting average. However, his reputation rests on the campaign he began in Toledo on that August day in 1883.

Notes:

1. *Toledo Blade*, August 11, 1883.
2. Ibid.
3. Robert Peterson, *Only the Ball Was White* (New York: McGraw-Hill, 1970), p. 30.
4. Toledo, the home team, batted first. In those days the home club was allowed to decide which team batted first.
5. *Toledo Blade*, August 11, 1883.
6. Peterson, p. 30.
7. Peterson, pp. 43-44.
8. David W. Zang, *Fleet Walker's Divided Heart* (Lincoln, NE: University of Nebraska Press, 1995), p. 43. This text comes from an interview with Mullane in *New York Age*, January 11, 1919.

The Legend of Wild Bill Setley

by Scott Fiesthumel

Throughout baseball's long history, colorful and eccentric characters have left their mark on our national pastime. Many major league players—including Dizzy Dean, Bill "Spaceman" Lee, and Mark "The Bird" Fidrych—added to the game's lore. There were also minor league players who were just as colorful (if not more so). But since they never made a name for themselves in the major leagues, history has forgotten them. One of the most unusual players in this group was William Warren "Wild Bill" Setley. Few people lead a life as eclectic as Wild Bill.

Bill Setley played ball for over 50 teams—ranging from the highest minor leagues in organized baseball to the lowest semi-pro or amateur teams—sometimes in the same season. After his playing days ended, he became an umpire, a policeman, a security man at the Oklahoma House of Representatives, and a promoter of exhibition games—including the game pitting the "Big Six" (Christy Mathewson) against the "Big Train" (Walter Johnson). He traveled to Cuba with the Cincinnati Reds and appeared on Ripley's *Believe It Or Not* radio show with Lou Gehrig. At the time of his death in 1956 (at age 97), he may have been the oldest living former professional baseball player—at least that's what he claimed.

Setley received the nickname "Wild Bill" around 1898, about a decade into his pro career. It was in ref-

erence to the stories he told about his time in the "Wild West" and to his general nature. Setley was playing in New York state (for about seven teams during that summer), and the newspapers loved the stories he told. One of the best was his description of growing up on a ranch near St. Joseph, Missouri. One of the neighboring ranches was that of Frank and Jesse James. Bill told an intricate tale about how the James boys used to come over to teach him to ride horses and shoot their pistols. Once the legend of "Wild Bill" was born, Setley wasn't about to ruin it by telling everyone that his stories were mostly just tall tales. He was actually born in New Jersey and grew up in Philadelphia—far from Frank and Jesse James.

He started playing ball in Philly, eventually developing into one of the finest amateur pitchers in the city. His fine performances pitching in exhibition games against the National League's Phillies led him to the minor leagues. He played some in the South (New Orleans, Savannah, Staunton, Richmond, and Charleston) and a lot in the East and Northeast—especially in Pennsylvania (Philadelphia, Altoona, Harrisburg, York, Allentown, Shenandoah, Reading, and more) and New York state (Amsterdam, Utica, Ilion, Canandaigua, Oswego, and more). Wild Bill's 1898 season was perhaps his finest, and also gives a good idea of what his entire career was like.

He started the season playing in the South for New Orleans and then Savannah. After being released, he made his way north, where he had played before. He

Scott Fiesthumel is the co-author (with Tony Kissel) of The Legend of Wild Bill Setley, *which is currently available.*

signed with Utica of the New York State League (NYSL) and had the finest six-week stretch of his career. Wild Bill went 10-2 for a Utica team that had won only 10 games in the six weeks before his arrival. But Bill's antics both on and off the field got him suspended and then released by Utica. He would pitch for a couple of semi-pro teams in the area before being briefly signed by both Oswego and Auburn of the NYSL. Finally, Canandaigua—his fourth NYSL team of the season—picked him up for their pennant run. The 38-year-old Setley captured the pennant for the Rustlers by leading them to four victories over Oswego in four days. For the season, he posted a 14-4 NYSL record.

After the season, he was playing a semi-pro game in Herkimer, NY, when he pulled his "potato trick" for at least the second time in his career. He would take a peeled potato to the mound with him. With a runner on first base, he threw over a couple of times to hold the runner close to the bag. Then he would take out the potato and throw it over the first baseman's head. The runner would see the overthrow and start for second—only to be met halfway there and tagged with the ball by Bill. In Herkimer, the umpire sent the runner back to first. A few years earlier, in Williamsport, PA, Wild Bill had pulled the potato trick in a Central Pennsylvania League game. The umpire called the runner out, saying there was nothing in the rules to prevent it, and if he didn't know the difference between a ball and a potato, he deserved to be out.

In an odd coincidence, the most recent time the potato trick was pulled in organized baseball occurred in 1987 by a player playing *for* a Williamsport team. Dave Bresnahan was a catcher for the Williamsport Bills who overthrew third base with a potato and tagged the runner out at home. The umpire called the runner safe, and Bresnahan was removed from the game and fined $50. He was released the next day, but was honored the following year when Williamsport held Dave Bresnahan Day. Admission to the game was one dollar . . . and a potato. Wild Bill would probably have appreciated that.

When not pitching, Wild Bill occasionally played outfield—displaying the same gift for eccentricity. He would catch pop flies behind his back (drawing fines) and once took his potato trick out with him. In one game, a player hit a line drive into the gap. Setley ran to field the ball and came up throwing, gunning the hitter down at second base. The batter couldn't believe Bill could get to the ball that quickly, so he

asked to see it. When he and the umpire checked the infielder's glove, they found a potato, which Bill had hidden in the outfield grass for just such an occasion.

But Bill could also be a smart ballplayer. In 1898, he issued perhaps the first intentional walk in NYSL history. In a game in Cortland, a good Cortland batter, Armstrong, came to the plate late in the game with two men on base. Here's how the *Cortland Evening Standard* described the scene, beginning with Setley's first pitch:

> "One strike", yelled Kelley, the umpire. Armstrong's teeth froze together, and he hit the rubber [home plate] an awful crack with his club. Setley beckoned to Toft to get away from behind the bat. He moved about five feet to the right and Setley threw him four easy ones. Armstrong did not attempt to reach any of them, and he was sent to his base on balls. The three bases were filled and the audience began to feel gloomy. Great things were expected of Shincel, who next came to bat. He fanned the air twice, and then Setley let him have a nice one. He hit it high in the air, but the ball dropped right into Mulhall's hands. The visiting team all said the play was one of the cleverest and most daring ever seen."

It was the first intentional walk any of them had ever seen. The intentional walk had been around for about a decade, but was very rarely used. One examination of major league games of the era found it was used less than one time per one hundred games. During his travels with many teams, Bill may have seen or heard about it. Or possibly he thought of it on his own. Setley's pioneering use of the strategy showed he had a good knowledge of the game. And to load the bases with the walk showed Bill was extremely confident—or foolhardy.

Bill Setley was also something of a lovable rogue off the field. More than once he was chased (or ran) out of town with accusations of bad debts, missing funds, or disputes with managers. But not only wasn't he banned from baseball, he often returned in later years to play in the same town or for the same manager. He seemed to be able to talk himself out of these incidents and from scrapes with the law. The most serious of these occurred in 1903, when he was arrested for bigamy and abduction.

With his career as a player completed, Bill needed work. He found it in a familiar place. In March 1903, Setley became the baseball coach at Hamilton College in Clinton, NY, just west of Utica. Less than three weeks later he would be in jail, disgraced.

Shortly after he arrived at Hamilton, Wild Bill put together a card game where hundreds of dollars changed hands. After winning several hundred dollars, Bill found himself in police court and was compelled to return most of his winnings. Things got worse (and really strange) after that.

On April 11, the 43-year-old Setley "eloped" with a 17-year-old Clinton resident, Veronica (Vera) Prockup, and they were married in Utica. She was a domestic on College Hill (according to the *Clinton Advertiser*) and Bill said she told him she was nineteen. When they returned home to Clinton, Vera's parents (who had learned that Bill was still married to his first wife) preferred charges of abduction against Setley and had him arrested. The Utica newspapers had extensive coverage of the many court dates and testimony by Bill's first wife, Alice. After Alice divorced him, and before he could go to trial for bigamy and abduction, the charges were apparently dropped. There is no mention of why in the newspapers. Just months later, in the spring of 1904, Wild Bill umpired an exhibition game for Utica's NYSL team. Not only was he free, he was as popular as ever.

Shortly afterward, the Setleys decided to get a fresh start, and Bill and Vera moved to the Oklahoma Territory. After rebelling against authority during his playing career, Wild Bill's next jobs were ironic. He became a policeman in Tulsa and an umpire for several western leagues. Oklahoma wasn't yet a state when the Setleys moved there—and an oil boom fueled huge population increases. Wild Bill was in the right place at the right time as he helped tame the "Wild West"—both on and off the baseball field. He umpired in several different leagues, including the "Three Eye," Western Association, Oklahoma State, Kansas State, and Southwestern.

As an umpire, Wild Bill earned a reputation for handing out $5 fines to players and managers who argued with his calls. Twice he was beaned by balls thrown by players and often was harassed or attacked by fans of the rough and tumble world of baseball in the "Old West." Setley was often called the best umpire in many of the leagues he worked in, although he would invariably make calls against teams that would get their hometown newspapers upset, leading to bad press and even implications that he fixed games as an umpire.

In 1908, the Cincinnati Reds made a barnstorming trip to Cuba to play several games against Cuban teams. Setley must have made a pretty good impres-

Hunting in Cuba with the Cincinnati Reds. From left; Frank Bancroft (Reds business manager), Bob Bescher, Larry McLean, and Bill Setley.

sion during games seen by major league scouts, because the Reds asked Wild Bill to accompany them to umpire all games the Reds played against Cuban teams and act as umpire. Setley and his wife and daughter all made the trip. Cincinnati won a series of games against a Havana team, but didn't fare as well versus the Almendares Blues club. The Reds went only 1-5-1 in the series with that powerful Cuban team. One of the leaders of Almendares was their 20-year-old pitcher, Jose Mendez. Mendez later earned the nickname "The Black Diamond," and once struck out Babe Ruth three times in a game. Against the Reds, he pitched two shutouts, with a no-hitter going into the ninth in one game, when he gave up one hit.

John McGraw later said that Mendez was the best pitcher in baseball. Setley recalled, "We saw something on that Almendares team. They had a pitcher, Mendez, a big Cuban Negro, and he pitched 24 consecutive shutout innings against the Reds. He set the Reds down with one hit in the first game. Frank Bancroft, the Cincinnati business manager, who was acting as manager on the trip, said, 'Whitewash that Mendez and I could sell him for $20,000."

Five years later, Wild Bill was involved with the organizing and promotion of an exhibition game between New York Giants and Chicago White Sox. The game was played October 28 in Tulsa—where it was cool enough to briefly snow. The exhibition game was played to raise money for the Giants/Sox round-the-world tour. Oklahoman Walter "The Big Train" Johnson was signed for $500 to pitch against "The Big Six," New York's Christy Mathewson. Johnson out-pitched Matty, winning 2-0 while allowing eight hits and striking out eight Giants. That the game was played at all was amazing, because just before it was scheduled to start, the first base section of the grandstand collapsed. Soldiers had been marching under the bleachers and one was killed instantly. More than 50 fans were seriously injured—some of whom reportedly died later. Yet after the wounded were taken away and the scene brought to some semblance of order, the game went on.

Wild Bill told (and was the subject of) many baseball stories. The most famous was the one about the "closest game ever played"—a game that ended with the score of 2½-2. There were several versions of the story, but the one he told on Ripley's *Believe It or Not* radio show was heard by the most people.

The game was played between two minor league teams, the Allentown Killers and the Pottsville Colts,

and the score was tied 2-2 in the bottom of the 11th inning. Mike "King" Kelly, the Allentown player/manager, had just broken the last bat that either team owned. Umpire Tim Hurst told Kelly that the game was over and would be a tie, but the stubborn player would have none of that and walked over to a nearby shed. Kelly returned with an ax, intending to bat with it. "You can't use that," said Umpire Hurst. "Sure I can," said King Kelly and he got his way. Kelly swung and missed at two pitches and then connected on the next one. The ax sliced right through the ball's center, with one piece flying foul over the grandstand, and the other half going out into left field.

Kelly circled the bases and headed for home with the winning run. The outfielder threw the ball in to the relay man, and he fired it in to the catcher, who applied the tag on the sliding Kelly at home plate. "You're out!" hollered Umpire Hurst, and Kelly answered, "The hell I am. I'm only half out. He's just got half of the ball!" The umpire pondered this for a moment, and then decided to give Allentown half a run to make the final score 2½ to 2 in Allentown's favor.

In some versions of this story, Wild Bill himself is the umpire or the outfielder. The teams and players involved also changed over the years. Extensive research by Tony Kissel and myself has failed to turn up any evidence that such an event occurred. If it did, the teams and players involved are almost certainly obscure semi-pro or amateur ones—not involving Tim Hurst or King Kelly.

Setley's appearance on Robert Ripley's radio program was sort of overshadowed by Lou Gehrig's famous on-air commercial mistake. When asked what cereal he ate for training, Lou replied, "Wheaties" (he had previous endorsed them) rather than the correct sponsor, Huskies.

Finding complete statistics for minor league players of Wild Bill's era is, as you can imagine, quite difficult. His record in organized baseball (at least what stats are available) was 65-56. In 1896, he posted a 20-16 record in professional games—with an additional 4-1 record in semi-pro or amateur games. That season just four National League pitchers topped his 113 strikeouts, and all of them pitched more games than Wild Bill. But Setley's career (and life) can't be measured by mere statistics. He did more in his lifetime than some men would in ten lives, and it is unlikely we'll ever again see a player/umpire/promoter/policeman like Wild Bill Setley.

Cyril "Cy" Buker

Coaching in Wisconsin and Pitching for the Dodgers in the '40s

by Jim Sargent

In 1941, the year the Japanese bombed Pearl Harbor and propelled America into World War II, the Brooklyn Dodgers won the National League pennant by two and a half games over the St. Louis Cardinals. But the New York Yankees won the World Series in five games, thanks in part to a critical error by Dodger catcher Mickey Owen in game four, with the Yankees ahead in the series, two games to one.

In the ninth inning of the fourth game, with the Dodgers leading 4-3 and two strikes on the batter, Owen let Hugh Casey's third strike on Tommy Henrich get under his glove and roll away. Henrich made it to first, the Yankees scored four runs to win the game, 7-4, and New York wrapped up the fall classic with a 3-1 victory the following afternoon.

The Dodgers recovered and contended all through the 1942 season, but the youthful St. Louis Cardinals, led by stars such as Stan Musial, Enos Slaughter, and brother battery mates Mort and Walker Cooper, finished first by two games. However, the talent-rich Yankees, again paced by greats like Joe DiMaggio, Charlie Keller, Joe Gordon, and Bill Dickey, won another World Series in five games.

In 1943, the first year that World War II seriously affected the manpower of the major leagues, Brooklyn finished third behind St. Louis and the Cincinnati Reds. But the Dodgers plummeted to 23½

games off the pace in 1943, while the Cardinals, with another year of experience, had become the league's powerhouse.

Brooklyn declined even further in 1944, finishing in seventh place, 42 games below the pennant-winning and World Series champion Cardinals. But the Dodgers began to improve in 1945, contending for the NL pennant and finishing in third place, 11 games behind the first-place Chicago Cubs and only two games in back of the Cardinals—the team hurt least by the wartime manpower drain.

By 1945 Leo Durocher, who began managing the Dodgers in 1939, was virtually the only man left from the pennant-winning 1941 club. With a mixture of younger and older talent, Durocher kept his team in the pennant race by using a variety of lineups and an assortment of pitchers.

In 1941, Durocher's lineup had included stars such as Dolf Camilli at first base, Billy Herman at second, future Hall of Famer Pee Wee Reese at short, Pete Reiser and Dixie Walker in the outfield, Owen behind the plate, and 22-game winners Kirby Higbe and Whit Wyatt on the mound.

For Brooklyn's last wartime season, Walker, who was drafted into the military, still played right field, and Eddie Stanky, whom the Cubs traded to the Dodgers a few weeks into the 1944 season, became the names most recognizable to Flatbush fans.

What was it like to pitch in the Dodger farm system and for the big league club during the mid-1940s?

Jim Sargent is a Professor of History and Dean of the Social Science Division of Virginia Western Community College in Roanoke. His last article for TNP was on June Peppas and the All-American League.

A good example is Cyril "Cy" Buker, a right-handed pitcher who compiled a 7-2 record for Brooklyn in 1945. During his only big league season, Cy showed that he was not the stereotypical "wartime" player.

Brooklyn's top winner in 1945 was Hal Gregg, a hard-throwing 24-year-old in his third major league season. Gregg led the National League in walks in 1944 and 1945. But in '45 the tall right hander produced his best season in a nine-year career, going 18-13 with a 3.47 ERA. In 1946, with many big leaguers returning from military service, Gregg had a 6-4 mark, but a sore arm kept him from surpassing that win total in five more seasons.

Brooklyn had three pitchers who won 10 games in 1945. Rookie Vic Lombardi had a 10-11 record with a 3.31 ERA. Considered small at 5'7" and maybe 160 pounds, the southpaw also reached double digits in wins in 1946 and 1947 with the Dodgers and in 1948 with the Pittsburgh Pirates. Overall, Vic posted a 50-51 ledger during his six-year major league career.

Curt Davis went 10-10 with a 3.25 ERA in 1945. A 6'3" right hander who won 19 games for the Philadelphia Phillies in his rookie season of 1934, Davis enjoyed three more seasons with 15 or more wins, making the NL All-Star team in 1936 and 1939. But the Greenfield, Missouri native had no record in 1946, his final fling at the majors.

Tom Seats, who first pitched in the majors for the Detroit Tigers in 1940, spent most of the war years as a shipyard worker while also hurling for San Francisco in the Pacific Coast League. Signed by the Dodgers in 1945, Tom was 10-7 with a 4.36 ERA. After failing to stick with Brooklyn in 1946, the 5'11" southpaw returned to the PCL for three seasons.

The Dodgers had two other hurlers who matched Buker's seven-win total. Art Herring, a 5'7" right hander who broke in with the Tigers in 1929 but who was out of the majors from 1940 through the 1943 season, went 7-4 with a 3.48 ERA. A good relief pitcher during past seasons, Art won all seven games in 1945 as a starter. The Oklahoma native also won seven times in 1946 but only once in 1947, his final big league season with the Pirates.

Les Webber, a right hander who first made it with the Dodgers in 1942, had a 7-3 mark with a 3.58 ERA in 1945. The California native, who was 4-F with a heart murmur, also won seven games in 1944. Later slowed by arm and rib injuries, Les was 4-4 in 1946 and had no decisions with the Cleveland Indians in 1948, his final year in the majors.

Other Dodger pitchers included young Ralph Branca, who was 5-6 with a 3.04 ERA, and Clyde King, a 6'1" right hander from Goldsboro, North Carolina. Both were second-year hurlers.

Branca, a hard-throwing right hander who would enjoy a 12-year major league career with a 88-68 lifetime mark, became best known for the gopher ball he threw to Bobby Thomson in the Dodger-Giants playoff finale on October 3, 1951. But he won 21 games for Brooklyn in 1947, plus he won game six of the '47 World Series. After the 1951 playoffs, Buker suffered an offseason pelvis injury that hurt his subsequent career.

King went 5-5 with a 4.09 ERA in 1945. Later a manager and coach in the majors, Clyde worked mainly out of the bullpen. His best of seven major league seasons came in 1951, when he went 14-7 for the Dodgers—recording 13 of the wins in relief.

A newcomer on Brooklyn's nine-man staff, Buker had to prove himself. He also had to fit into the mentality of the times, a mind-set where big league clubs used contracts with reserve clauses to control players as if they were property. The independent-thinking Cy would not prove to be a good "company man."

Born February 5, 1919, in Greenwood, Wisconsin, Cyril grew up thriving on sports. He played several positions in sandlot ball and at Greenwood High, graduating in 1936. Playing for the University of Wisconsin, he mainly pitched.

"I had a pretty good arm when I was a kid," Buker explained in a 1999 interview, "and I just kept on throwing, that's all. I started out in the county leagues, and in high school, and eventually at the University of Wisconsin."

An all-around athlete, Buker graduated from Wisconsin with a bachelor of science degree in 1940. With the German blitzkrieg raging in Europe, Cy lined up a job teaching and coaching for the fall. He also decided to give professional ball a shot.

Signed by New York after Wisconsin, Buker was sent to Clinton, Iowa, of the Class B Three-Eye League. "I was signed by Heinie Groh of the Giants out of Wisconsin. I started at Clinton in the Three-Eye League, and I hurt my elbow right away. They didn't have any surgery for that kind of thing, and I thought I was done," he said in 1999.

"I won my first game, 7-1, against Moline. But the next time out, I couldn't throw the ball up to the plate. My elbow was locked.

"They sent me over to Wausau in the Northern League. I told them, 'I can't throw.' So I jumped the ball club and came home at the beginning of August.

I went to work, teaching and coaching all sports at Sturgeon Bay, Wisconsin."

Cy played semi-pro baseball in 1941:

"I didn't go back to organized ball until 1942. I liked to play, so I played second base in semi-pro ball. I didn't have much of a throw there. By golly, by the end of 1941 I noticed that my arm was getting stronger! At the end of the season, I pitched a ball game and did real well. I decided I would give it another try."

In 1941, Cy took a job at Shullsburg in southern Wisconsin. The following summer he got a better offer from Eau Claire. For three years he coached all sports and taught a variety of classes at Eau Claire, until signing with Brooklyn in early 1945.

"It's a funny thing, but I never put in a full season with any ball club. When I started out, I was in the lower minors. I would teach until we got into the latter part of May or early June, and I would join the ball club. Then I'd jump the ball club and come back to school when football started.

"In 1942 I started out with the White Sox at Wisconsin Rapids in the Class D Wisconsin State League, and I did pretty well."

Considering that he was coming off arm problems, Buker produced a solid season for seventh-place Wisconsin Rapids, going 5-5 with a 6.88 ERA.

"We had a bad ball club. I managed to win a few, but my arm got stronger as the year went along. At the end of the season, with World War II and everything, the league blew up and I was a free agent again.

"So I went back to coaching and teaching full-time. I didn't go into organized ball in 1943. I stayed up at Eau Claire. I was coaching at Memorial High, which at that time was the biggest high school in the state. I had a good job. I made $2,000, which was a lot of money in those years.

"When I started out in the Wisconsin State League, I got $80 a month. I got an extra $10 for driving the bus. We had a center fielder by the name of Decker at Wisconsin Rapids. He was married and had two kids, and he made $35 a month.

"Those were the days when you stayed in fleabag hotels with no air conditioning and sometimes slept three to a bed. We got a dollar a day for meal money!

"We liked to play ball. That's why you played in the 1940s. That was baseball in the lower leagues. Today, nobody would go through that kind of stuff."

After concentrating on coaching during the 1943 season, Cy signed with St. Paul in 1944:

"In the spring of 1944 I got a call from St. Paul in the American Association. I told them I couldn't join the club until the 3rd or 4th of June. I threw batting practice and they liked what they saw.

"From June until the end of the year, I went 13-3. Two of those are playoff games, and they don't show up in the record. But I had a real good year."

Working in 25 games, Buker came through with a 3.23 ERA to go with his 11-3 regular-season mark. Fourth-place St. Paul defeated Toledo in the semifinals, four games to three, and Cy won two games. But Louisville beat St. Paul in four straight games to capture the league title.

In early 1945 Buker, still teaching at Eau Claire, talked it over with his father and decided to give it a shot with Brooklyn.

"I got a leave of absence from Eau Claire and joined the ball club. I wasn't there two days before I was in the Army. The Army finally released me about May 15. I was in what they call the observation unit. I had asthma, and I was wheezing up a storm.

"I got in my first game for the Dodgers just after the middle of May. From then until the end of the year, I was in the game quite a bit.

"The thing I want to stress is that there was no early man, no middle man, no late man. If you went to the bullpen, you got up in the first inning to warm up, or the second, or any other inning. It went that way through all nine innings.

"We had a bunch of young, hard throwers like Ralph Branca, Hal Gregg, Vic Lombardi. They were wild as hell. If you went to the bullpen, you could crank up for nine innings and never get in the ball game. The next day it would be the same thing all over again. That's the way Leo Durocher ran things."

Still, Buker made the most of his opportunity with the Dodgers. Pitching mainly in relief in 1945, he produced a 7-2 record with a 3.30 ERA. Brooklyn contended for the pennant until July, finishing third with an 87-67 record, behind the Cubs and the Cardinals.

The 5'11" 190-pound right hander pitched whenever he was needed. For example, he recalled one memorable afternoon in Cincinnati when he lost and won games in both ends of a double-header. On Tuesday, September 11, with the temperature near 100 degrees at Crosley Field, Buker came on to relieve Art Herring in the bottom of the eighth. Cy pitched scoreless ball for two innings.

But in the Cincinnati tenth, Kermit Wahl led off with a single. Pitcher Joe Bowman advanced the runner with a groundout. Dain Clay was safe on an error by Dodger first sacker Eddie Stevens. Buker walked pinch-hitter Dick Sipek to set up a force at any base. Instead, Al Libke bounced one through the legs of second sacker Eddie Stanky.

The Reds won, 5-4, and Buker left the field:

"I'm in the clubhouse taking a shower after the game and taking my time, figuring my day's over," Buker recalled. "Here comes Charley Dressen, whistling that shrill whistle he had, saying, 'Cy, get out in the bullpen. Leo wants you right now!'

"I didn't have any choice. It was either go out there or go back to St. Paul. So I put my uniform back on and went to the bullpen."

The first-game loss lowered Buker's record to 4-2. In the second game, he relieved Clyde King in the fourth and allowed one run on a two-out wild pitch. After that, he hurled scoreless ball and the Dodgers came from behind to win, 11-6.

The victory upped Cy's mark to 5-2, thanks to nine-plus innings of relief on a sweltering afternoon. The next day he spent much of the afternoon warming up in the bullpen as Brooklyn lost, 3-2, to St. Louis at Sportsman's Park. And so it went in 1945 for the stocky right-handed ace.

Buker hurled 87⅓ innings spread over 42 games. By mid-July, one *New York Times* story called him "Durocher's fireman."

The 26-year-old rookie won twice as a starter, earning his first victory by beating the Phillies in Philadelphia, 9-2, on Thursday, June 21, with relief help in the eighth and ninth frames from Vic Lombardi.

On Wednesday, July 18, in the second game of a double-header at Wrigley Field, Cy started and pitched the first 6⅓ innings and beat the Cubs, 9-5, with relief help from Tom Seats and Ralph Branca.

That lifted the Wisconsin hurler's record to 4-0. Mostly, however, he worked out of the bullpen, often two or three innings at a time.

Two examples illustrate the ups and downs of a relief pitcher. On Tuesday, July 24, in St. Louis, Cy, pitching in relief of Lombardi and Gregg, suffered his first loss (making his record 4-1), as the Cardinals beat the Dodgers, 7-6.

With the score tied at 6-all in front of a ladies night crowd of 15,543, Cy entered the game in the ninth inning and gave up a leadoff single to Marty Marion. Pitcher George Dockins laid down a sacrifice bunt, moving the runner to second. Marion scored the game winner on a line single to right by Augie Bergamo.

Four days later at Brooklyn's Ebbets Field, Buker saved Hal Gregg's 13th victory, a 2-1 triumph over the Boston Braves, with one pitch. A rainy-day crowd of 10,688, including 5,000 youthful war-bond salesmen who received free tickets, saw Gregg falter in the ninth. With the Dodgers ahead, 2-0, the right hander yielded two-out singles to Butch Nieman and Whitey Wietelmann.

Manager Leo Durocher summoned pint-sized Vic Lombardi to put out the fire. But Lombardi walked Chuck Workman and Tommy Holmes to force in one run. Buker got the call with the bases loaded. He fired a fastball to Bill Ramsey. Ramsey lined a shot above the head of third baseman Frenchy Bordagaray, who leaped high and made a great catch, allowing Buker to walk off the mound with a save.

Cy won his seventh victory in Flatbush on Wednesday, September 19, pitching in relief of Lombardi. Called from the pen in the top of the seventh with no outs, the bases loaded, and the Dodgers ahead, 3-2, Buker induced Danny Gardella to ground into a force-out—but Bill Jurges scored the tying run. When shortstop Eddie Basinski booted a routine ground ball, Leon Treadway scored the go-ahead run.

Buker retired the side and pitched scoreless ball for the last two innings. In the bottom of the seventh, his teammates rallied for two markers, with Frenchy Bordagaray's single knocking home the eventual game winner.

With the season nearly over, Buker returned to teaching and coaching at Memorial High. When Branch Rickey sent the right hander a 1946 contract with a raise of $500 above the major league minimum of $5,000, Cy reacted by tearing it up and mailing the pieces back to Brooklyn.

A month later, Rickey sent another contract, this one with a $1,500 raise. But this contract was contingent upon Buker surviving the cut-down date. Deciding to pursue his baseball dream and place his coaching career on hold, he resigned from Memorial High. Buker recalled arriving at spring training three weeks late:

"I could see that everyone was mad at me. Nobody would even talk to me. I was assigned to the B squad immediately, without throwing a ball. It went that way throughout spring training and into the season.

"I sat on the bench. I never pitched one ball in 1946. They didn't want anyone to see me. I sat on the bench until the final hour of the last day before cut-down, and, you guessed it. I was optioned to Montreal.

"I got no $1,500 and no chance to pitch. I did not

throw a single ball in the majors in 1946!"

In fact, the Wisconsin native never pitched another game in the big leagues. In 1946 the Dodgers, stockpiling players in the minors under tight-fisted general manager Branch Rickey, optioned the right hander to Montreal of the triple-A International League.

Moving to Montreal, Buker produced a fine season, getting off to a 10-2 start. But he was involved in a collision at home plate and injured his pitching arm and hand. Sidelined for several weeks, Cy finished the season with a 12-7 record and a 3.81 ERA.

"I didn't pitch much for six weeks. But when I came back, I didn't have the same kind of stuff. I ended up winning only two more ball games the rest of the year, and I lost five. But my earned run average was around 2.00 in the first part of the season."

Buker liked playing ball with Jackie Robinson. Cy recalled that Robinson was installed as the second baseman:

"As the season moved on, Jack started to improve. As the season progressed, he got better and better. He was a pretty good ballplayer by the end of 1946.

"Jack could run, and at the end, he could turn the double play as well as anyone. He got a lot of 'leg hits.' Anything on the ground on the left side, he'd beat it out.

"We had a heck of a club. We won that league by something like 18 or 19 games!"

Buker, however, never fully recovered from the hand injury. When the Dodgers optioned him to Montreal in 1947, he refused to go. Brooklyn then sent him to St. Paul, where Cy came through with an 8-8 record and a 5.31 ERA. He started the 1948 season with the Milwaukee Brewers and finished with Kansas City. Going 4-4, he saw his ERA rise to 8.51.

In 1949 Buker refused to report and was suspended for the season. He signed to teach and coach at Greenwood, Wisconsin, where he stayed 12 years. In the summer of 1951, Cy took a final fling at the game he loved. Pitching and working with young players in the single-A Western League, he compiled a 2-6 record with three clubs.

After he retired from teaching and coaching in 1970, the Wisconsin native was inducted into the state's High School Football Coaches Hall of Fame. Over the years he has kept active by doing bodywork and painting on classic automobiles.

Sports card entrepreneur Larry Fritsch, who played football, basketball, and baseball at Spenser High in the 1950s against Buker-coached teams, recalled, "When I learned that Cy had played in the big leagues, I searched for a photo of him and included it in our first One-Year-Winner card set. I respected him as a coach and a man, and I thought a Buker card would be a welcome addition to the set."

One of the best relief pitchers in the National League in 1945, Buker was seldom hit hard. The fast-balling right hander remembers giving up only two home runs, one to Andy Pafko of the Cubs and another to Whitey Kurowski of the Cards.

Proving to be more than a wartime player, Cy Buker made a major contribution to a Brooklyn club that contended for the pennant much of the summer. Despite his value to the team in 1945, when the veterans returned in 1946, he was not given a chance—due at least in part to his contract dispute with the Dodgers.

Surviving the stiff competition of the big leagues and the upper minors, the longtime coach and teacher has few regrets about his accomplishments. He loved baseball, and he loved coaching young men. But after his 7-2 mark and strong relief pitching in 1945, he deserved a chance to make the Dodgers or another team in 1946.

Despite the ups and downs of his diamond career, Cy Buker recently observed, "I wouldn't trade those days in baseball for anything in the world."

George Brace
Baseball's Foremost Photographer

by James D. Smith III

George Brace officially retired from his vocation as a baseball photographer at 65. That number would hardly seem remarkable except for one fact: it wasn't his age, it was his years of service as a visual chronicler of America's national pastime. Through 1994, from his home base in Chicago, Brace captured more than half of major league baseball's years in pictures, leaving a priceless legacy to fans everywhere.

His technical skills were beyond question. In a January 2002 interview, Brace rehearsed for me the speed graphics used with a 55mm lens accommodating sunlight conditions at the 1933 All-Star Game. Closer to his heart, however, was the sport itself. He remembered with fondness corresponding as a kid with Hall of Fame immortal George Wright, reaching back to the 1869 Cincinnati Red Stockings. He also loved playing the game, recounting with delight days with the Westwood Badgers of 1924 (which he helped organize) and later teams. "I was always a big fan," he recalled, "and had a great time wherever I went."

George Brace was born on Chicago's South Side on April 11, 1913. His parents, Fred and Margaret (Ward) Brace, were die-hard Sox followers. Gradually, he became partial to the Windy City's more successful team, the Cubs—and in 1929 his big break came. That team needed photographs of the

Jim Smith has been a SABR member since 1982, and has contributed to a variety of publications. He would like to thank Mary Brace for her kindness in supplying photos and captions for this remembrance.

players in their street clothes, and had previously worked with a local photographer named Francis Burke. Their phone call, however, reached George Burke, who (knowing little about baseball) took on Master Brace at 16 as an assistant. Together, until his mentor's death in 1951, they formed a partnership taking photographs of the Cubs, White Sox, and football's Chicago Bears. "For the first two years, I was in charge of the files, and then really got to know the craft." With Burke's passing, respect for Brace as a freelance photographer gained him continued access to Comiskey Park and Wrigley Field.

Brace and Burke teamed up as photographers for baseball's first official All-Star Game (NL vs. AL) in 1933. Held at Comiskey, "it was great, brand-new, and there was quite a bit of interest. Arch Ward organized it, but I never met him. I was about 20 years old, and Mr. Burke stationed me on the first base side with the camera. I was the closest one to Babe Ruth as he went back and forth from right field. And I was just behind my favorite player, Lou Gehrig." The memories flowed.

That game was a landmark in baseball history and began a cordial relationship with the Iron Horse which would last the remainder of his career. "He was the nicest guy you'd ever want to meet—didn't talk much, but was so considerate. I took a profile picture of him which Lou liked so much he ordered dozens of eight-by-tens. Another time, there were about 60 kids who had won a contest and showed up (from

1933 NATIONAL LEAGUE ALL~STAR TEAM

HARTNETT, WILSON, FRISCH, HUBBELL, WALKER, WANER, ENGLISH, SCHUMACHER, TRAYNOR, LOTSHAW.
HALLAHAN, BARTELL, TERRY, McKECHNIE, McGRAW, CAREY, HAFEY, KLEIN, O'DOUL, BERGER.
HASBROOK, MARTIN, WARNEKE, CUCCINELLO.

1933 AL/NL All-Stars: "Dad always paid close attention to detail, and the uniforms for the game caught his eye. The National Leaguers wore the league designation instead of their home team jerseys, and so he and Mr. Burke offered to take photos of each individual as a keepsake. It was the only year they did that with uniforms. History was being made right here in Chicago, at old Comiskey."

Connecticut, I think) at a game and he posed with every single one."

Meanwhile, on Chicago's diamonds, Brace played ball through 1936. There was that late 1920s streak in which his team won 21 consecutive games, and CYO championship experiences to remember. There was also the 1933 tourney (coinciding with the World's Fair) in which someone "introduced me as the world's greatest official scorer." Then there was softball—and employment which made possible his activities as a photographer. Brace worked during the swing shift at a Durkee Famous Foods processing plant on the North Side, leaving him free for day games. His goal was to attend at least one game in each Cubs and White Sox series—and the longtime Logan Square resident's record was remarkable.

Over the years, Brace's shutter captured an estimated 13,000 subjects on their trips through Chicago (players, managers, umpires, groundskeepers, ball boys, mascots, concessionaires, announcers, et al.), and historic moments such as the building of the bleachers and scoreboard at Wrigley Field and the 1937 ivy planting. "If they came to Chicago, I got 'em," he told everyone, leaving hundreds of thousands of images.

In 1996, two years after eye and leg problems caused his retirement, Richard Cahan and Mark Jacob presented a selection of these gems of the times in *The Game That Was: The George Brace Baseball Photo Collection*. Jacob recalled the experience: "The thing most striking to me was how George viewed baseball as fun—not just a career, not just a way to make money, but simply as a beautiful sport that brought enjoyment to people."

Even Brace couldn't be everywhere. "The Negro Leagues brought some great teams to Chicago, and the East–West Classic was wonderful. But they had all their own photographers," he told me. "So now and then I'd go down to the park on 39th and Wentworth just to watch games. I remember some early discussions about the Chicago Americans ordering lights."

A World War II U.S. Army veteran, with his passing on June 15, 2002, Brace was survived by Agnes, his wife of 60 years. His son John and daughter Mary (who continues as proprietor of the collection) have vivid memories of baseball as part of their upbringing. Following the appearance of *The Game That Was*, there was long-deserved recognition (including the taping of an oral history at the Hall of Fame). Current Cubs photographer Stephen Green drew on George Brace's half century of experience when he started

the job in 1982. "He had a reverie for the game and for photography that always impressed me. He taught me to approach these players not as stars but as people, like you and me, playing the world's best game."

The photographs in this article are from the George Brace Collection, and are available at www.bracephoto.com.

Bob Feller & Jeff Heath: "This was taken in the late 1930s. He came out from behind the camera to pose with two of Cleveland's best—ballplayers and people. This shot became a sort of trademark for my dad. Anytime there was an article written about his work, he liked to have this photo used—so here it is one more time!"

Lou Gehrig: "This became Lou's favorite photo of himself to give out to the fans. Sometimes he'd order 500-1,000 at a time. Lou seemed to like the warmth that it conveyed, and he became Dad's favorite player . . . a very kind-hearted and wonderful man. His illness and death were such sad news to my father."

Charlie Grimm & Cub: "Dad really had a great sense of humor, and especially enjoyed the promotions and 'doings' at Wrigley Field. Bill Veeck and the whole gang certainly had some ideas. Hey, like the book says, it was a game. There's so much fun in his pictures, something for all types!"

Wartime baseball: "The only time Dad missed an entire White Sox or Cubs series was during World War II, while he was in the U.S. Army in the Pacific. Even there, in New Guinea and the Philippines, he was snapping pictures. These are pretty rough, maybe taken with a box camera— and he used whatever was available to develop the negatives."

Ernie Banks: "From the first day of his rookie year in 1953, Ernie Banks was a special subject. And after that wonderful career with the Cubs, he asked Dad to come to the Hall of Fame with him and photograph his favorites. Mr. Banks visited our home several times to pick up photographs."

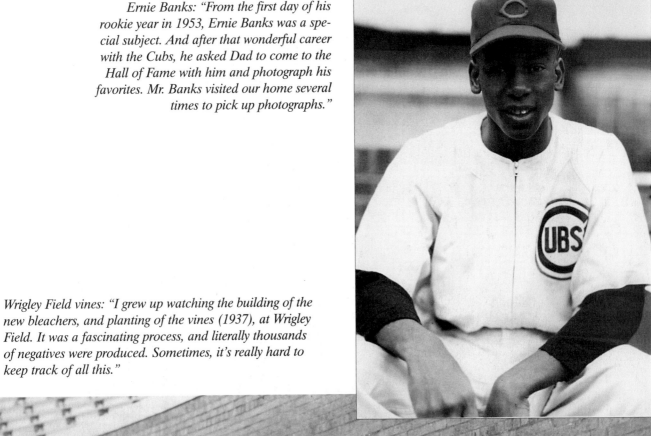

Wrigley Field vines: "I grew up watching the building of the new bleachers, and planting of the vines (1937), at Wrigley Field. It was a fascinating process, and literally thousands of negatives were produced. Sometimes, it's really hard to keep track of all this."

Mr. & Mrs. Babe Ruth: "Dad always referred to Claire as Babe Ruth's second wife, for clarity or whatever reason. This was taken at Comiskey, and reminds me that she traveled with the Yankees on road trips at times. He was an amazing player and personality."

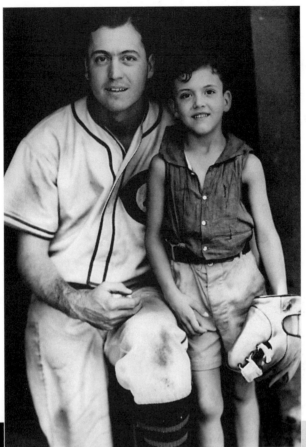

Billy Herman & son: "He loved to take pictures with a family sense at the ballpark—players with children, brothers, fathers and sons, and so on. In his career, Dad went from the Waners to the Ripkens! He'd dress kids up (like Billy Jr. here) in little uniforms with equipment . . . isn't this a beautiful picture?"

Ted Lyons Day: "Because I've worked with these photographs since I was a kid, a lot of these old players are just recognized as friends. But Dad had greater personal contact and love for the game—and he really respected Ted Lyons. I started out drying pictures, then printing the black-and-whites. I'm still finding shots in the files I wish I could ask him about."

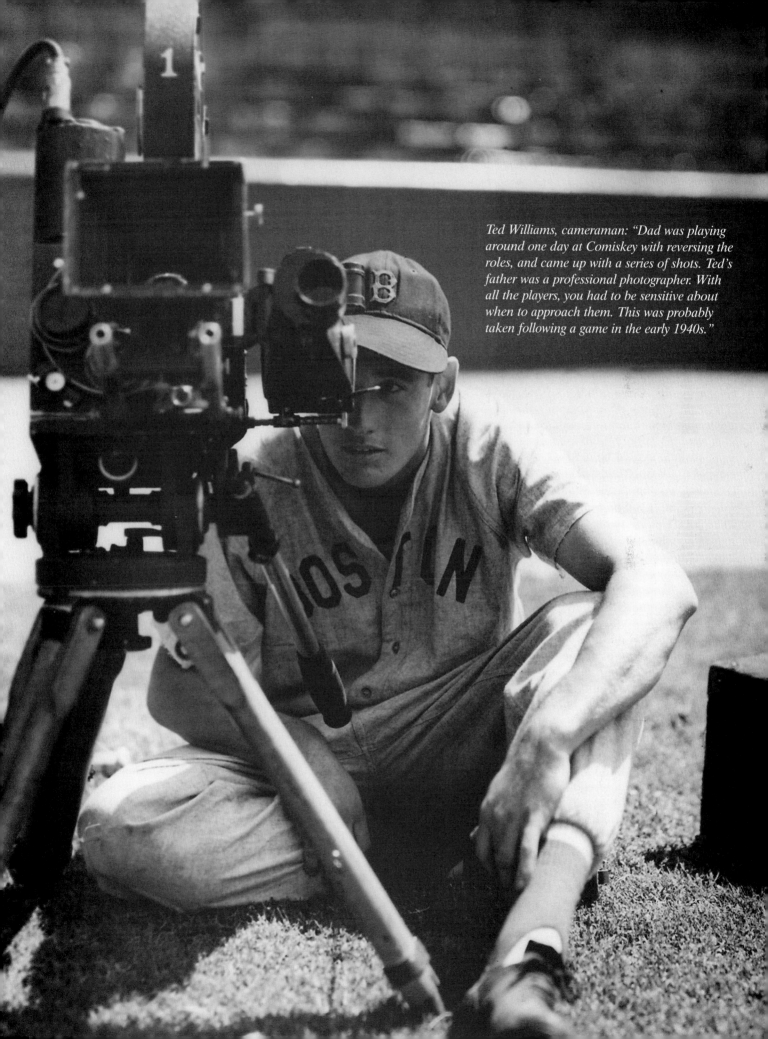

Ted Williams, cameraman: "Dad was playing around one day at Comiskey with reversing the roles, and came up with a series of shots. Ted's father was a professional photographer. With all the players, you had to be sensitive about when to approach them. This was probably taken following a game in the early 1940s."

Let's Play Three!

by David McDonald

Late in the summer of 1914, Doc Reisling, the ball-playing dentist from Ohio, found himself at the center of one of the most bizarre pennant races in baseball history. It was September 6, the penultimate day of the Canadian League[1] season, and Reisling's London Tecumsehs[2] trailed their arch rivals, Shag Shaughnessy's Ottawa Senators,[3] by two games.

Seven weeks earlier, the Tecumsehs had led the Senators by ten, and appeared to be a shoo-in to avenge a final-day pennant loss to Ottawa in 1913. The Tecumsehs had got off to a 46-23 start in 1914, but had won only 23 of their next 43 games. They stood at 69-43. The Senators, meanwhile, had made up for a sluggish 34-32 start by going on a 41-13 tear,[4] which brought their record to league-leading 75-45.

September 6 was an off-day for the Tecumsehs, as it was a Sunday, and Sunday ball was not permitted in the Methodist-dominated province of Ontario. Catholic Quebec was a different story. Of Canadian League clubs (all Ontario-based in 1914 except for the Erie, PA, Sailors), Ottawa was uniquely situated to take advantage of Quebec's tolerance of Sunday fun. And, since the beginning of the season, the Senators had been playing Sunday doubleheaders to good crowds at Dupuis Park in Hull, Quebec, just across the Ottawa River from the capital.

On this last Sunday of the season, Ottawa was slated to play two against the third-place Sailors. A sweep by the Senators would give them a three-game margin over the Tecumsehs with only a Labor Day doubleheader remaining for each team. Now, in most circumstances, a three-game lead with two games to go would have the leaders popping champagne corks. But not in the Canadian League in 1914.

The arithmetical anomaly was the result of a marked disparity in the number of games each of the contenders had played that summer. London, because of an inordinate number of rainouts and ties,[5] had recorded only 112 decisions, compared to Ottawa's 120. Going down to the wire, the difference in games played actually favored the Tecumsehs, even giving rise to the possibility of London finishing the season in first place one game behind Ottawa. A Senators split of their final four games, combined with a Tecumsehs sweep of their Labor Day doubleheader, would leave Doc's boys a game back of Ottawa. But it would also hand them the pennant by virtue of a superior winning percentage, .623 to .621. It was shaping up to be a strange weekend.

In Hull, it poured down rain all day Sunday, and the games between Ottawa and Erie were called off. With that, the balance shifted very slightly in favor of the Senators. Certainly, in the event of a virtual tie atop the standings—which would result from a pair of London wins and a pair of Ottawa losses on Labor Day—the Tecumsehs would still emerge victorious, .623 to .615. But now, because of the Sunday washout, an Ottawa split of its remaining games would trump a

David McDonald is a writer and filmmaker. He lives in Ottawa.

London sweep, and the Senators would capture their third title in three years by perhaps the closest margin in baseball history, .62295 to .62281. That much was relatively clear.

But outside there lingered a major element of uncertainty. A sluggish low-pressure system had blanketed the lower part of the province for several days, from London all the way to Ottawa, 350 miles to the northeast. What if either team were unable to play one or both holiday games on account of the weather? Again, some of the more exotic meteorological scenarios favored Reisling's teams. If, for example, London won one game on the field and lost the other to the weather, and Ottawa dropped two, the Tecumsehs would finish first by five percentage points. Or, if London swept a pair, and Ottawa lost a single, the Tecumsehs would win by three percentage points. Or, if London didn't play at all and Ottawa lost two, the Tecumsehs would win the pennant by a single percentage point, .616 to .615. Still, any sort of bet on London didn't seem very wise.

But Doc Reisling had something up his sleeve. It was the notion of playing a third game on Labor Day against visiting St. Thomas. Ostensibly, the additional game would be a makeup for a late August rainout with the fifth-place Saints. A third contest would guarantee nothing, but it would provide Doc with an extra piece in this most intricate of pennant endgames: whereas, for example, a doubleheader sweep by the Tecumsehs wouldn't be enough to overcome a Senators split, a tripleheader sweep would be.

At the same time, there were some tripleheader traps Reisling would have to be mindful of. If, for example, London won a pair, while Ottawa played only a single game and lost, the Tecumsehs would be on top by three percentage points. In this event, a third game was to be avoided, because a loss would simply hand the flag back to the Senators. For Reisling then, it would be a tripleheader if necessary, but not necessarily a tripleheader.

But first the Tecumsehs would have to get the blessing of the Saints. St. Thomas, no doubt welcoming an opportunity to pick up a little extra gate money and perhaps also a chance to stick it to Ottawa's overbearing Shaughnessy, agreed to go along with the scheme. Whether Reisling was aware of them or not, there were certainly precedents for desperation tripleheaders, even at the major league level.[6] On September 1, 1890, Bill McGunnigle's Brooklyn Bridegrooms had beaten the hapless Pittsburgh Alleghenys three times on their way to the National League title. And on September 7, 1896, Ned Hanlon's pennant-bound Baltimore Orioles had swept a Labor Day triple bill from the doormat Louisville Colonels. In the minor leagues, games had been played in even greater multiples.[7] On September 15, 1889, Sioux City of the Western Association had swept baseball's first quadrupleheader from visiting St. Joseph. In 1903, the Hudson club of the Hudson River League had also won four in a single day, beating up the Poughkeepsie Giants.

Then there was the rabidly contested New England League pennant race of 1899, which had seen Manchester, in a wild attempt to overtake league-leading Newport, stage a season-finale sextupleheader against Portland. The Manchesters had won all six, including a final-game forfeit when the punching bag Portlanders finally threw in the towel and walked off the field. Rival Newport, meanwhile, had countered with a triple bill of their own, and had swept the Taunton club. In the end, though, an unimpressed league executive had recognized only a single win for each of the contenders, and the league title had gone to Newport.

On Labor Day morning[8] in Ottawa, the rain finally let up, and the Senators, still oblivious of Doc Reisling's gambit, took the field at Lansdowne Park against the sixth-place Peterborough White Caps. Almost immediately, the skies opened up again. There was nothing to do but get the tarps out and wait. In London, the weather lifted in time for the morning game and the Tecumsehs beat the Saints 4-1, behind the solid pitching of Carlos Hammond (10-7).

Back in Ottawa, the rain finally stopped about one o'clock. Shaughnessy, knowing he had to win at least one to nail down the pennant, sent his groundskeeper out to round up 20 gallons of gasoline, which they sloshed over the soggy infield. Then someone tossed a match in, and they burned off some of the damp. When the smoke finally cleared, umpire "Buck" Freeman[9] examined the scorched infield and gave the go-ahead. And with the smell of burnt gasoline hanging in the air, Ottawa's 23-year-old rookie sensation Urban (but everyone called him Herb Shocker[10]) slogged out to the mound in search of his 20th win and the Canadian League championship. The sun even came out for a moment.

In London, Reisling decided to go with his hot hand and brought back first-game winner Hammond to face the Saints in game two. But a tired Hammond faltered early, and sore 19-game winner Bobby Heck had to step in to nail down an 8-3 victory. So far, so good. In Ottawa, the Senators knocked out 14 hits in support of Shocker and beat the White Caps 6-2. And, as far as anyone in the capital knew, the defending champs had just clinched another pennant. Shaughnessy's gamble of starting his ace, Shocker, in the opener appeared to pay off. Now he wouldn't have to count on his last healthy hurler, struggling journeyman Hank Gero, to beat Peterborough flash Louie Schettler (20-12, with a league-leading 174 strikeouts) in the finale. Gero had won just four of ten decisions since being purchased from Brantford at the end of July for $525. Schettler, on the other hand, had won 10 of his last 12 decisions for the second-division White Caps. The former Phillie had already recorded several wins over the Senators that season, including a two-hit shutout in late May.

With Ottawa's victory in game one, there were now three things that would have to happen in order for the Tecumsehs to overtake the Senators. The rain would have to hold off in both cities, the Tecumsehs would have to beat the Saints a third time, and Schettler would have to shut down the Senators.

In the end, all three conditions were met—no rain, a 9-3 London win in game three, and Schettler's continued mastery of the Senators—and yet Doc Reisling's Hail Mary play still fell short. What happened was this: after a couple of scoreless innings in the capital, umpire Freeman decided to call the game—on account of the cold, he said, although it was reportedly no colder than it had been all day. And so ended one of the strangest pennant races in baseball history. With the no-decision, Ottawa had finished at 76-45 (.628), compared to London's 72-43 (.626). Shaughnessy and the jubilant Senators adjourned to a hotel to get warm.

"It is more likely that Shag had cold feet when he called off that second game in Ottawa," the *London Free Press* said in speculating on who was really responsible for the truncated match between the Senators and the White Caps. The rival *London Advertiser* grudgingly conceded: "Shag is a foxy boy and if you win any pennants from him, you have to sit up nights and dope out a fancy line of stunts to get ahead of him."

Whether it was Shaughnessy's foxiness that saved the day, or just dumb luck, is not clear. Certainly, the Ottawa skipper would have kept himself apprised as best he could of the goings-on in London over the course of that final day. But at what point he might have become aware of Doc Reisling's tripleheader is not clear. The evidence at least suggests that

Shaughnessy realized Reisling's ruse about the second inning of game two, and, understandably anxious about the prospect of beating Schettler, he somehow prevailed upon umpire Freeman to call it a day. Otherwise, why start a second game at all, especially one the participants understood to be meaningless?

At least, that's the way the *Free Press* saw it. Their writer complained about the appearance of "fix up baseball" in Ottawa. He pointed to the fact that "there was no complaint of cold weather during the playing of the first game," and that none seemed to arise until "the discovery of what a loss to Peterboro [sic] in the second game meant."

The speculation was rendered moot the following day, however. Canadian League president James Fitzgerald,[11] perhaps miffed that Reisling hadn't sought his blessing to play three, announced that London's final game would not count in the standings. The club's record would be rolled back to 71-43. Fitzgerald cited a little known rule of organized baseball, apparently inspired by the infamous New England League sextupleheader of 1899, that no team could play more than two games on one day.[12]

Had Reisling appealed to the league beforehand, Fitzgerald might well have done what National League President John Heydler did six years later when he overruled the two-game limit to allow Pittsburgh to host Cincinnati in the major leagues' most recent triple bill. The October 2, 1920, triple was staged to decide who would take home the share of World Series money allotted in those years to the club finishing third in the standings. However, the Reds quickly snuffed the day's drama by beating the Pirates 13-4 in the first game to clinch third spot. The teams then clowned their way through two more, now meaningless, games. Somewhere, Doc Reisling must have been grinding his teeth.

Notes:

1. The Canadian League was founded in 1911 as an all-Ontario, Class D outfit. Thanks to the addition of larger centers Ottawa (1912) and Toronto (1914), the Canadian operated as a Class B league in 1914 (Class A being the highest minor league designation of the day). Or, at least, it thought it did. The league was apparently unaware that it was supposed to remit an increase in dues to the National Association for its upgrade to Class B—at least until it received only Class C fees for the players it lost in the 1914 draft. The league decided not to press the issue because it felt it would be better off operating as a more modest Class C circuit in subsequent years. However, the economic upheaval of the Great War caused the league to suspend play after 1915. It never resumed.

2. The London team, also called the Cockneys in the press, took their nickname from Tecumseh, war chief of the Shawnees, who allied his people with Britain and her Canadian colony against the United States in the War of 1812.

Tecumseh was killed in the Battle of the Thames in southwestern Ontario in 1813. Among Doc Reisling's Tecumsehs was one future hall of famer, speedy, hard-hitting (.325 in 1914) center fielder Edmund Lamy, the world professional speed-skating champ. Lamy was elected to Speed Skating Hall of Fame in Minneapolis a year before his death in 1962.

3. Two more hall of famers—this time Hockey Hall of Famers—were involved with Shaughnessy in the ownership of the Ottawa Senators. They were Frank Ahearn and Tommy Gorman, later elected to the Hockey Hall in the builders category. The Senators began play in 1912, and, in four seasons in the Canadian League, they won four pennants, making them probably the most successful short-lived franchise in baseball history.

4. An eventful period during which Canada declared war on Germany (August 4), and Babe Ruth hit his only minor league home run, at Toronto's Hanlan's Point park (September 5).

5. Ties being a far more common result in the days before ballpark lighting allowed late-running games to be played to a conclusion.

6. Thanks to SABR members Mike Emeigh, Joe Haardt, Clifford Blau, and Dave Smith for providing information on major league tripleheaders.

7. Thanks to SABR members Mike Welsh, Bill Deane, Wayne McElreavy, and Josh Raisen for providing information on minor league multipleheaders.

8. Doubleheaders in the Canadian League were generally morning-afternoon, separate-admission games.

9. Not *the* Buck Freeman, the two-time major league home run champ, but one of a number of Freemans in baseball in those years—including at least four major leaguers—who, thanks to the old slugger, sported a secondhand nickname.

10. Shocker spent one more season in Ottawa, as the Senators cruised to a fourth pennant, this time by a comfortable 12½-game margin. Shocker won 19 and lost 10 in 1915, with a league-leading 303 innings and 186 strikeouts, and was drafted that fall by the Yankees.

11. Fitzgerald was also the "sporting editor" of the *Toronto Telegram*.

12. Probably the last tripleheader in organized baseball was played August 13, 1972, when the Cocoa Astros of the Florida State League swept the Orlando Twins, with Eleno Cuén throwing a no-hitter in the middle game.

BOXING AND BASEBALL *For generations before Billy Martin socked a marshmallow salesman, the sports of baseball and boxing were entwined. Back in 1883, then reigning heavyweight champion John L. Sullivan, pitched the first of several exhibition games, winning 20-15 against a semipro team at New York's old Polo Grounds. He had three hits and made four of his team's 10 errors. Critics also charged that he deliberately served up gopher balls, but Sullivan pocketed a hefty $1,595 from the gate. Sullivan's boxing career ended in 1892, when Gentleman Jim Corbett knocked him out to win the heavyweight crown. Later, the portly pugilist was an ardent Boston Americans fan, and he would occasionally sit in the dugout during American League games.*

In 1894, Corbett defended his heavyweight crown against Englishman Charlie Mitchell, knocking him out in the third round. The referee for the match was "Honest John" Kelly, a former major league player, manager, and umpire, who later refereed two more championship fights. A contemporary of Kelly's was Tim Hurst, who managed the 1898 St. Louis Nationals to a last place finish. Hurst was also a boxing referee, matchmaker, and promoter.

Gentleman Jim Corbett was a great gate attraction, as well as a good ballplayer. He made appearances in 37 minor league games, the first in 1894. He played first base for a Scranton team in an Eastern League victory over Buffalo, collecting 2 hits and 2 RBI. His brother Joe, a future major league pitcher, played shortstop. The champ appeared in another 36 minor league games, the last for Binghamton in 1901. Like his heavyweight predecessor, Corbett attended many major leagues, but at the Polo Grounds.

A Chicago grand jury in 1920 indicted former featherweight champ Abe Attell as a go-between in the Black Sox scandal. In the minds of many this confirmed the unsavory character of boxing. Two years later, AL president Ban Johnson persuaded AL owners to prohibit boxing matches in their parks. The National League declined to go along with it.

In January 1930, Commissioner Landis banned boxing for all baseball players following the brief boxing career of White Sox first sacker Art "Whataman" Shires. Shires lost a desultory five-rounder to Chicago Bears center George "The Brute" Trafton, but it was his challenge to Hack Wilson that purportedly prompted the ban. Shires fought several suspected bouts that resulted in his being suspended by the boxing commissions of 32 states.

The brother of Dodgers first sacker Dolf Camilli was killed in the ring fighting future heavyweight champ Max Baer. Camilli fought under the name of Frankie Campbell. Another future heavyweight champ was offered a contract by the Chicago Cubs, but Rocky Marciano's mother refused to allow him to sign it saying, "I didn't raise my son to be a catcher." Years later, however, the Milwaukee Braves signed Peter Marchegiano, Rocky's brother, to a minor league contract. — JIM CHARLTON

The Sporting News During WWII

by Eric Moskowitz

"No nation that has had as intimate contact with baseball as the Japanese," *The Sporting News* wrote in an editorial shortly after Pearl Harbor, "could have committed the vicious, infamous deed of . . . December 7, 1941, if the spirit of the game had ever penetrated their yellow hides."[1] Today, 60 years removed, the writing is racist and the message ridiculous, promoting a notion that a collective national understanding of a game, even baseball, could instill a value code that would morally preclude a nation from a military sneak attack. It's ludicrous and jingoist. And it's consistent with the wartime tone and agenda of America's baseball newspaper.

Sandwiched around Pearl Harbor, 1941 and 1942 form the period when America first confronted the second World War, a time of preparation and patriotism, unbridled enthusiasm and uncertainty. They were also the final years when *The Sporting News* covered only one sport, a time when the so-called "Bible of Baseball" presented the nation's pastime as both essentially American and essential to America's war efforts.[2] This article will examine the different ways in which *The Sporting News* (hereafter TSN) conveyed that message in the year before and after America's entrance into the fighting, embracing a tone and style aimed at selling the game of baseball as patriotic and vital—a time when the pages of TSN were laden with an air of importance, for the idea that baseball might be fatuous would mean a threat to the survival of the game and the very newspaper itself during wartime.

Sportswriter Alfred Henry Spink founded TSN in St. Louis in 1886, covering everything from American baseball to British wrestling. By the turn of the century, though, TSN had turned itself exclusively to baseball, establishing a position not merely as documenter of and commentator on the game, but also as essential player in the inner workings of the national pastime; by the 1920s it had become sufficiently ingrained as part of the establishment to earn the sobriquet "Bible of Baseball."[3] As promoter of the sport, it offered news, features, and commentary on baseball in a self-conscious fashion; the front-page flag billed it as "The Base Ball Paper of the World," while a box in the upper corner sandwiched BASEBALL between "From All Points of Compass" and "News • Gossip • Comment." In the pre-television dawn of U.S. involvement in the war, TSN was unquestionably the leading source for all things baseball. And as such, it relied entirely on baseball for its own existence.

As the war approached, professional baseball faced an apparent crossroads; after years of struggling to recover from the throes of the Depression and achieve stability, 1941 finally saw a return to the kind of prosperous season that major league baseball had known during the Roaring Twenties. Now, though, baseball's immediate future was in question: How

---

Eric Moskowitz is a newspaper reporter at the Concord Monitor *in New Hampshire. In 2001, he graduated Phi Beta Kappa from the University of Pennsylvania, earning honors in American History.*

would the sport handle the inevitable loss of many of its top players? Would interest in baseball wane during the war? Would it be able to continue during wartime as a nonessential industry? TSN wasted little time in embracing the war effort, seizing an opportunity to transmit a message of baseball as an integral part of American culture and a key to patriotism; at the same time, it promoted the sport as something not merely tangental to the war effort but crucial to an American and Allied victory.

Examining issues of TSN one full year before Pearl Harbor reveals some foreshadowing of what would lie ahead. An unsigned editorial on December 19, 1940, stated that:

> Baseball, like the remainder of the nation, faces many grave and troublesome problems. It casts an anxious eye toward Europe's battlefields, it realizes the delicate situation in Asia and it hears rumors and threats that on some front the United States will be drawn into an international war. Already it is preparing to send many of its finely trained young men to the colors for a year's training in the nation's armed forces, wants to do its duty, willing and to the full. It joins with the country as the selection of its motto, "Be Prepared."[4]

Although the grammar in the third sentence is awkward, the message is clear: Baseball is aligned with the rest of the nation in its fears and concerns;

baseball must gird itself to lose many of its stars to the looming war; and baseball is ready to do its patriotic duty to the fullest.

This kind of pro-baseball propaganda was hardly confined to TSN's op-ed page. Simply by reporting the deeds of baseball players and personnel, TSN was able to let the game do the talking, with the news stories selling the game as patriotic without need for editorializing. In January 1942, after America had entered the war, Tigers manager Delmar Baker faced the prospect of preparing for the season without knowing which members of his team would be showing up for spring training and which players would be drafted; rather than complain, though, he accepted the facts in an upbeat manner. "The country comes first," he said. "We'll have to do the best we can with the boys who are left after the government's needs are taken care of—and no squawkin'."[5] Likewise, those players eligible for the draft but deferred or rejected—particularly before direct U.S. involvement, when 4-F medical rejections were far more common—were quick to assert that the army was where they wanted to be. Giants outfielder Morrie Arnovich, removing his bridge work as evidence,

J. G. Taylor Spink, publisher of The Sporting News *from 1914-1962.*

maintained that he had actually tried to volunteer but was rejected for his lousy teeth. "He never at any time asked for a deferment and, on the contrary, he tried to enlist. As a Giant, he doesn't like being called a *dodger*, particularly a draft dodger."[6] Finally, TSN depicted baseball players as patriots through their on-field actions as well. Legendary foul ball hitter Luke Appling, a TSN writer predicted, would make "life brighter for the [soldiers], sailors and marines" thanks to the American League's policy of collecting foul balls and sending them to the camps: "Now that there will be a worthy cause to support, you can depend on 'Butterfoot' to go 'all out' and chip off probably a boxful every time he comes up."[7] Worthy? Collecting foul balls amounted to a highly visible but minimally efficient act on the part of the American League; simply shipping boxes of balls to the camp without the production of collecting foul balls would have been simpler and easier but far less dramatic. Still, TSN found plenty of opportunities to mention the donations.

More often than not, though, TSN did not simply report and present the news so much as massage and mold it in baseball's image. In some cases, this meant editorials that were prescriptive in nature. On March 6, 1941, TSN wrote, "The draft, like rain, falls on the just and unjust, on those prepared for it and those unprepared, and baseball, as one that stands or falls on the attitude of public opinion, cannot and must not ask for special favors."[8] The following year, during the war, it advised players not to expect the usual sympathy from fans when butting heads with stingy owners: "The fans of this country are definitely in no mood for holdout squabbles. The fans are in no frame of mind for reading about extended scraps relating to sums which these fans could not earn in five years— some of them in a decade. LET'S HAVE NO MORE OF THIS NONSENSE!"[9] At times these advisories dipped into the realm of the sentimental or maudlin. In one of the few signed editorials by publisher J.G.T. Spink, fans were asked not to be too harsh in their outbursts should a player make a gaffe, as his mind may be on other, more pressing matters. Rather, fans should be appreciative of baseball's war efforts and "be glad to accept the run of [the] 1942 baseball season as the product of the gods." Thus, "look well at these heroes, for they go. They go to make a fairer, a brighter, a safer world. . . . They go, hoping to return. But if, on some distant shore, they meet their Maker—and so many doubtless will—Baseball will do no less than canonize the spirit with which these combatants went from fields of peace to the charnel house."[10] Spink's editorial appeal is mawkish and overdone. But while it may not have weathered the decades well, it must be considered that such lines, when they rolled hot off the presses, undoubtedly set the hairs standing on the back of more than a few readers' necks. Whether Spink believed this in his soul and bled it out through his typewriter, or simply thought it made good copy, the intention is clear—to elevate baseball onto a sacred, God-given pedestal, a sport played by men devoted to their country.

This prescriptive piece from Spink broaches the realm of another slate of TSN editorials, those crafted to equate baseball with patriotism and make it seem integrally associated with everything that is good and just about America and being American. Likewise, TSN promoted a sense that baseball was duty bound to do whatever was asked of it and more to aid the war effort. In an editorial written immediately after Pearl Harbor, TSN exclaimed: "The message—to which all in the game, from the majors to the smallest minors, will give their whole-hearted endorsement—will be: 'Uncle Sam, we are at your command!'"[11] In an editorial on April 9, 1942, TSN touched upon a theme it would revisit frequently— that baseball could provide both entertainment for the American people at home and a healthy, clean diversion for soldiers overseas, particularly as an alternative to the vices which might distract young men away from home for the first time. As TSN was wont to do all so frequently during this period, the editorial utilized capital letters for emphasis: "BASEBALL CAN PLAY A USEFUL ROLE IN THIS WAR. THIS IS NOT MERELY A TRITE WINDUP TO AN EDITORIAL IN A PUBLICATION DEVOTED TO BASEBALL. IT IS A SINCERE CONCLUSION BASED ON INCONTROVERT-IBLE FACT."[12] Clearly, TSN was serious about promoting the perception that baseball had a duty in the war, yet this editorial offered little by way of fact or evidence. The capital letters make the piece seem particularly self-conscious, as if TSN knew what it needed to do, and knew that there were those who might criticize baseball, but could nonetheless not come up with concrete reasons; instead, they simply dressed up and reinforced the same message of baseball as vital.

In a similar vein, while TSN had long been known as the "Bible of Baseball" for its reporting on the hallowed pastime, during the war it actually went so far as to paint baseball with the brush of religion. But TSN began conjuring up an image of baseball as

TWO UNCLE SAM TEAMS THAT COULD MAKE MAJORS SAY 'UNCLE'

sacred and virtuous and even blessedly thankful without calling attention to the change; take, for example, this editorial from 1942's Thanksgiving issue, in which "Baseball" thanks:

> A benevolent Providence which placed the game's natal setting . . . in this, our grand America. Just think of the situation if somebody in Germany had evolved this sport and today its virtues were confined largely to the terrain over which Adolf and his Gestapo terrorize. Baseball thanks a heavenly Protector for having given it to America, and to the sort of people who are in this, our country. . . . Baseball thanks the fans, the players, the club owners, the baseball writers. . . . Baseball thanks an all-pervading Providence for its clean face, its clean body, its splendor and its outlook, its abiding faith in God. . . . And as Baseball thanks the Lord and thanks America, this great country of ours thanks our Heavenly Father for the glories of its achievements, the justice of our cause, the might of the right—and Baseball.[13]

Here, Spink & Co. have elevated the game of baseball into Baseball, a proper noun, and one which has the ability to issue its own thanks to a higher authority. Furthermore, the piece acknowledges the importance of everyone involved, from fan up through sportswriter and all the way to owner, not wanting to alienate any readers—each one a current or prospective subscriber. In some senses, the message is a bit ambiguous. Is TSN thankful for the fact that baseball had not been squandered on Germany, never to reach beyond a Third Reich divide to the United States, or is TSN suggesting that had the game been played in Germany, a set of cultural values and mores might have developed that would have prevented Hitler's rise? Of course, prompting the reader to scour for subtext was never the point. This was all about wrapping baseball in a distinctly American banner,

advancing the notion that a game, in other hands, might have meant national virtues that would have steered the world in a more peaceful direction.

In addition to presenting baseball as a positive diversion for the troops overseas or a morale booster for the home front, TSN also made apparent efforts to trumpet the game as a force more closely linked even to the actual fighting effort. In an April 2, 1942, editorial entitled "The Game and That Old Navy Spirit," TSN quoted Jack Troy, sports editor of the *Atlanta Constitution,* who said, after watching a game at the Jacksonville, FL, Naval Air Station: "AND I KNOW NOW FOR CERTAIN THAT THOSE WHO CRITICIZE BASEBALL JUST DON'T KNOW WHAT THEY'RE TALKING ABOUT." The editorial clearly highlighted how the game provided entertainment for the soldiers and also built their spirit. But this was more than a mere matter of morale, as Troy wrote, "They'll carry this same spirit into battle—and the Japs will remember Pearl Harbor."[14] In yet another editorial, this one coming almost a year after Pearl Harbor, TSN endorsed baseball for the well-suited physical training it provided, citing an Italian "broadcast explaining the debacle in North Africa," which declared the "Americans threw too many baseballs." This was "grudging tribute from an enemy," explaining how "skill developed on the diamond has been transformed into hitting and pitching power, as well as teamwork, that will help our soldiers, sailors and marines contribute to victory for the United States."[15] Could the Americans' baseball training have meant the difference in battle? Impossible to prove, but unlikely. Still, the mere fact is that this Italian quote snippet surfaced, and TSN embraced it as a means of heralding baseball as integral to preparing American soldiers for war.

In line with this notion, one also discovers a wealth

Baseball thanks an all-pervading Providence for its clean face, its clean body, its splendor and its outlook, its abiding faith in God. Baseball knows that to America belongs only the best, and it likes to think that it is a vital part of that best.

And as Baseball thanks the Lord and thanks America, this great country of ours thanks our Heavenly Father for the glories of its achievements, the justice of our cause, the might of the right—and Baseball.

•   •   •

of headlines, stories, and feature photos that on one hand described baseball in military terms and on the other wrote about the military effort (and players turned soldiers) in terms once employed only for baseball. In the case of the former, this was done both by analogy and by direct description. For example, the lead to a spring training story in the pre-war year of '41 likened baseball's biggest-ever spring training program to "Uncle Sam['s being] engaged in the biggest preparedness campaign in the history of the nation."[16] Meanwhile, TSN frequently employed headlines like "New Pelican Leader Has Army of Backers," or "Conscripted for Service • In Game's Big Tent," to preface such innocuous and non-war-related stories as the hiring of a popular new manager or a bevy of minor league call-ups.[17] On the flip side, by 1942 one item had seemingly become a weekly fixture—a feature photo of an ex-player in military uniform accompanied by a caption employing baseball terminology to describe war. For example, under the headline "Hitting High in Tough Loop," TSN ran a photo of former Senator Buddy Lewis leaning against a fighter jet; he wrote to his teammates to tell them he was "aiming at a new slugging record against the Japs." TSN added, "Lewis doesn't see how the little brown men can be any harder to hit than some of the American League's southpaw chunkers," and that Lewis will be taking to the sky in flight school as his teammates try to "take off from the sixth rung" of the American League ladder.[18]

The single most classic example of mixing baseball and military metaphors, so to speak, occurred in the January 22, 1942, issue, in which President Roosevelt's now famous "Green Light" letter urging organized baseball to continue during the war was reprinted front and center. The banner headline, "Stay In There and Pitch—F.D.R.," ran across the top of the page, while "Player of the Year" and "'Green Light' from No. 1 Umpire Rallies Game Throughout Nation" prefaced accompanying stories, celebrating Roosevelt while beating the analogy into overuse.[19] Meanwhile, the quintessential example of this type of writing being employed not just for a headline but for a standard news result can be found in the write-up of the fund-raising all-star extravaganza held between the American League All-Stars and a team of service all-stars in 1942, which the AL team won 5-0. Frederick Lieb's final sentence reads: "As for the servicemen—they lost, but their training had been for a bigger game! Their victory will come later." This story actually embodies several of TSN's tactics; Lieb

wrote, "The game, and its attending spectacle, proved conclusively the value of baseball as a wartime activity," and also its patriotic significance: "As though it were a contagion, one could feel the patriotic fervor of the entire 65,000 . . . it made one murmur to one's self: 'I'm proud to be an American!'"[20]

One of the most interesting aspects revealed in studying TSN over this period is the way in which the publication, prior to U.S. entry into the war, tried to present baseball as something uniquely American that served to differentiate the U.S. from war-torn nations. In April 1941, before the U.S. entered the war, TSN ran an opening-day editorial proclaiming: "War broke loose on many fronts in America this week—war in which no quarter is asked and none expected—but instead of a war of rifles, bayonets, cannon, machine guns and airplanes, it is a battle of bats and balls. . . . That is the American way—the Baseball way. . . . God has blessed America in many ways and, happily, baseball is one of His numerous manifestations . . . it offers a common meeting place, where freedom of expression is unfettered, class distinctions are leveled and rivalries can be settled without bloodshed or slaughter of innocents. PLAY BALL!"[21]

But then the United States went to war, and TSN did not skip a beat, reconciling the fact that America was now involved in both a "battle of bats and balls" and a "war of rifles" by promoting baseball as something the Japanese could and would never understand but the people of the Allied nations could doubtless grow to appreciate. This Japanese situation, however, presented baseball-equals-American advocates with a particularly vexing dilemma. American missionaries had introduced the game to Japan in the 1870s; by the early 1930s the Japanese had erected huge facilities for their college teams rivaling all but Yankee Stadium in size, and even TSN was proclaiming that Japanese acceptance of baseball proved "we wear the same clothes, play the same game and entertain the same thoughts. In other words that we are all brothers."[22] Post-Pearl Harbor, TSN's editors directed a new spin:

> In this strange land, where militarists are as strong as the old Samurai of the Hermit Kingdom before Commodore Perry, and where college-educated men believe their humorless, sallow-faced Emperor to be the Son of Heaven, baseball became the outstanding sport of the colleges. . . . Having a natural catlike agility, the Japanese took naturally to the diamond

pastime. They became first-class fielders and made some progress in pitching, but because of their smallness of stature, they remained feeble hitters . . . it was always a sore spot with this cocky race that their batsmen were so outclassed by the stronger, more powerful American sluggers. For despite the brusqueness and braggadocio of the militarists, Japanese cockiness hid a national inferiority complex.

The editorial continues, saying that in retrospect, "this treacherous Asiatic land was really never converted to baseball," citing the evidence that the Japanese never grasped the concept of good-natured American bench jockeying and umpire razzing— apparently, as TSN claims here, "the very soul of baseball." The editorial suggests that this is much preferred to "stab[bing] an 'honorable opponent' in the back" or "crush[ing] out his brains while he is asleep." Finally, it concludes that although the Japanese may have acquired some baseball skill, they were never touched by the soul of the game, because (as stated earlier) "no nation that has had as intimate contact with baseball as the Japanese, could have committed

the vicious, infamous deed."[23] This is pure racist pap, a revisionist history reinterpreting the effects and questioning the embrace of baseball in Japan. But it also served as a powerful way for TSN to instill pride among readers that baseball was ingrained in the spirit of Americans but proved a maddening enigma to the treacherous Japanese.

Meanwhile, TSN frequently asserted the growing understanding of the game among Allied nations. Under the British banner, Canada entered World War II well before Pearl Harbor. Thus, in May 1941, TSN revealed that Montreal Royals games had a decidedly military flavor, with hundreds of soldiers in attendance. Air Vice-Marshal L. S. Reader said, "[Sport] is the life of our people, stands for everything we're fighting for, and its value right now can't be overestimated," adding, "I don't think anything appeals to [our men] like baseball."[24] Furthermore, TSN published a slew of letters from British readers, some writing on scraps of wallpaper, others mentioning bombs falling overhead, who had become avid fans of the game and cherished the copies of TSN that made it through to England. One classic three-paragraph sketch, set in a front-page box, told how RAF squadron leader James G. Hanks had taken in a Buffalo Bison game; catching on quickly, he was cheering, "Well done, blighter!" by the seventh inning—the first time he had cheered, or let go of his emotions, since the war started."[25]

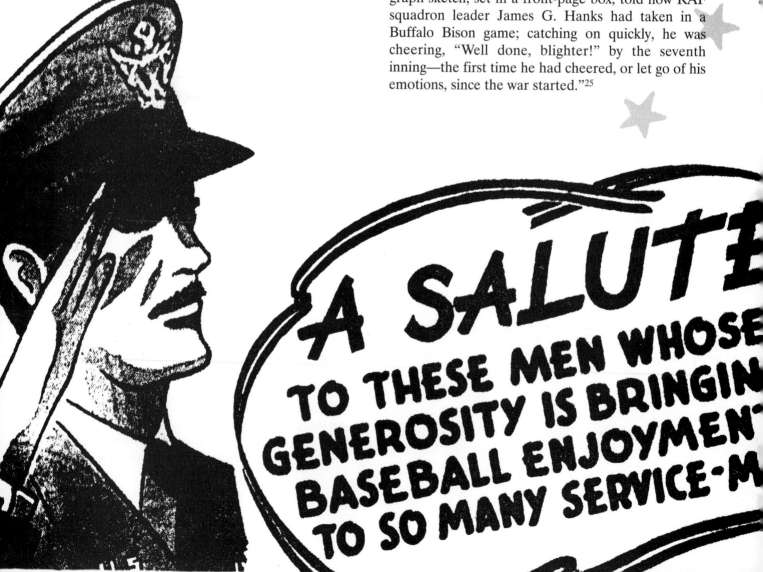

During this period TSN's editorials typically did not engage in any true editorializing, any defense or criticism of an issue. By and large, they either praised something baseball had done, predicted what would happen, or prescribed some course of action that baseball should, and most likely would, take. On occasion, though, TSN's editorials did venture into a defensively critical mode, springing to attention if anyone dared suggest that baseball was not of utmost consequence to either winning the war or feeling patriotically American. Immediately after Pearl Harbor, Cleveland fireballer Bob Feller enlisted in the Navy. According to TSN, some "arm-chair critics" saw fit to snipe at Feller nonetheless, grumbling that he "failed to select an especially hazardous branch of the service." Given that Feller enlisted for training as a physical instructor, one would think it was a legitimate gripe to suggest that his status as a major league star may have facilitated his entry into a non–life-endangering role. But TSN wrote: "Perhaps these criticisms are to be expected . . . about those who have attained prominence in any walk of life. Some persons resent any success attained by others and search for flaws in their armor." The piece went on to paint baseball in a humble, just-doing-its-duty light, seeking no cheers or expecting any "unjustified criticism of the patriotic efforts of its members."[26]

As stated above, on July 7, 1942, the American League All-Stars met a team of service all-stars, with Feller pitching, in a contest at Cleveland that drew 62,000 fans and netted $193,000 for the Army and Navy Aid Funds.[27] But to former heavyweight boxing champion Gene Tunney, then serving as the director of the Navy's physical fitness program, such activity was purely fatuous; he labeled these Army-Navy sports extravaganzas as "athletic boondoggling" and a return to an "era of wonderful nonsense." While it would be hard to argue against such a tremendous fund-raiser and public morale booster, a practical thinker like Tunney could conceivably have viewed a group of soldiers spending valuable time flying around the country to play games as frivolous or in-essential to the war cause. Nonetheless, TSN thoroughly skewered the once venerable champ, mocking him for having recently delivered "a violent pronunciamento against the humble cigarette" which so many millions of troops cherished; they also suggested that "the Commander" would be better served spending his time mastering navigation and naval combat than wrongly painting service athletes as shirk-

ers of duty.[28]

Finally, TSN never failed to barrage the reader with a bevy of subtle and not so subtle house ads, promotional gimmicks, staged photos, and press releases. In a moment of pure, unadulterated propaganda, TSN ran a small box on the bottom of its back page just two weeks after Pearl Harbor, entitled "$50,000 Lick by Babe." Explaining how the ultimate baseball icon, Babe Ruth, had purchased defense bonds, the "story" said, "Babe Ruth drove another home run out of the park . . . one worth $50,000," and featured the following (obviously manufactured) quote from the Babe: "One safe and sure way of knocking the other boys out of the league is to buy defense bonds."[29] TSN also frequently ran reproductions of self-serving letters, such as the following: from Hall of Famer Ty Cobb, calling it the "only real baseball publication we've had," and signing up for a lifetime subscription at the special rate of $25; and from Hank Greenberg, a hero TSN had previously milked as the subject of as many as four stories a week during his initial conscription, writing once to say how much the troops cherished TSN and again later to sign up for his own lifetime subscription. At times TSN filled space in random sections—between box scores, perhaps, or set off by a border within an unrelated story—with photos or thumbnail notes that were not quite house ads but not quite true news either. Take, for example, the feature photo on June 4, 1942, of baseball equipment juxtaposed over a warehouse; the headline stated

"Game's Gift to Fighters," while the image itself bore the words: "For Our Armed Forces: Baseball Equipment Fund." The caption told how the recreation needs of the fighting men are not being forgotten, thanks to organized baseball's Ball and Bat Fund. Examination of the photo, however, reveals that all of the products can be identified—Hillerich & Bradsby Louisville Sluggers, baseballs by Wilson and Spalding—as frequent advertisers in TSN; meanwhile, TSN-produced rule books were also included in the photo of items being mailed.[30] Technically, such a photo is newsworthy in the sense that it feeds readers information about the Ball and Bat Fund, but there is also an underlying ulterior motive, innocent or not—that hyping patriotism was good for the game and consequently healthy for TSN; images of sponsors and of TSN itself were also far from harmful to the publication. Last, TSN continuously ran promotions aimed both at bolstering its image as a desirable propagator of feel-good American patriotism and at improving its circulation figures. Promoted as "How We Can Do Our Bit," TSN offered readers a chance to order gift subscriptions at reduced rates for soldiers; on November 20, 1941, atop the front page, on a line normally alluding to a story inside, TSN advertised that a free carton of Chesterfield cigarettes would be sent with every gift subscription headed to a military base; and a full-page ad in 1942 aimed at getting companies, teams, and organizations to order blanket subscriptions covering all of their men who had or would enter the service featured testimonies from base librarians on how much the soldiers enjoyed reading TSN.

It is clear that TSN embraced the war effort from the earliest moments of American preparation through the country's full-fledged entrance into the fighting. Beginning with the first volunteers from the professional ranks and the impact of conscription on those ball players with low draft numbers, TSN began running a regular column updating the whereabouts and happenings of baseball players and the military, entitled "From Army Front." By January 29, 1942, with the U.S. at war, the column had been replaced for good by a full-page dubbed "In the Service." The same format as "From Army Front" was maintained with the addition of several new features. Every week TSN ran one or two photos of former ball players now in the service; space was also devoted to an increasing number of war-related baseball briefs and, on occasion, a lengthy feature looking back at baseball, patriotism and World War I for those nostalgic older fans.

But the war's influence on the pages of TSN hardly remained fixed under the "In the Service" banner. A disproportionate number of letters in the "Voice of the Fan" section, even those free of war content, seemed to come from servicemen. Perhaps this is just a reflection of the demographics of TSN readers, many of whom were young men, and thus many of whom were in the armed forces. But given that when a letter from a soldier was printed, the header would make that known (e.g., an April 10, 1941, letter regarding Grover Cleveland Alexander was prefaced: "Soldier Goes to Bat for Alex"), while TSN never tagged "Civilian" above the equivalent letters, it is more than an educated guess to suggest that TSN favored running letters from soldiers, war content or not, because it played to the image of baseball, and consequently TSN, as a diversion and a morale booster at the military base.

It is worth noting that in 1942 every single issue but one had at least one editorial relating to the war, baseball's duty, or patriotism; that one war-free page came on August 6, 1942, when the lead editorial was a lengthy piece entitled "No Good Raising the Race Issue," which stated that baseball was better off without integration because the current system was satisfactory—integration would only undermine black businesses in the form of the Negro Leagues while creating inevitable riots when so many blacks and whites came together. The irony here is thick; these same editors so valiantly trumpeting patriotism and making claims of baseball as a God-given blessing, of baseball epitomizing America's greatness as a land of democracy, and of baseball serving as notice of our stark differences from the dreaded, narrow-minded Axis peoples, are also casting their vote for the maintenance of a Jim Crow, "separate but equal" America. In an unaware editorial less than two months later (one Spink himself wrote entitled, "Look Well at These Heroes, for They Go") TSN praised baseball players going off to war; Spink wrote "[they] go to make sure the playgrounds of the future, that men may not be slaves and Lincoln's Emancipation Proclamation may envelop the white races too, as well."

What, then, should one make of this particular case of hypocrisy? What about other, lesser contradictions appearing in TSN during this period? Alternately, the newspaper condemned publications using photographs depicting ballplayers holding bats as if they were rifles, then ran a cartoon of its own depicting Ted Williams in this very pose, and then later ran an almost identical editorial condemning photos of that nature.[31] Likewise, some of the claims they made—that night ball games drawing 30,000 people were conservation-minded because the lights consumed less electricity than would 30,000 people at home all using reading lamps; that being at a modern stadium was safer than being at home in the event of an air raid—seemed to be trying too hard to make baseball appear in line with the war effort on the home front.[32]

Was it all just a journalistic charade? The defensive nature of some of the writing suggests that the TSN editors were well aware of the potential threat of baseball being deemed inessential to the war effort; furthermore, the TSN staff worked calculatedly not only to promote the game but to ensure their own livelihood. After all, if baseball was to suddenly take on the stigma of insignificance, of being frivolous in a time of war, and the game were to be put on hold, TSN would have no reason to exist. It was in the best—and only—interest of TSN to promote baseball as integral to American identity, as a key to maintaining morale on the home front, and as a consequential piece in the formula aimed at winning the war. Helping to establish baseball's validity would solidify the publication's claim to existence during the war; constantly trumpeting a voice of patriotism could also boost readers' morale and lead those newsstand purchasers to feel good enough to opt for subscriptions. Take TSN's "how we can do our bit" campaign; while undoubtedly patriotic, such direction to readers could also be construed as a calculated maneuver to tug at the reader's patriotic strings and lead to increased subscription sales, for fear of a reader missing the next installment on how to aid the war effort through the national pastime.

But the mere act of documenting TSN in the early years of the war does not necessarily mean to condemn it, not by any means. If there was an ulterior motive at play, it was a love of the game of baseball. Through the lenses of history, the writing seems over the top, even comically so at times. It veered into ugliness and racism, in the name of baseball and America. But this reader believes that the editors and writers firmly believed in and stood behind what they were printing. A true passion for the game of baseball pours forth from the dusty old pages, a spirit that cannot accurately be conveyed here through selective quoting and extraction but which comes through in viewing the entirety of the newspaper. Though the prose was often exaggerated, the pages of TSN in 1941 and 1942 form a gold mine of baseball history and literature, rich in heartfelt infatuation with the game. Did the writers actually buy into the extremist nature of what they were writing when it came to Japanese baseball and Pearl Harbor? That can't be surmised from the text itself. But it should not be forgotten that the same passages that seem ludicrous and offensive today could well have raised goose bumps on the flesh, and put stars and stripes in the eyes, of readers during the war.

At times TSN's rhetoric capitalized on a hatred of the enemy as subhuman, but it also was predicated on a sense of baseball as divine gift. Yes, the writers of TSN depended on baseball for their livelihood and relied on transmitting pro-America, pro-baseball propaganda, but that does not mean that it must be dismissed as phony. There is a reason that these men were writing about baseball for TSN; they cared about the game sufficiently to make a life of it. More than that, although TSN required baseball to stay afloat, some of the words and themes on the sports pages of independent newspapers were no different. As evidence, see the "Scribbled by Scribes" column in TSN that ran every week on page four; decades before the Internet provided access to every major paper in the country, "Scribbled by Scribes" offered a "best of" compilation of poignant excerpts from baseball beat reporters and sports editors at newspapers around the country—pieces culled from papers that reported on all subjects, with wartime circulation figures and revenues hardly tied to a game. And yet across the nation, writers embraced this style of sheer baseball promotion—albeit perhaps with fewer capital letters and exclamation marks—that the reporters and editors of TSN adopted in attempting to elevate the status of the game of baseball as patriotic, as fundamentally American, and as crucial to the Allied effort. And baseball, *The Sporting News* and America survived the war.

Notes:

1. "It's Not the Same Game in Japan," *The Sporting News,* December 18, 1941, p. 4.
2. From the "The Vault: History of the Sporting News" at *The Sporting News* Web site (http://www.sportingnews.com/archives/history/).
3. Ibid.
4. "The Game's Own Unity Program," *The Sporting News,* December 19, 1940, p. 4.
5. "Uncle Sam 'Piloting' Tigers for Present," *Ibid.,* January 1, 1942, p. 6.
6. "Arnovich Sets Fans Right on Army Aims," *Ibid.,* February 27, 1941, p. 3. Italics added for emphasis.
7. "Appling 'Foul' Friend of Service Men," *Ibid.,* January 15, 1942, p. 4.
8. "In the Service of their Country," *Ibid.,* March 6, 1941, p. 4.
9. "Fans in No Mood for Holdout Debates," *Ibid.,* February 26, 1942, p. 4.
10. "Look Well at These Heroes, For They Go," *Ibid.,* September 24, 1942, p. 4.
11. "Uncle Sam, We Are at Your Command!" *Ibid.,* December 11, 1941, p. 4.
12. "Here We Go Again; May Best Teams Win," *Ibid.,* April 9, 1942, p. 4.
13. "The Game Has Cause for Thanks," *Ibid.,* November 26, 1942, p. 4.
14. "The Game and the Old Navy Spirit," *Ibid.,* April 2, 1942, p. 4.
15. "America Threw Too Many Baseballs," *Ibid.,* November 19, 1942, p. 4.
16. *Ibid.,* February 13, 1941, p. 5.
17. *Ibid.,* October 23, 1941, p. 1, and October 9, 1941, p. 5.
18. "Hitting High in Tough Loop," *Ibid.,* April 16, 1942, p. 6.
19. *Ibid.,* January 22, 1942, p. 1.
20. *Ibid.,* July 16, 1942, p. 5.
21. "Battling Begins on the American Front," *Ibid.,* April 17, 1941, p. 4.
22. As quoted in Richard C. Crepeau's *Baseball: America's Diamond Mind 1919-1941* (Orlando: University Presses of Florida, 1980), p. 198. Interestingly, Zoss and Bowman write (p. 98) that National League President John Heydler went so far as to say that he hoped to see a Japanese World Series winner in the near future.
23. "It's Not the Same Game in Japan," *The Sporting News,* December 18, 1941, p. 4.
24. "Montreal Has a Mixed Program; It's Game in Army, Army at Game," *Ibid.,* May 8, 1941, p. 3.
25. "RAF Vet Now a Fan," *Ibid.,* July 9, 1942, p. 1.
26. "Sniping at a Patriotic Action," *Ibid.,* December 25, 1941, p. 4. Surprisingly, TSN did not mention the fact that Feller enlisted only after being deferred from the draft because his father was dying of brain cancer.
27. *Ibid.,* July 16, 1942. To put that figure in perspective, a state-of-the-art Flying Fortress bomber cost $300,000 at the time (according to *Diamonds in the Rough*).
28. "Commander Tunney Shoots Wide of Mark," *The Sporting News,* September 3, 1942, p. 4. Of course, this was an era of smoking naivete, when magazine ads declared, "More doctors recommend Camels than any other brand."
29. "$50,000 Lick by Babe." *Ibid.,* December 25, 1941, p. 12.
30. *Ibid.,* June 4, 1942, p. 11.
31. *Ibid.,* May 1, 1941, p. 4, January 29, 1942, p. 1, and March 12, 1942, p. 4.
32. "Throw the Right Switch," *Ibid.,* June 12, 1941, p. 4, and "In Case of Air Raid," *Ibid.,* February 5, 1942, p. 2.

On April 15, 1918, a disappointing crowd of 7,000 plus turned out on a lovely spring day to see the Boston Red Sox open their season with an easy 7-1 victory over the Philadelphia Athletics. For the third consecutive year Babe Ruth, the American League's best lefthander, drew the opening day assignment, and for the third consecutive year he responded with a well-pitched victory. Ruth allowed just four hits, and the only bad inning he had was the second, when a hit, two walks, and a sacrifice fly gave Philadelphia its only run.

Elmer Myers, loser of thirty-nine games over the previous two seasons, was manager Connie Mack's choice to open for the Athletics. Myers and Willie Adams, who relieved him were touched for nine hits by the Red Sox, including two each by Everett Scott and Harry Hooper. Both of Hooper's hits were doubles.

Fans in Boston remember 1918 as the last time the Red Sox won the World Series. But to most baseball fans, 1918 was the year when Babe Ruth, one of the game's greatest pitchers, began to be Babe Ruth, the game's greatest slugger. The Babe had won twenty-three games in 1916, and twenty-four in 1917. But in 1918 he appeared on the mound in only twenty games, winning thirteen and losing seven, while playing seventy-five games in the outfield and at first base. He hit eleven home runs, which was good enough to tie Tilly Walker of Philadelphia for the league lead.

Making full use of Ruth's hitting ability was the idea of Boston manager Ed Barrow. The United States was fully engaged in World War I in 1918, and Barrow was managing because player-manager Jack Barry was in the service. Because of the war the season was cut short, ending on Labor Day.

The Red Sox with a record of 75-51 won the pennant by two and a half games over Cleveland. In the World Series, which began on September 5, they defeated the Chicago Cubs four games to two. Ruth won two games including a shutout in the opener. Until the Cubs scored against him in the eighth inning of the fourth game, he had set a record of 29⅔ consecutive scoreless innings pitched in the World Series.

In 1919, playing most of his games in the outfield, Ruth hit twenty-nine home runs to establish a new major league record. The following winter the Red Sox sold him to the New York Yankees and the face of baseball changed forever.

— LYLE SPATZ

The Robinsons in Montreal

by Alain Usereau

We didn't feel like we belong with them.
—Lucille and Edgar Méthot,
Jackie and Rachel
Robinson's neighbors in
Montreal in 1946.

Lucille and Edgar Méthot were bundles of nerves the morning of Wednesday, September 3rd 1986, waiting at the corner of DeLorimier and Ontario streets in Montreal. With some help from the Expos, the Méthots were meeting Rachel Robinson, who, with Jackie, lived next to them 40 years ago.

Jackie Robinson and his wife lived at 8232 DeGaspé Street, between Guizot and Jarry. That area is located in the northern part of the city, a predominantly French residential area. The Méthot family was at 8234 and shared a veranda with the brilliant Montreal Royals rookie. In fact, from that very veranda, the Méthot couple could see the flashy limos carrying Jackie's friends stopping in front of their place. They still talk about the day Roy Campanella came in a long white car to visit the Royals' second baseman.

The Méthots were often identified as the French-Canadian family that helped the Robinsons adapt to this new environment in 1946. Numerous Jackie Robinson stories praise the warm welcome and the moral support he got from Montrealers. And each time, their neighbors are mentioned as among the people who helped Jackie to keep it going, while he was breaking the color barrier of organized baseball in the International League.

"The Robinsons were real good people, humble, and they remained so, even after Jackie became a local star," remembered Lucille Méthot. Her husband has another story to support it, as related by Lucille. "Edgar will never forget the day Jackie Robinson came back to Montreal to play in an All-Star game. He was determined to see Jackie, but they met one another in the middle of Ontario Street! Jackie was crossing the street with Campanella and after seeing Edgar, started running towards him in the middle of the street! The tramway almost run them down while they were embracing each other."

After one season in Montreal, Jackie made the team in Brooklyn with the Dodgers. For three or four years, the wives did write to each other before distance and circumstances impeded. "The Robinsons were way too important. We didn't feel like we belonged. That's why I stopped writing" explained Lucille.

It was quite a time for whites to admit that they didn't feel up to par with blacks. But for the Méthots and other residents of the area where Jackie lived, there was no white or black. Just a great athlete and his wife.

"When I think about it, I don't think there was racism here. I never heard of any difficulties that the Robinsons might have had in the neighborhood. People couldn't care less about racism. They brought attention because their social standing was above ours. Financially, we felt they were at ease. We were impressed. Sometimes, they talked about coming back to Montreal. (I was so scared to see them back at home. You know, we are ordinary people. It's rather modest here, at home)," Lucille says.

Lots of things were said and written about the Robinson's adap-

Alain Usereau is a radio journalist for NTR in Montreal, the French audio arm of Canadian Press. He has a degree in mathematics and certificate in journalism, and is a fan of the Expos since their beginning. He has been preparing for their departure for the past ten years.

Jackie Robinson hit .349 in his only minor-league season in 1946. He had just three home runs, his lowest season total.

tation to Montreal. It was said that their children were taken care of by neigbors so they could go out, that they had interpreters among the neighbors to help them in their daily tasks, etc. Nothing is further from the truth. "We were really the only ones to see them regularly. It was normal since we were living in the same building. I remember sewing part of a Rachel's dress, when she was pregnant. The night, we were waiting for them to shake hands before going back in our apartment. Today, we think it was a little foolish to act this way, but we liked them," Lucille relates.

After David's birth, in Los Angeles, the Méthots got a telegram from Jackie the next day. They kept that telegram along with a ball signed by Jackie which reads: "To the Méthots, thanks for all." That ball is not for sale, said Lucille, "not even for a million dollars!"

The Méthots will be remembered as simple people who were fortunate enough to live a great experience in the surroundings of one of the most influential athletes in the history of North American sports. The greatest moment of all came when the Méthots gave the Robinsons a laminated photo of the couple taken in front of the building where they lived. They remember the happiness felt then by the Robinsons.

"We only have good memories. We still see Jackie striding on the street, coming back home. We can see him back from the theater and telling us that he probably didn't understand the movie in French. Jackie really enjoyed romantic movies. With his big black hands, he took our baby and rocked him in his arms. The sad thing is that we never took shots of these moments. Our son reproached us sometimes for this but we had no idea that it would become that significant," Edgar recalls. He has one more regret in that he never asked Jackie for an autographed bat. " I really thought about it, but I was too shy. Even today, I still can not forgive myself for that!"

The Nashville Seraphs, 1895

by Bill Traughber

Like most Southern cities, baseball was introduced to Nashville, Tennessee during the Civil War. With the Union army's occupation of the city in 1962, the troops showed the city's citizens how to play the game of "base ball."

One of the first professional baseball teams in Nashville was the Nashville Seraphs. Nashville also fielded teams in 1885-86 (Americans), 1887 (Blues), and 1893-94 (Tigers). But the 1895 Nashville baseball club, from the original Southern League, won the city's first professional baseball championship.

The Seraphs' 1895 season was controversial, but not necessarily on the field. Protested games and fights with umpires were not uncommon in this era when the national pastime was evolving.

Sulphur Springs Bottoms was an area of Nashville that attracted picnickers on holidays. So named because of the nearby natural spring, which contained sulphur. The odorous liquid was used for medicinal purposes. The first ballpark in the city was nearby.

Seraphs' games were played at Athletic Park, which later became Sulphur Dell. Legendary sportswriter Grantland Rice is credited for renaming the ballpark Sulphur Dell. Rice was born in nearby Murfreesboro, Tenn., and began his writing career for

Bill Traughber is a Nashville sports historian who researches and writes stories on Nashville sports history. As a Nashville native he has had over 200 stories published in several Nashville publications. Currently he is a contributing writer for The City Paper *in Nashville.*

a Nashville newspaper in the early 1900s. He was also a graduate of Vanderbilt University.

Exhibition games were played in the preseason against major league teams, local athletic clubs and Vanderbilt University. These major league teams would pass through Nashville by rail on their northward journey home from their spring training camps in the South.

An ad was located in an old Nashville newspaper announcing an April exhibition game with Nashville vs. Ted Sullivan's Wild Texas Steers. Admission prices included: Ladies—Opera Grand Stand 50 cents, Smokers—Grand Stand 40 cents, Bleachers 25 cents. Ladies accompanied by gentlemen, admitted to Grand Stand free on Fridays.

Members of the league at this time were Atlanta, Evansville, Little Rock, New Orleans, Memphis, Mobile, Montgomery, and Nashville.

Leading Nashville was player-manager George Stallings, who had a brief major league career as a player with Brooklyn and Philadelphia of the National League. Stallings had a successful 13-year managing career with four different teams sprinkled between 1897 and 1920. He led the Boston Braves to the 1914 World Series championship.

In the Southern League, one umpire was assigned to each game, and he stood several feet behind the catcher. When there was a baserunner, he positioned himself behind the pitcher.

Obviously, this situation would be a cause of bad

calls and frustration by both players and fans.

Newspapers of that time would print box scores and the stories would include the player's last name only. Occasionally, a first name would be mentioned in an extended story. Southern League records of this period are unavailable or primitive, and sometimes research includes scanning the local newspapers for information.

The home team usually batted first, which was optional in the Southern League. Therefore the line score placed the visitors at the bottom, unlike modern baseball.

This 1895 season opened for Nashville on an April afternoon at Evansville, IN Seraphs' fans in Nashville could receive details of the games by telegraph at the Merchants' Exchange (corner of Church and College Streets) and at the Grand Opera House (Ryman Auditorium), built in 1892.

Nashville lost the opening game, 17-10, and Nashville's daily morning newspaper of that day, *The Nashville American,* gave a detailed summary of the game. The following paragraph reveals the passions and emotions about baseball in that era and what lay ahead for the season:

> The principal feature of the game was the work of Umpire Keller. His decisions were disgusting, and gave both clubs reasonable excuse for a vast amount of kicking. The Nashville infield with the exception of Stallings seemed to be suffering from a severe case of "stage fright."

By the middle of August, Nashville trailed Evansville and Atlanta in the standings. An apparently ordinary game in Nashville against Atlanta on August 10, would later be pivotal in determining the Southern League championship. The Seraphs lost the game 10-9 at Athletic Park behind the pitching of their ace starter, Sammy Moran. More than 1,000 fans witnessed the poor pitching performance, but the villain of the game was, of course, the umpire.

With Nashville trailing 10-8 in their ninth inning at-bat, they scored one run. With two outs, runners were on first and second with the Seraphs catcher, Dan Sweeney at bat. Clark (no first name given) was the umpire, and *The Nashville American* reports on Sweeney's plate appearance:

> Two strikes had been called when he hit a high foul fly toward the grand stand. Wilson got under it, but his foot slipped and he did not get his hands under it at all. Just as he went to reach for it some boy in the

grounds threw a glove or a cap past his head. For this alleged interference Clark called Sweeney out. Then pandemonium reigned supreme. A howling mob went after Clark and he doubtless would have been subjected to the rough treatment which his robbing tactics had earned for him but for the interferences of a package of Chief Clack's regulars and detectives. As it was, one enthusiastic fan gave him a sound nose pulling.

George Wilson was Atlanta's catcher and Clack was Nashville's chief of police. The game would be meaningful three weeks later.

With the help of a remarkable 20-game winning streak, Nashville vaulted into first place in the standings. At this time only a few games remained on the schedule. Nashville stood at 65-35 (.650), Evansville 61-33 (.649) and Atlanta was third at 62-34 (.646).

With the teams traveling by train, games that were postponed due to rain were not rescheduled this late in the season. Percentage points determined the Southern League champion.

The season was scheduled to close after the games of September 2. However, Atlanta won a game on September 3 (which they played on their own) against New Orleans. The extra game gave Atlanta a tie with Nashville. Nashville was 71-35 while Atlanta finished at 69-34. Nashville played three more games than Atlanta, but each team finished with the same percentage, .670.

Nashville claimed the pennant and protested the final standings due to these reasons:

They claimed that the August 10 "Glove Game" should have been thrown out due to the umpire's incorrect call. New Orleans used a player who was ineligible after he was suspended from Pennsylvania State League. Nashville insisted that the games he appeared in should be forfeited. And third, Atlanta played a game one day after the season was officially over and believed that the game shouldn't count in the standings.

If New Orleans were to forfeit the games in question, Nashville would be the beneficiary. The president of the Nashville team, Mr. White, gave his opinion of the controversial season ending:

"I do not think there is any necessity for talking about playing off a tie, for there is none to play off. The Nashvilles are winners of the pennant and it should be awarded to them. I would rather see that flag fly over the Nashville Base Ball Park than to be presented with a $1,000 bill as the proceeds of playing off of a tie, or from any other source.

"The action of the association may be necessary in order to officially decide the award of the pennant but of result of that action no reasonable being can have any doubt. I have only the kindest feelings for Atlanta. It is a very nice country town, and if she keeps her club together might be able some day to successfully contest with Macon and Milledgeville, Ga."

A few days later, a meeting was held in Chattanooga with the league and team representatives to determine the winner.

The American reported the results of that meeting.

> The Nashville Base Ball Club of Nashville, Tenn., the club which won more games than any other club in the Southern Association and won them all fairly, not a forfeited game or an irregular game of any description being included, has justly and rightfully been declared the championship pennant winners for the season of 1895, and the pennant for which the Nashville team so earnestly fought and so fairly won by their magnificent line of twenty consecutive victories at the close of the season, will fly from the grounds of the Nashville club.
>
> The game of Aug. 10, between Nashville and Atlanta, played at Nashville, was by unanimous vote, thrown out. This game is now the now-famous "glove game," which Clark gave to the Atlantas because some small boy in the audience threw a glove in front of Catcher Wilson while he was in the act of attempting to catch a foul ball, which he could not have possibly reached. The ground upon which the game was thrown out was that Clark's decision was an illegal one, there being no rule providing for the punishment of a club for the offense of an outsider.

George Stallings, looking much like the successful Georgia plantation owner that he was, managed the "Miracle Braves" of 1914, as well as the Highlanders of 1910. Stallings was convinced that first baseman Hal Chase had tried to throw a 1910 game, but he could not make the charge stick. Chase replaced Stallings for the last 11 games of the year.

The league also voided Atlanta's September 3 game played after the season. With the loss (Glove Game) taken away from the Seraphs and a win taken away from Atlanta, Nashville's percentage jumped to .676. Atlanta's percentage fell to .667. Nashville withdrew its protest of New Orleans' ineligible player.

Nashville's franchise folded after that 1895 championship season. The Southern League folded in 1899 and the Nashville Vols would be charter members of the newly formed Southern Association in 1901. The Vols remained in the association until 1961.

The records of baseball in the early years were so disorganized and unavailable that some records reveal that Atlanta was the official Southern League champions. Since that time researchers have uncovered many mistakes concerning the recording of games. Standings and players' batting averages have been altered, but since the organizations folded decades ago, only the researchers can change history.

In case you didn't know, the dictionary defines a Seraph as: one of the six-winged angels of the highest rank believed in ancient Judaism to guard God's throne with sacred ardor, or one resembling or befiting an angel.

The Biggest Little Town in Organized Ball

Majors Stadium Welcomed Big Crowds for Minor League Baseball

by Dr. J. M. Dempsey

An industrial lot on the eastern edge of downtown Greenville, Texas, covered with heavy equipment, gives no sign of its grand history, except for one feature: a brick and concrete arch still stands with the welded metal inscription "Majors Stadium," coated with a layer of primer paint, across the top. It takes an excellent imagination to visualize Joe DiMaggio ranging across the lot, as he did one day in 1949.

In the late 1940s and early 1950s, the site was the home of the Class C and Class B Greenville Majors. The Majors' story epitomizes the boom and bust of small-town, independent minor league baseball in the postwar years.

At Majors Stadium, originally known as Phillips Field, crowds representing up to one-seventh of the city's population routinely passed through the elegant archway on summer nights, sharing a communal experience that would quickly disappear with the advent of television and air conditioning. Such was the city's enthusiasm for the Majors that it once attracted attention from *The Sporting News*. Community pride in the Majors led city leaders to build what was then considered a state-of-the-art minor-league facility. But with remarkable swiftness interest in the team faded. Now few citizens in the town of 25,000 know the rich history of the Greenville Majors and Majors Stadium.

J.M. Dempsey is an assistant professor of journalism at the University of North Texas. He holds a Ph.D. from Texas A&M University, where he announced Aggie baseball on radio for seven seasons.

MINOR LEAGUE BOOM

In the euphoric atmosphere immediately following the end of World War II, the number of minor leagues jumped from 12 in 1945, to 41 in 1946, to 59 in 1949.[1] Attendance boomed from 10 million in 1945, to 32 million in 1946, and more than 40 million in 1949. *The Sporting News* noted that the record-setting attendance reached down to the lower minors. The Class D Evangeline League drew 575,000 in 1946, and the Class B Western International League drew 780,443.[2] But just as quickly, the bush-league boom faded:

> Television boomed, but it was not baseball on TV that was keeping the fans at home. For an evening's entertainment a family could watch "Milton Berle," "I Love Lucy," and have the novelty of a dozen other shows. Earlier, people were looking for a way out of hot, stuffy houses; now, with air conditioning being perfected there was no need to leave home.[3]

The rise and fall of the Greenville Majors mirrored the national minor league boom and bust. But the Majors' rise was more metoric and their fall more abrupt than that of other small-town teams.

Ironically, in the era of the Internet and satellite television, minor league baseball has staged an incredible comeback. Obviously, many people are now looking for reasons to get out of the house. In 2001, the minors drew 38.8 million fans, the second-highest total in history, and the most since 1949, when seemingly every small town had a team. In 2002, another 38.6 million paid their way into minor league parks.[4]

Even in major league markets such as Dallas-Fort Worth, Kansas City, and, yes, New York, fans are attracted to minor league baseball—even more improbably to independent minor league games—by outrageous promotions, low ticket prices, seats close to the field, and the family-oriented atmosphere.

Some cities and ballparks somehow defied history. Minor leaguers have played ball at Wahconah Park in Pittsfield, Massachusetts, since around 1892. But, more typically, the revival of minor league ball has represented a rebirth. Since 1995, 78 new minor league ballparks have been built.[5] What baseball fans of the early 1950s abandoned as obsolete, their grandchildren have reclaimed, too late for the Greenville Majors and many other teams like them.

Class D minor league teams had played in

ORIGINS OF PHILLIPS FIELD

Greenville in 1905-07, 1912, and from 1921 to 1926. The teams had been known by various names, including Hunters, Highlanders, Togs, and Staplers, and played in various leagues, including the North Texas, Texas-Oklahoma and East Texas Leagues.[6]

The 1906 Greenville Hunters played in the Texas League, then Class D, with big-city teams in Dallas and Fort Worth. Joseph W. Gardner, the owner of the Dallas franchise, put up the money to place the team in Greenville. Low attendance caused the league to drop the Greenville and Temple franchises for the second half of the season. Don Curtis, who later became a St. Louis Cardinal scout and signed Dizzy Dean, managed the Hunters.[7]

These early teams played at the "Younger lot" on East Lee Street; Haynes Park, northeast of Majors Stadium, "clear across the railroad"; Morrow Park on the city's far northwest side; Pickens Park (which burned) and later Urquhart Park on "Puddin' Hill" on the far southeast side of the city; and the old Hunt County Fair Grounds on East Stanford Street.[8]

By the end of the booming 1920s, the citizens of Greenville decided that the city needed an athletic facility that compared favorably with rival cities. In 1929, Mrs. F. J. (Eula Lasater) Phillips made a $3,500 donation to the Greenville Athletic Council to buy the property. It was named for her and her late husband, Frank, a local bank president. Unlike today's

tax-supported projects, funding for the new stadium came entirely from citizen contributions. At the meeting in which Mrs. Phillips' donation was announced, "enthusiasm ran riot," and immediately Athletic Council members pledged $1,400 for the project.[9]

The Greenville Baseball Club, a citizens group that was contemplating the acquisition of a new minor league team, donated $1,800 that remained from the liquidation of the previous minor league team three years before to the Greenville Athletic Association. Individual citizens donated the remainder of the necessary funding.[10]

Although the facility was created to serve the immediate needs of the high school football team, planners conceived from the beginning that it might also serve a minor league professional baseball team at some point. "[The Building and Grounds] committee voted that the next step in the stadium program should be the erection of a baseball grandstand," the *Greenville Morning Herald* reported.[11] The newspaper did not report how the field would accommodate both football and baseball, with separate grandstands.

Phillips Field, with an original seating capacity of 2,960, hosted its first event on October 4, 1929, when the Greenville High School Lions hosted Dallas' Oak Cliff High School Leopards in a football game.[12] On December 31, the Greenville Athletic Association turned Phillips Field over to the city of Greenville, but the property was to be managed by the Greenville Public Schools.[13]

Coach Henry Frnka led the Lions in the undefeated, state championship season of 1933.[14] At the time Texas high school football teams played for a single state championship; no classifications based on school enrollment existed. They defeated Dallas Tech 21-0 for the championship at the Cotton Bowl (then "Fair Park Stadium") in Dallas.[15]

Frnka coached the Lions from 1931 to 1935, then left Greenville to begin college coaching, serving as an assistant coach at Vanderbilt and Temple Universities from 1936 to 1940. He later was named to the Texas High School Coaches Hall of Honor.

MINOR LEAGUE BASEBALL RETURNS TO GREENVILLE

In the postwar boom of 1946, a minor league professional team finally took up residence at Phillips Field. The Greenville Baseball Club raised $22,000 in the sale of stock from local businesses and individuals to place a team in the Class C East Texas League.[16]

The team was named the "Majors" in honor of the first young man from Greenville killed in World War II, Truett Majors.[17] "We had just emerged victoriously in World War II," Joe Phillips, the grandson of Frank and Eula Phillips, baseball historian and collector, remembered. "We were proud of that and had local guys like Monty Stratton, who was still trying to pitch with one leg, and Audie Murphy, the most decorated soldier in World War II. There was a lot to celebrate and feel good about."

The club bought Phillips Field from the school district for $6,000. For the 1946 season, the long, straight wooden football grandstand on the west side of the property served as the ballpark's primary seating. The visitors' bleachers on the east side were razed to make way for the baseball outfield. "Home plate will be directly in front of the old 50-yard-line marker on the west side with the playing field to the east," a *Greenville Morning Herald* article explained. The park's symmetrical dimensions were about 320 feet down the left and right field lines and 400 feet to center.[18] The outfield fence was "of metal construction and is there to stay, with no possibility of destruction by fire," the newspaper reported.[19] The 75-cent reserved seats were located between the 20-yard lines. The Greenville High School football team played the 1946 season at the park, and then moved to a new stadium across town, also named Phillips Field, which still stands.

In Greenville, a city infamous for the well-intentioned but thoughtless slogan "the blackest land, the whitest people" ("whitest" meaning "most honest" or "most decent"), segregation still ruled the day in 1946. The newspaper article describing the conversion of the football stadium into a baseball park explained that the lumber from the razed visitors' bleachers was "being stacked for use in erecting a Negro bleachers at the north end of the playing field."

Hungry for baseball and good times after four years of world war, Greenville fans attended Majors games in droves, despite a slow start that kept the team in the second division of the East Texas League until the latter part of the season. The regular-season attendance of 160,186 (reported by some sources as 167,000) has been reported as a Class C full-season attendance record.[20]

Unfortunately, the attendance record is doubtful. A record book of minor-league baseball shows that Greensboro, North Carolina, of the Class C Carolina League, reported attendance of 171,801 in 1946.[21] But the Greenville fans' support of the Majors in 1946

is remarkable nonetheless. U.S. Census figures show Greensboro had a 1950 population of more than 74,000, and it surely would have been several times larger than Greenville in 1946. The Majors averaged 2,460 fans per game in 1946, meaning about 17% of the city's 1946 population of 14,000 attended a game on any given night. By comparison, if 17% of New York City's 1950 population of more than 7.8 million attended a single baseball game, the attendance would have been more than 1.3 million.

A *TSN* article on the Majors attendance referred to Greenville as "the biggest little town in Organized Ball." The article noted that the Majors' attendance was more than the total attendance for the entire East Texas League in the last two seasons before World War II, and that the attendance was greater than that of several Class AA Texas League teams, all playing in cities at least six times larger than Greenville. Thanks largely to Greenville, in 1946 the East Texas League led Class C baseball in attendance with 700,000.

The Majors made a strong impression on at least one veteran baseball fan. In a note to a friend, an unidentified writer remembered going to a Greenville Togs game in 1922. "They sure play a classier brand of ball here now than in 1922. This is big-time stuff now," the writer enthused.[22]

Greenville fans showed a fierce passion for baseball in 1946-47. The Majors met the Henderson Oilers in a best-of-seven East Texas League playoff series in 1946. Rabid fans from both cities traveled with their teams, and tempers flared on both sides. In the first game, played at Phillips Field, an overflow crowd estimated at 5,000 turned out to see the Majors win, 5-3. The seventh game of the series had to be moved from Henderson to the neutral site of Texarkana after near-riot conditions in Henderson at the sixth game. League president J. Walter Morris ordered the change, calling the Henderson fans' abuse of the Greenville players "a disgrace to organized baseball." At least one Greenville player was attacked by a Henderson fan.[23]

But apparently the Greenville fans themselves had been less than perfect models of decorum. Prior to the sixth game, a reporter with the Henderson newspaper, anticipating that the Oilers would win and force a seventh game in Henderson, wrote: "The seventh and deciding game will be played at the Oiler stadium, in a city where fans have a sense of fair play and decency. There will be no more games this year in Greenville."[24] Two thousand Greenville fans traveled more than 120 miles to Texarkana for the deciding game, only to see their team lose to Henderson, 12-6.

"When the playoffs came against Henderson, there absolutely was a fever about the town," Joe Phillips remembers. "Dad was afraid to take me to the home games because there had been fights at the games in Henderson. A person couldn't buy a ticket for the playoffs. Prior to that I had taken my good friend to the games with us. I had already asked him to go with me to the game, but Dad couldn't take him. I lost a friend after he came over to the house and we had to tell him that we didn't have a ticket for him."[25]

"My favorite players were power hitter Dean Stafford and Gibby Brack, who had played in the major leagues during the 1930s," says Phillips. Brack played in 315 games for the Brooklyn Dodgers and the Philadelphia Phillies from 1937 to 1939, hitting .279 with 16 home runs. "Center fielder Eddie Palmer was the 'Frank Sinatra' of the team. A nice-looking guy, he was a fast runner with a head-back style. He would run out from under his cap regularly, to the delight of the fans and especially the girls." Forty-four-year-old Sal Gliatto, who spent the 1930 season with the Cleveland Indians, pitched for the Majors and managed the club early in the season. On June 1, first baseman Alex Hooks replaced Gliatto as manager.

The support for the local team seems quaint by today's standards. Before the series with Henderson, the newspaper reported that a group of 30 businessmen had pledged to reward the players. "Each Major player will get $5 for each hit he gets during the series. He will also get $5 for a sacrifice hit or an outfield fly that advances a base runner," the paper reported. Pitchers would share $25 for a win. A pitcher going the full game would keep the whole $25 for himself.[26]

"After supper, we would sit back on the porch and talk," Majors fan Marie Heidmann told the *Greenville Herald Banner* many years later. "A little after seven p.m., we would hear the sounds from Phillips Field. It would start with 'Take Me Out to the Ballgame.' So up we went to the ball game. That really was a wonderful, wonderful time. People didn't have to pay a lot to see a baseball game. [In 1946, Majors general-admission ticket prices were 25 cents for children and 50 cents for adults with reserved seats going for 75 cents. Season tickets were $4.] It was family entertainment. Those were the nicest boys and they could play, too." Mrs. Heidmann remembered once deciding to stay home and listen to the game on the radio, but the announcer's excited description of a Gibby Brack homer proved too much to stand; the family headed to the ballpark.[27]

MAJORS STADIUM REPLACES PHILLIPS FIELD

For the 1947 season, the Greenville Baseball Club demolished the old wooden football stands. Baseball stands, built of steel and concrete in a semicircle from third base to first base and seating about 3,600, were constructed. The Greenville Baseball Club sold stock to raise the money to build the concrete and steel grandstand, which was modeled after Burnett Park in Texarkana.

The new park, christened Majors Stadium, was considered one of the most modern in this part of the country. "I recall that the stands were painted in forest green," Phillips said. "There were [open] concrete areas where folding chairs were set up for reserved box seats, close to the field. There were two entrances to the seats behind home plate and entrances and ramps on the first- and third-base sides. A roof protected those in the upper part of the stands from the rain. The press box seemed large and adequate to accommodate radio and print news with a fine view behind and above home plate.

"It never dawned on me that we had a 'state-of-the-art baseball park until later when I visited and/or played in the ballparks in places like Paris, Gainesville, Sulphur Springs, Sherman, Denison, Tyler, and Marshall. I was told by one source much later that Greenville and the park in Kilgore were the prettiest and nicest minor league parks in East Texas."

Joe Phillips recalls the fun of hanging around the ballpark as a boy. A favorite pastime was collecting used soda bottles. "Those were the days when there were no paper cups and the bottles could be returned for refilling to the plant," he remembered. "I think we got one or two cents a return and it seemed like a lot of fun. Of course, trying to get foul balls before the 'official ball chaser' — Hilly Brown — was challenging, and always rewarding if you could get a ball."

With a brand-new ballpark in place, the Majors rose to the Class B Big State League for the 1947 season. Although finishing the regular season in second place, one game behind Texarkana, the team won 100 games. Greenville again led the league in attendance, but, ominously, with an excellent team and a new park, attendance fell to 154,356. Still, the Majors far outdrew the Austin franchise of the Big State League.

An overflow crowd of 4,101 turned out for the Majors' 8-3 win over the Wichita Falls Spudders. The big attraction was the wedding of Stafford and

All that remains of Majors Stadium is the Stone Arch.

Frances Erwin. The couple walked beneath an arc of bats held aloft by an "honor guard" of players from both teams. The Majors lost a playoff series to Wichita Falls, four games to two.

DiMAGGIO, YANKEES GRACE MAJORS STADIUM

As suddenly as the passion for the Majors began, it cooled. In 1948, the Majors fell to last place in the Big State League, and attendance accordingly fell by more than half, to 67,334. The Majors, who led their league in attendance by a wide margin in each of their first two years, attracting national attention, suddenly found themselves dead last in paid admissions.

"Greenville had a very bad baseball team in 1948," Phillips explained. "Earlier stars had departed and there was dissension among the fans and loyal team backers. Greenville was not going to support a loser."

But on a chilly Sunday afternoon, April 10, 1949, the little ball yard enjoyed its greatest glory, playing host to big-league royalty, the New York Yankees.

Casey Stengel, in his first season, managed the team, and the immortal Joe DiMaggio roamed center field.[28] Hall of Fame broadcaster Mel Allen described the game for radio listeners in New York. But the Majors were not content to simply set foot on the same field as the perennial world champions: The minor leaguers actually beat the Yanks that day, 4-3.

In those days it was common for major league teams to barnstorm their way through the south in the last days of spring training, prior to moving north for the start of the regular season. Following the disappointing 1948 season, the Greenville Baseball Club entered into a lease agreement for the Majors and the ballpark with George Schepps of Dallas, the longtime owner of the Dallas Texas League team and several other clubs. Schepps had enough influence to bring the Yankees to Greenville.

Tellingly, the game did not draw a capacity crowd to Majors Stadium. A crowd of 2,951 attended the game, considerably less than the stadium's capacity of about 3,600. A heavy rain the night before had soaked the field, and rained out a scheduled game against a

Chicago Cubs B squad. Apparently some believed the Yankee game had also been rained out. A *New York Times* account of the game said: "Rains and unseasonable cold resulted in a disappointing crowd." The weather report in the *Dallas Morning News* the following day said the day's high temperature in Dallas, 50 miles west, had been 59 degrees.

Despite the weather, the Majors earned their victory. DiMaggio started in center field, and had a single and scored a run in two at-bats. Ace pitcher Allie Reynolds started on the mound for the Yankees, and pitched five innings, giving up three runs on five hits. Other well-known Yankees, such as second baseman George Stirnweiss, shortstop Jerry Coleman, third baseman Bobby Brown (who went on to become president of the American League), and right fielder Gene Woodling played in the game. But the Yanks, perhaps wary of playing on a soggy field, committed four errors. Still, they apparently gave it their best. "The Yankees took a full session of batting practice . . . and a regular infield workout despite the wet grounds and in every way possible put on a show for the fans that was well-appreciated," a local sportswriter wrote.

The game produced a mystery that remains unresolved. Playing center field that day for the Majors was Pepper Martin. Whether this was the former St. Louis Cardinals "Gashouse Gang" third baseman and outfielder John Leonard Roosevelt "Pepper" Martin, nicknamed the "Wild Horse of the Osage" for his exuberant, reckless play, is questionable. Martin scored the winning run for the Majors in the bottom of the seventh inning, and had one hit and two RBI.

Pepper Martin had played for the old Greenville Hunters minor league team in 1924 and 1925 before going on to a legendary career with the Cardinals from 1928 to 1944. He would have been 45 years old in April 1949, but in those days, many major-league players continued to play in the minors long after their glory days had ended.[29]

The playing field and seating at Majors Stadium in the late 1940s.

Contemporary accounts of the game suggest that it was not *the* Pepper Martin who played for the Majors that day. The Greenville newspaper accounts make no special reference to Martin. The very brief *Dallas Morning News* account of the game makes no reference at all to Martin, but the story on an exhibition game between the Majors and the Texas League Dallas Eagles in Greenville on Friday night, April 8, 1949, refers to a "Charlie 'Pepper' Martin," rather than John "Pepper" Martin. The *New York Times* story on the Yankees-Majors game refers to "Pepper Martin (not of the Osage)." Records show that Martin, whoever he truly was, did not remain with the Majors during the regular season. John "Pepper" Martin managed the Miami International League team in 1949.

However, some believe that the Martin who played for the Majors that day indeed was longtime major leaguer. "The chances of another Pepper Martin playing for Greenville are slim to none, but neither the (Baseball) Hall of Fame nor (Texas A&M University-Commerce historian Dr. James) Conrad could guarantee the same Martin scored the winning run against the Yankees," a newspaper article said.[30]

Joe Phillips attended the game as a boy, and until recently held a baseball that was autographed by several of the Yankees and Majors, including Pepper Martin. Phillips, a baseball collector, sold the ball recently and is confident the Martin autograph was genuine. "I've got to think that was our daring John 'Pepper' Martin. He signed on the sweet spot of our baseball and the signature looks like his," Phillips wrote. Phillips believes George Schepps probably brought Martin in to bolster the Majors' lineup just for the exhibition game with the Yankees. Indeed, the *New York Times* article indicates the Majors brought in some reinforcements for the game.

One other player in the Majors lineup that day played in the major leagues. Second baseman Elmer "Red" Durrett played in parts of two seasons, 1944 and 1945, for the Brooklyn Dodgers, hitting just .146.

The game foreshadowed the end of DiMaggio's career. The Yankee Clipper reinjured a heel that had been operated on the year before. The nagging heel injury finally caused DiMaggio to retire after the 1951 season.

THE SWIFT DECLINE

The 1949 Majors improved only slightly, placing sixth in the eight-team league, and attendance fell even further, to 58,500. The lease agreement with George Schepps apparently was not profitable for either party. At a board meeting of the Greenville Baseball Club on August 25, 1949, the directors passed a motion "not to be lenient any longer with G. Schepps and that the money that he now owes is now due," although apparently the lease continued in effect. Apparently to keep the team afloat, the club later voted to borrow "a maximum of $7,500" prior to the 1950 season.

Majors Stadium enjoyed another day in the sun when the legendary Monty Stratton, a Greenville-area native and former Chicago White Sox star, pitched a game for the home team. A popular 1949 movie starring Jimmy Stewart and June Allyson, *The Stratton Story*, celebrated Stratton's comeback from losing a leg in a hunting accident. On June 17, 1950, Stratton, using an artificial leg, pitched for the Majors in a game against Austin at Majors Stadium. Expected to pitch only a few innings, Stratton went the distance, giving up 11 hits, striking out five, and walking one in an 11-6 Greenville victory in front of a crowd of 2,951.

In 1950, still operating under the lease agreement with Schepps, the Majors regained their winning form, finishing 75-71, but it did not stop the attendance decline. As part of what was by now a general dip in minor league attendance, only 50,511 fans made their way to Majors Stadium, fewer than 700 per game. A crowd of 801 saw the team sweep a doubleheader from the Sherman-Denison Twins, 11-8 and 6-1, on Labor Day. It would be the final bow for the original Majors.

The team folded prior to the 1951 season. George Schepps and his partners paid the Greenville Baseball Club a settlement of $2,500, terminating the lease. The club turned down an offer to stage stock-car races at Majors Stadium, and instead allowed the park to be used for various amateur baseball leagues including the Hunt County League and the Little League games.

"I firmly believe that air conditioning and television were major factors [in the attendance decline]," Joe Phillips said.

"Instead of going to the baseball games, my parents and my family were now watching television at home or visiting friends where we'd gather to see wrestling or the fights. Before air conditioning, the ballpark offered a great place to 'cool' off before television. At least you could be moderately cooler and be surrounded by friends."

Phillips also believes a general darkening of the post-war horizon played a role in the Majors' decline. "By the late 1940s, Russia had dropped its first A bomb and the Cold War was just beginning to mount up. The Korean War was starting, and the optimism of the immediate postwar era had now turned to worry over the nuclear threat and Communism."

Marie Heidmann felt a personal loss in the original Majors' demise. "We [friends] would all sit in the same area, just like you do at church," she recalled wistfully. "It was the thing to do in Greenville. But little by little, attendance went down. It really was sad."

The remarkably tenacious Greenville Baseball Club remained active and brought professional baseball back to the city. Greenville again fielded a Big State League team in 1953. The Greenville Baseball Club took over the Longview Cherokees franchise.

THE LAST GASP

Dick Burnett, the owner of the Dallas Texas League team, operated the team under a deal similar to the earlier one with George Schepps. A strong opening-night crowd of an estimated 2,500 saw the new Majors defeat Texarkana, 6-3, but the crowd for the second game nosedived to 331.

Despite a good start that had the Majors in first place, the Greenville fans did not respond to the new team. The Majors moved to Bryan midway through the season. The team drew only 30,051 for the season in the two cities combined, and after moving to Bryan slumped to a 70-77 record. The team retained the name of "Majors" for the remainder of the 1953 season, and then took the name "Indians" in 1954. It played at Travis Park, which is still in use as a baseball facility today.

Greenville's last gasp in minor league baseball came in 1957. The Greenville Baseball Club took over the McAlester Rockets franchise of the Sooner State League. The Rockets had a long-standing player-development agreement with the New York Yankees, which continued in Greenville. Again, the new team received the name of "Majors." An estimated crowd of 700 turned out for the Majors' first home game, a 6-2 win over Paris, and newspaper accounts show most games drawing about the same size of crowd. The Majors drew only 23,066 fans, but that was third best in the eight-team league. The Sooner State League folded before the next season.

The final season of minor league ball at Majors Stadium brought black players to Majors Stadium for the first time, at least as members of minor league clubs. One of them turned out to be a future Hall of Famer, Ponca City's Billy Williams, who went on to enjoy a great career with the Chicago Cubs.

Unlike today's minor league teams, the Majors of the 1940s and 1950s rarely held splashy promotions to help fill the stands. The 1947 wedding of outfielder Dean Stafford and the 1950 appearance of Monty Stratton were the rare exceptions. The Greenville Baseball Club typically would run a full-page, or even a two-page, ad in the newspaper for the season opener, but no more advertising would appear after that. "I've tried to recall if the Majors held any 'special event' nights, like cow-milking contests, donkey baseball, and so on, but I can't recall that they did," Joe Phillips said. Even in 1953 and 1957, the Majors enjoyed good daily coverage in the local newspapers, but, with minor league ball fading across the country, the exposure did not generate enough support for the Majors to buck the trend.

Years later, sportswriter Bob Franklin put the demise of the Majors in perspective. Musing on overflow crowds for youth-league games in Greenville, Franklin theorized that, in addition to the emergence of television and air conditioning, changes brought about by the postwar baby boom also doomed small-town minor league ball:

> For a fleeting moment, it makes an ardent baseball fan like me want to bring back the professional game, the exhilarating past when the Greenville Majors rode high in the Big State League and the diamond sport was a paying proposition. . . . Could baseball make a successful return? Would people surrender the price of admission? The answers are no. Baseball in the minor leagues is dead. . . . There's just too much competition for the entertainment dollar. Go-carts, trampolines, bowling, miniature golf, skating, movies that are better than ever, and what have you have dispersed the entertainment dollar.

Admiring the family togetherness engendered by "kids baseball," Franklin concluded: "There was family togetherness back in the days of the Greenville Majors too, but boys bustling with energy would rather play than watch. And parents, overflowing with pride, would rather watch their own children play than the adroit professionals"[31]

In early 1958, the Greenville Baseball Club finally dissolved and sold Majors Stadium to the Majors' original president, automobile dealer J. P. "Punk" McNatt. McNatt bought the ballpark for $15,000, allowing the club to pay off its debts and donate the remainder to local charities. McNatt leased the park, renamed "Punk McNatt Stadium," to the Greenville YMCA for $1 per year. In 1961, McNatt sold the property to the YMCA, also for $1.[32]

For several more years Hunt County League semi-pro and youth-league teams played on the field. Joe Phillips believes he played in the final game at Majors Stadium, a semi-pro affair, sometime in the early '60s. "Felan Monk hit the last ball out of the ballpark down there," Phillips said. "I'm sure that was the last game." Charles and Billie Pickens, owners of the Greenville Transformer Co., bought the Majors Stadium property in May 1964, and soon razed the stands. The company still occupies the site. A building that stands at the northwest corner of the property on the corner of Houston and Church streets is part of the locker rooms for the old stadium. The brick entry that remains—ghostlike—at the southwest corner of the stadium site was constructed as part of a Works Progress Administration (WPA) improvement project in 1940.[33]

Mrs. Pickens told the *Commerce Journal* in 1986 that she maintains the arch "for old times' sake." Little League teams still come each year to have their team pictures made in front of it. Mrs. Pickens has rebuffed attempts to move it to a new, more prominent location.

The Greenville Majors—like other small-town minor league teams of the late '40s and early '50s—existed in a tiny niche of time, never to be seen again. It was the exuberant, optimistic period immediately following World War II, just before television cast its spell on the country, isolating neighbors in their homes. The children of the baby boom were still toddlers, and the grim specter of the Cold War had not fully emerged. It was all over almost as soon as it began, but for a brief time, the Majors created something very close to major league excitement in a small northeast Texas town. Life in Greenville and other one-time pro-baseball cities might improve in other ways, but it would never again be so colorful. As Joe Phillips recalls: "The '46-47 team seemed to pull Greenville together tightly, a rallying place. I don't think the city ever recovered that feeling."

Notes:

1. Johnson, Lloyd and Miles Wolff (eds.). *The Encyclopedia of Minor League Baseball,* first edition (Durham, NC: Baseball America, Inc.) 1993.
2. "Tops in Attendance," *The Sporting News,* November 6, 1946, p. 20.
3. Johnson and Wolff, pp. 219, 263.
4. "Minor league baseball draws third-highest attendance mark," Associated Press, September 25, 2002.
5. Pochna, Peter. "Majoring in family fun; Minor league ballparks go above and beyond baseball," *The Bergen County, NJ, Record,* August 4, 2002, p. A-1.
6. "Galaxy of Baseball Stars Paraded on Greenville's Diamonds," *Greenville Morning Herald,* May 9, 1950, Section 16, p. 1; Johnson and Wolff; Phillips, Joe. "Professional Baseball in Greenville, 1900-2000," unpublished manuscript, 2002.
7. O'Neal, Bill. *The Texas League, 1888-1987: A Century of Baseball* (Austin, Texas: Eakin Press, 1987), p. 255-56.
8. "Greenville Fans Have Modern Baseball, Football Playing Fields," *Greenville Evening Banner,* May 7, 1950, p. 4.
9. "Mrs. Frank Phillips Contributes $3,500 for Purchase Permanent Athletic Field," *Greenville Evening Banner,* February 26, 1929, p. 1.
10. "Select Site for New Phillips Field," *Greenville Morning Herald,* April 25, 1929, p. 1; "Executive Committee Selects Site for Phillips Field, Accepts Donation from Baseball Club," *Greenville Evening Banner,* April 25, 1929, p. 1.
11. Contracts to be Let for Phillips Field Stadium," *Greenville Morning Herald,* July 4, 1929, p. 3.
12. Ibid.; "Phillips Field Be Dedicated With Game With Oak Cliff On Oct. 4," *Greenville Morning Herald,* September 11, 1929, p. 3.
13. "City Accepts Phillips Field," *Greenville Morning Herald,* January 1, 1930, p. 1.
14. "Frnka, former Greenville coach, dead," *Greenville Herald Banner,* December 20, 1980, p. 1; Dan Bus, "Only the Memories Remain," *Greenville Herald Banner,* February 11, 1968, Walworth Harrison Public Library, Greenville, Texas.
15. "1933 Football Team Wins State Title to Thrill Fans," *Greenville Evening Banner* (Centennial edition, sports section), May 7, 1950, p. 6.
16. "$22,000 In Hand Local Baseball Club Organized; J.P. McNatt is President," *Greenville Morning Herald,* January 23, 1946, p. 1.
17. "Baseball Club Be Known As Greenville Majors," *Greenville Morning Herald,* 7 March 1946, p. 1.
18. "Conversion Phillips Field Baseball Park Under Way," *Greenville Morning Herald,* February 22, 1946, 5.
19. "Committees Are Named to Sponsor Opening Game Here," *Greenville Morning Herald,* April 17, 1946, p. 8; "Baseball At the Old Phillips Field" (photo cutline). *Greenville Evening Banner* (Centennial edition, sports section), May 7, 1950, p. 4.
20. "160,186 Paid See Majors Play Here During Season," *Greenville Morning Herald,* September 25, 1946, p. 3; "Baseball At the Old Phillips Field," 4; "Galaxy of Baseball Stars," Section 16, 1; Harrison, *History of Greenville.*
21. Johnson, Lloyd and Miles Wolff (eds.). *The Encyclopedia of Minor League Baseball,* Second edition (Durham, NC: Baseball America, Inc., 1997).
22. Newspaper clipping. Collection of Erica McKenzie, Rowlett, Texas.
23. "President J. Walter Morris Says Final Game on Neutral Field Wednesday Night," *Greenville Morning Herald,* September 17, 1946, p. 1.
24. Ibid.
25. Phillips, personal communication with author, January 3, 2003.
26. "Local Fans Make Cash Awards for Majors Series," *Greenville Morning Herald,* September 10, 1946, p. 3.
27. Press, Brad. "One victory put Majors into 'League of their Own,'" *Greenville Herald Banner,* July 10, 1992. Collection of Erica McKenzie, Rowlett, Texas; "Committees are Named to Sponsor Opening Game Here," *Greenville Morning Herald,* April 17, 1946, p. 8; Heidmann, Marie. videotape of speech to Hunt County Museum, July 1992.
28. "Majors Win Surprising 4-3 Victory Over New York Yankees Here Sunday," *Greenville Morning Herald,* April 12, 1949, Walworth Harrison Public Library, Greenville, Texas.
29. Herman Scott, "Blackland Footprints," March 8, 1965, *Greenville Herald Banner,* p. 1; "Pepper Martin." (August 3, 2002).
30. Press, Brad. "One victory."
31. Franklin, Bob. "Poor Robert's Almanac," *Greenville Herald Banner,* August 2, 1960, 8.
32. "Punk McNatt Buys Majors Stadium—YMCA leases field," *Greenville Herald Banner,* April 17, 1958, p. 3; *Direct Index to Deeds, L-R, 1/1/54-1/1/65,* Hunt County, Texas, Clerk's office, "McN" section, 54.
33. "Donation made Phillips Field," *Greenville Morning Herald,* March 17, 1940, p. 6.

IN-THE-PARKA HOMERS *World War 2 brought an abrupt shift in spring training rituals when Commissioner Landis ruled that teams had to forgo their annual trek south, and instead practice close to home. For the springs of 1943, 1944, and 1945 Indiana replaced Florida as the state with the most training sites. Seven teams—the Browns, Tigers, Reds, Indians, Cubs, Pirates, and White Sox—warmed up in such towns as Muncie, Terre Haute, and French Lick. The Cardinals stayed closer to home, venturing to Cairo, Illinois. The Red Sox trained at Tufts College, while the Braves prepped at the Choate School in Connecticut. The Phillies went to Hershey, then to Wilmington in 1944. Connie Mack took his A's to Wilmington, and then to Frederick, MD.*

The Dodgers went north to chilly Bear Mountain, New York. After one March blizzard the pitchers practiced by throwing snowballs. The Giants and Yankees went to New Jersey, with the Giants practicing on the grounds of the old Rockefeller estate in Lakewood. In 1945 the Yankees lived in the mansion, which had 47 color-coordinated rooms, 17 baths, and a nine-hole golf course. But this was nothing new to the Giants, who had trained in Lakewood in 1895-96. One can only imagine where the Blue Jays, Expos, and Twins would have had to spend their springs! — JIM CHARLTON

Joe Borden

The First No-Hit Pitcher and National League Winner

by Rich Westcott

Ask nearly any baseball fan to identify Joe Borden, and the response is predictable. Joe Who? It's true, Joe Borden is not a name that is instantly recognizable. To most people, in fact, it isn't even remotely familiar. But, although he wallows in the depths of obscurity, Borden does, nonetheless, have an important place in baseball history.

There was a time when Borden was briefly one of the premier pitchers in professional baseball. That was in an era long before we ever heard of Sandy Koufax or Nolan Ryan. It was even way before Walter Johnson and Christy Mathewson ascended the stairway to baseball deity. Borden's time was in the 1870s. In that decade of professional baseball's infancy, the 5-foot, 9-inch, 140-pound right hander not only hurled the first major league no-hitter, he also won the first National League game ever played. The two landmark events in major league history occurred less than one year apart and were the highlights of Borden's short-lived baseball career.

In Borden's day, pitchers had to keep their arms below the belt when they delivered a pitch. They stood just 45 feet from home plate. And batters could request where they wanted a pitch to be thrown. Pitchers had to keep both feet on the rubber, it took

Rich Westcott has been a writer and editor for 40 years, and was the founder, editor, and publisher of Phillies Report. *He is the author of 15 baseball books, including* No-Hitters: The 225 games, 1893-1999 *(with Allen Lewis) and most recently* Great Home Runs of the 20th Century *and* Winningest Pitchers: Baseball's 300-Game Winners.

nine balls to walk a batter, and catchers received pitches while standing several feet behind home plate. Although the rules favored the hitter, Borden and other pitchers found ways to get around the restrictions imposed on their craft. They learned to throw underhanded fastballs, curves, and drops. They even started using pitchouts and brushbacks.

Born May 9, 1854, in Jacobstown, New Jersey, Joseph Emley Borden learned the art of deceiving hitters at an early age. By the time he was 21, having been plucked from an amateur team in Philadelphia, he was pitching in the big leagues with the Philadelphia Pearls of the National Association, the first of baseball's major leagues. At the time, the Pearls were one of three Philadelphia teams (the others were the Athletics and the Centennials) playing in the National Association.

According to *The Great Encyclopedia of 19th Century Major League Baseball* by David Nemec, Borden replaced Cherokee Fisher, who had been cut from the Pearls for "drunkenness and general misbehavior." Borden made his big-league debut on July 24 for a Pearls team that would go on to a fifth-place finish in the 13-team National Association. Because his family, a prominent one in mid–New Jersey, did not approve of his playing baseball, Borden initially used pseudonyms, pitching under the name of Nedrob (Borden spelled backward) or Joe Josephs. On July 28, 1875, pitching as Joe Josephs, the rookie fired major league baseball's first no-hitter while blanking the Chicago White Stockings, 4-0, at Philadelphia's Jefferson Park. It would be the only no-hitter in the National Association's five-year existence.

The numbers of Borden's strikeouts and walks against a Chicago team that eventually finished in sixth place, losing 7 of 10 games to the Pearls, are not known. But a report in a Philadelphia newspaper claimed, "Borden tossed the Chicago team up and down in a blanket." The game was played in one hour and 35 minutes and was umpired by Nicholas E. Young, who later served as president of the National League from 1885 to 1902. Absorbing one of his seven losses (against six wins) that season, Chicago pitcher Mike Golden gave up seven hits—all four Philadelphia runs were unearned.

Borden finished the season with a 2-4 record in seven games, each of which he started. He finished all seven, and both of his victories were shutouts. Working in 66 innings, he gave up 47 hits, struck out nine, and walked seven (statistics from *Total Baseball*).

When the National Association folded after the 1875 season, Borden moved to the Boston Red Caps in the newly formed National League. Unimaginable as it may seem for so long ago, some accounts claimed that Boston, believing it had obtained one of the best pitchers in the country, gave Borden a three-year contract.

History visited Borden again on April 22, 1876, when manager Harry Wright named the slender hurler as his opening day pitcher against the Philadelphia Athletics. The Athletics were one of several teams that over the years carried that name. This particular version, however, failed to finish the season, getting thrown out of the league after refusing to make a late-season road trip. The game, also played at the 5,000-seat Jefferson Park, which was located in the north side of Philadelphia in an area that was crammed with notable ballparks, was the first National League game ever played.

With an estimated crowd of 3,000 watching, Borden, now playing under his own name, pitched the Red Caps to a 6-5 victory, giving him and Boston the distinction of earning the new league's first victory. Borden went on to post an 11-12 record in 218 innings and 29 games for the fourth-place Red Caps. While registering a 2.89 ERA , yielding 257 hits, and striking out 34, he led the league with 51 walks (statistics from *Total Baseball*). But at the age of 22, he was curiously released before the end of the season. In a brief biography by Randy Linthurst in SABR's *Nineteenth Century Stars* he is said to have received a cash settlement. Joe wound up serving as a groundskeeper at South End Grounds, the Red Caps' home park.

The little pitcher who made baseball history never appeared in another major league game. Having lived in Yeadon, Pennsylvania, during his brief career as a player, Borden eventually found his way to West Chester, another Philadelphia suburb. There he established a business manufacturing boots and shoes. An article in the *West Chester Local News* said that Borden married Henrietta Sebastian Evans on February 4, 1891. The bride was a member of a prominent local family. Her father was the publisher of another West Chester newspaper and also served two terms each in the state assembly and the state senate, and her grandfather was a highly regarded botanist, historian, and financier.

Eventually Borden closed his shoe business and took a job as first assistant to the secretary of a major bank in Philadelphia. The former pitcher died October 14, 1929, at the age of 75 at his daughter's home in Lansdowne, Pennsylvania. He was buried in a cemetery in West Chester. Borden's grave site was unkempt and unnoticed for many years until located by SABR member Tom Taylor. The unadorned tombstone at the site makes no mention of a baseball career in which Borden was the first no-hit hurler in major league baseball and the National League's first winning pitcher.

BORDEN'S NO-HITTER

PHILADELPHIA	R	H	O	A
Murnane, 1b	0	1	13	0
McGeary, 2b	1	1	5	4
Addy, rf	1	2	0	0
Meyerle, 3b	1	2	0	0
Snyder, c	0	0	4	1
Fulmer, ss	0	0	0	4
McMullin, crf	0	0	3	0
Josephs, p	0	0	1	2
Treacy, lf	1	1	1	0
TOTALS	4	7	27	11

CHICAGO	R	H	O	A
Higham, c	0	0	5	2
Devlin, 1b	0	0	13	0
Hines, cf	0	0	2	0
Glenn, lf	0	0	3	0
Peters, ss	0	0	0	7
Miller, 2b	0	0	1	2
Golden, p	0	0	2	1
Warren, 3b	0	0	1	0
Bielaski, rf	0	0	0	0
TOTALS	0	0	27	12

	1 2 3	4 5 6	7 8 9		
Chicago	0 0 0	0 0 0	0 0 0	–	0
Philadelphia	1 2 0	0 0 0	1 0 X	–	4

Earned runs – None. Errors – Chicago 4, Philadelphia 1. Umpire – N. E. Young. Time - 1:35.

The Boston Pilgrims Never Existed

by Bill Nowlin

In reading accounts of the 1903 World Series, I so often came across the team name "Boston Pilgrims" that I accepted this on faith as one of the names by which the team was known. I even used it myself, presenting it as fact (see page 1 of *Tales from the Red Sox Dugout*). I find that I helped perpetuate a myth. That's all it appears to be: a myth. The official name was (perhaps) the Boston American League Ball Club, if we are willing to go by the team name provided for the signature line on the contract to play the World Series which was signed by the Pittsburgh Athletic Co. and the Boston club on September 16, 1903.

I cannot find any contemporary indication that the Boston American League baseball club was ever known as the Pilgrims in 1903. It's a fairly widespread myth, though, which has taken on the appearance of fact. Late in 2002, a quick survey of key baseball Web sites finds the American League entry in the 1903 Series almost always termed the "Boston Pilgrims." Among these sites are those of Major League Baseball and baseball-reference.com.

There also exist a number of standard baseball reference books. *Total Baseball* has always been my favorite. Unfortunately, the seventh edition describes the Boston Pilgrims as facing the Pittsburgh Pirates on page 280. No wonder I used the name when writing and while proofreading *Tales from the Red Sox Dugout*. No wonder other researchers do the same.

The Pilgrims keep cropping up. Burt Solomon's *The Baseball Timeline* (2001), produced in association with Major League Baseball, consistently refers to the "Boston Pilgrims." *The Sporting News* book *Baseball*, edited by Joe Hoppel, which was also published in 2001, says the 1903 World Champions were "the Red Sox (also known as the Pilgrims, Puritans and Americans.)" I've scoured the Boston newspapers of the day, though, and find nothing which even suggests that there was a team known as the Boston Pilgrims in 1903. Or, for that matter, the Puritans. They're both wonderful names, but I can't find even a shred of evidence that they were names used by anyone in Boston at the time.

The team was also not named the Boston Americans. That was perhaps the most common nickname—to distinguish it from the older NL club in town—but "the Bostons" was a nickname used interchangeably and about as often in the contemporary press. The Boston Red Sox might be in a position to know. They have a Web site, but according to their site the team was always named the Red Sox, from their founding in 1901 right up to the present! They should know better than that.

The Red Sox actually do know better. Their media guide, for example, details the story of how the team first became known as the Red Sox, though in the process gives the incorrect impression that the team was known as the Red Sox during the 1907 season.

Bill Nowlin has co-authored six books and nearly 100 articles on baseball, virtually every one of them about Ted Williams and Boston's American League baseball club.

(see page 282 of the 2003 media guide). It was not until the following year, 1908, that players donned red hosiery and played under the name "Red Sox."

Despite this awareness, though, the media guide is internally inconsistent. On page 340 of the same edition, the name Red Sox is applied to the 1903 club. On the cover, however, the "Boston Americans" are recognized. The Library of Congress Web site, by contrast, seems to get it right: "On October 1, 1903, the Boston Americans (soon to become the Red Sox) of the American League played the National League champion Pittsburgh Pirates in the first game of the modern World Series. Pittsburgh won the game by a score of seven to three, but lost the best of nine game series to Boston, five games to three."

Last things first. As mentioned above, the Red Sox media guide provides the 1907 date as the first for the "Red Sox." Describing them as adopting that moniker in 1907 would seem to imply that the team was known as the Red Sox during the 1907 season. They were not. That began with the 1908 season. Glenn Stout and Dick Johnson in *Red Sox Century*, the most definitive history of the team, report that Boston's AL team owner John I. Taylor made the decision to name the team the Red Sox on December 18, 1907 and ordered new uniforms with bright red stockings from Wright and Dixon, the sporting goods supplier.

Stout and Johnson then quote the reaction of both the *Boston Journal* newspaper and *The Sporting News*. Tim Murnane, writing in *The Sporting News*, said, "Well, what do you think of that? The Boston Americans have a new name . . . the 'Red Sox.'"

There are two points of note here. One, if the team was given this name only in mid-December, it would seem misleading for the Red Sox media guide or other sources to suggest that it was their team name for the 1907 season, as opposed to just the last two weeks of December. Second, the veteran writer Murnane suggests that the team was known as the Boston Americans up until the time the change was made. Murnane doesn't say the "Pilgrims" have a new name. He says the "Americans" have a new name.

Of course, they could have been the Pilgrims in 1903 and the Americans in 1907. Murnane actually adds more context when he elaborates, "Ever since Boston became identified with the American League an effort has been made to give the team an appropriate nickname which would sound good in print . . . but no two writers will agree on any one name. It was consequently up to John I. Taylor to re-christen his bunch and he has done so effectively."

In *Red Sox Century*, Stout and Johnson note what I found in my own reading of the several Boston daily newspapers of this era, regarding both the AL and NL teams in Boston: "Neither team had a nickname, nor would they for several more seasons. Both were simply called 'the Bostons,' although to differentiate between the two clubs, fans, sportswriters, and players commonly began referring to the NL entry as 'the Nationals,' and their American League counterparts as 'the Americans.' Other nicknames, such as the Pilgrims, Puritans, Plymouth Rocks, Somersets (so named after owner Charles Somers), or Collinsmen (after manager Collins) for the AL team and the Beaneaters, Triumvirs, or Seleemen (after manager Frank Selee) for the Nationals, were convenient inventions of the press. Their subsequent use by many historians is misleading. None of these nicknames was ever widely used by either fans or players."

Precisely. In fact, the nicknames were not always convenient inventions—in that both the Boston Nationals and the Boston Americans were sometimes dubbed the Beaneaters! Even within columns by the same sportswriter in the same newspaper, these casual nicknames were changed from day to day. Late in 2002, I completed a game-by-game chronology of the entire 1903 season, and found that the nickname used most consistently for the AL team—the only one which was really widely used at all—was the "Americans." Their 1902 uniforms reflected this terminology to some extent. Photographs show "B. A." on front of the uniform. This confirms what Tim Murnane reported just a few years later.

Almost all today's standard reference books list the 1903 team as the Boston Pilgrims, but it's hard to know why—other than that it really is a nice nickname, and a name that sounds good in print is appealing to many people. But the record of the day would indicate that "Pilgrims" was not used all that often in the press. How often was it used, though, really?

ANALYSIS OF BOSTON NEWSPAPER SPORTS COVERAGE IN 1903

The *Boston Herald* was the biggest newspaper in town in 1903. I decided to perform a content analysis of the game accounts as run in the *Herald*. A careful survey indicates that the team was indeed referred to by a number of names.

On some occasions, more than one team name would be used in a given day's newspaper—sometimes one name would appear in the headline and another one in the body of the text. I counted only one usage per game account. Assuming that texts were written by reporters closer to the game, and headlines often written by editors, I decided to choose the name used in the text unless no name was used, in which case I used the name from the headline, if there was one.

I read every game account for the entire 1903 season. There were nine accounts where no team name or nickname was used in either the headline or the text. The content analysis revealed that the name "Boston Americans" was used 57 times, while the term "Bostons" to describe the team was used in 54 game accounts. Interestingly, though, of the 54 game texts where "Bostons" was used in the story, 29 times the name "Boston Americans" was used in the headline or sub-head. The general impression is that the two terms were used fairly interchangeably, though with far more frequency than any other nicknames.

There were four game accounts in which the AL team was referred to as the "Beaneaters." There were two game accounts in which the only named characterization was "Bostonians," and there was one game account that referred to the team as the "Collinsites." There were a number of other collective phrases used as aggregate descriptors to "name" the team. These were: the locals Collins' club, the Boston side Boston Club, Collins' men, Collins' tribe, men from the Hub, the Boston team, the local team, and, of course, simply "Boston."

In early September 1903, when the American League pennant seemed within their grasp, there were a couple of stories which referred to them as the "coming champions" (the sportswriters of the day were not snakebit, the way Red Sox fans have learned to become) and once they clinched, there was at least one story referring to them collectively as the "American League champions." How many times was this team referred to as the "Pilgrims" or "Boston Pilgrims" in the *Boston Herald*? Not one time.

SAMPLING OF OTHER BOSTON NEWSPAPERS

One might conclude from this reading of the *Boston Herald* that there was no 1903 Boston team called the Pilgrims, or that for some perverse reason the *Herald* chose to ignore the name. I didn't want to have to read every game account in every other daily Boston newspaper, but I decided to sample them.

I looked at four other daily newspapers and read each of their game accounts for the month of September 1903. I picked the last month of the season, figuring that coverage would be fuller as the season progressed and as it became clearer that Boston's American League team—whatever it was called—would become the champions. I read each day's September 1903 coverage (whether there was a game or not) in the *Boston Post*, *Boston Globe*, *Boston Journal*, and *Boston Record*.

The *Boston Post* results were as follows: Boston Americans, 16; the Collins team, 5; Bostons, 3; Boston, 3; Collinsites, 1; the Collins boys, 1; the champion Boston nine, 1. On several occassions the "Boston Americans" were mentioned in the headline but not in the story. Sometimes the only mention was in the headline, while otherwise the team was listed as "Boston." As I read the *Post*, I counted such occurrences as "Boston Americans." More often than not the headline read "Americans" but the text simply referred to "Boston" as a collective entity, as in "Boston played a good game today."

Other teams, such as the Senators, White Sox, Athletics, Browns, and Highlanders were referred to by nicknames or by city name (e.g., the Detroits). Even when the *Post* used the term "Americans" in their headline, though, it was clear in the accompanying text that they more formally referred to the team as "the Boston American League club." The *Post* typically termed the other league's Boston entry as the Boston Nationals.

When describing the upcoming World Series, the September 1903 *Post* referred to the Pittsburgh National/Boston American series. How many times was this team referred to as the "Pilgrims" or "Boston Pilgrims" in the *Boston Post*? Not one time.

Analysis of the *Boston Globe*'s daily coverage produced the following results: Boston, 18; Americans, 6; Bostons, 1; Collins' men, 1; Bostonians, 1; the Boston boys, 1. There were two days where I could not find any mention at all of the team—and they were both in the final week of the season. The *Globe* seemed to be very cautious in giving the team any nickname at all.

As we can see, the use of the city name alone was the predominant usage. I tried to err in favor of finding a team nickname. If one story used "Boston" two times and "Boston Americans" two times, I would tend to "award" that game story to the "Boston Americans" tally. In most instances, there was no decision to be made, in that mixed messages as to team name were not conveyed. How many times was this team referred to as the "Pilgrims" or "Boston

Jimmy Collins

Pilgrims" in the *Boston Globe*? Not one time.

Anyone begin to detect a pattern here?

The *Boston Journal* had very good coverage of ball games, too. They often followed the practice of putting the nicknames of other teams into quotation marks, e.g. "Senators" and "Tigers." The content analysis in the *Journal* showed: Boston, 12; Bostons, 7; Americans, 2; Collins' men, 1; the Collins team, 1; Boston American club, 1; champions, 1; no reference, 5. Interestingly, a few days after Boston clinched the pennant, the *Journal* began to refer to the team in the headlines as the "champions," though only once did the story text apply that designation.

The *Journal* also included a column composed of quotes from fans on how they rated their team's chances, but not a single fan referred to the Pilgrims, either. How many times was the team in question referred to as the "Pilgrims" or "Boston Pilgrims" in the *Boston Journal*? Not once.

The last newspaper I read for September 1903 was the *Boston Record*. The *Record* always presented a header over its league standings. "The Americans' Record" was the box title for the league standings and "with the National Leaguers" for the senior circuit. As to daily coverage of the Boston entry in the AL, the *Record*'s stories broke down in these quantities: Americans, 11; Boston, 6; Collins and his pets, 1; Collins and his charges, 1; Jimmy Collins' men, 1 (the same story also referred to "the Boston boys"); Boston American League baseball team, 1; no reference, 2. How many times was this team referred to as the "Pilgrims" or "Boston Pilgrims" in the *Boston Record*? Not one time.

One might note, parenthetically, that the name "Puritans" also never appeared once in any of the daily newspapers sampled. A survey of these five major daily newspapers in Boston in 1903 failed to turn up even one reference to the alleged "Boston Pilgrims."

Where did this name come from? Agreed, it's a nice name, but it doesn't seem to have been this team's name. When a paper like the *Journal* included a column composed of quotes from fans on how they rated the team's chances in the 1903 World Series, not a single fan referred to the team as Pilgrims. The only reference I've yet found for the "Pilgrims" shows up in a *Boston Journal* article in December 1907—well after the 1903 season was concluded.

THE NATIONAL PASTIME

It is hereby agreed by and between Pittsburg Club of the National League and the Boston American League Club of the American League as follows:

1,- That a post season series shall be played between said base ball clubs consisting of a series of 9 games, if it be necessary to play that number before either club should win 5 games, said series however to terminate when either club shall win 5 games.

2,- Said games to be played at the following times and places: At Boston, Mass., Oct. 1, 2, & 3 (Thursday, Friday and Saturday) At Pittsburg, Pa., " 5, 6, 7 & 8 (Monday, Thuesday, Wednesday and Thursday) At Boston, Mass., " 10 and 12 (Saturday and Monday); providing however, in the event of the weather being such as to prevent a game being played on either of said days, such game shall be postponed until the next succeeding day when the weather will permit such game to be played at the city where scheduled. And in that event there shall be a moving back of the aforesaid schedule for the day or days lost on account of said inclement weather.

3,- Each club shall bear the expense of the games played on their respective grounds, excepting the expense of umpire.

4,- Each club shall furnish and pay the expenses of one umpire to officiate during said series and it is agreed that the umpire so agreed upon to be furnished shall be O'Day from the National League and Connelly from the American League.

No player to participate who was not a regular member of team Sep 1. 1903.

5,- The minimum price of admission in each city shall be 50 cts. and the visiting club shall be settled with by being paid 25 cts. for every admission ticket sold.

6,- A statement to be furnished the visiting club after each game, final settlement to be at the close of the series.

The respective captains of each team shall meet with the umpires above designated before the beginning of the series to agree upon a uniform interpretation of the playing rules.

IN WITNESS WHEROF the parties hereto have caused these presents to be signed by their respective Presidents this *16* day of September, A. D. 1903.

In Presence Of)
) by PITTSBURGH ATHLETIC CO.
_____)
) *Barney Dreyfuss*
) President.
) BOSTON AMERICAN LEAGUE BALL CLUB
) by
_____) *Henry J. Killilea*
     President.

SAMPLING OF OTHER NEWSPAPERS FROM CITIES WITH AMERICAN LEAGUE TEAMS

I also read every September 1903 game account in newspapers from three other cities which hosted American League baseball teams. I read through the daily coverage provided by the *Chicago Tribune*, *New York Times* and *Washington Post*.

The *Chicago Tribune* typically used the straightforward designation "Boston" in its game stories. No other name was used more than once—except for the name "Beaneaters," which was used in three accounts. In addition, the *Tribune* described the team as Collins' aggregation, Collins' men, the Americans, the Bostons, the Bostonians, and also, in one instance, the Plymouth Rocks.

The *New York Times* never really used any designation other than the city name: Boston. In accounts datelined from Boston itself, game stories would sometimes referred to "the local baseball team," "the local men," or, in one case, "the local Americans." After clinching the championship, the *Times* once referred to the Boston club as "the new American League baseball champions."

More than half the time, the *Washington Post* also simply used the city's name to describe the team. The *Post*, like the *Tribune*, employed "Beaneaters" (four times); they used "Americans" twice and "champions" twice. In general, the feeling I was left with was that the team really did not have any name, nor did it have a common nickname.

Even though the team was often described as the "Boston Americans," that was more often in the headlines than in the story. Even then, one did not get the impression that this was meant to be taken as the name of the time; it seemed more simply a way to distinguish the column presenting the AL team's coverage from that of the NL team's. Though it's convenient (and enjoyable) to have team nicknames, I believe that, in this case and the team's 1902 uniforms notwithstanding, it would be inaccurate to state definitively that the team nickname was the "Americans"—the designator "Bostons" was used as often.

We are probably better off concluding that the team really had no nickname until "Red Sox" became established prior to the 1908 season. All in all, the team was described in newspaper columns as "Boston" or "the Bostons" and, when more clarity was necessary, the "Boston Americans." The Boston Pilgrims, though, never existed, not in the minds of the sportswriters, or in the minds of the fans (as best we can tell).

Over the course of 2003, as we begin to celebrate the 100th anniversary of the first World Series, hopefully many Web sites and standard reference sources will begin to effect changes to correct the historical record. As a result of this research, STATS Inc. has agreed to change its data, as has baseball-reference.com and the *Baseball Almanac*. The Pirates have already corrected their Web site.

Over time, the names Pilgrims and Puritans will probably tend to disappear. It seems like sort of a shame, because someone once went to the trouble to invent these more colorful nicknames and they caught on. History is often rewritten, but there is merit to sticking more closely to contemporary facts.

There is a fascination in reading these 1903 sportswriters, how they covered games and how they occasionally labored to find alternative nicknames to describe these early teams that awkwardly lacked more formal names or nicknames. Pittsburgh was typically spelled without the "h" in 1903. As Louis Masur notes in *Autumn Glory*, the United States Board of Geographic Names dropped the "h" between 1890 and 1911.

The 100th Anniversary of "Dummy vs. Dummy"

by Randy Fisher
and James Goodwin

On May 16, 1902, an unprecedented and unparalleled event occurred in baseball history. It was the first and only time two deaf professional athletes—Luther Haden "Dummy" Taylor and William Ellsworth "Dummy" Hoy—competed against each other in an epic encounter at the Palace of the Fans, home of the Cincinnati Reds. A diverse crowd of 5,000 deaf and hearing people witnessed this once-in-a-lifetime event. The Reds were celebrating the opening of their new concrete stadium. Weber's Band provided the music for the occasion. Mayor Julius Fleischmann and Judge Ferris gave short speeches complimenting the club and the public for the opening of the grandstand and expressing the hope that the season would be very successful.

Luther Haden "Dummy" Taylor took the mound for the visiting New York Giants. William Ellsworth "Dummy" Hoy played center-field and was the leadoff hitter for the Cincinnati Reds. At the age of 40, Hoy was in his last season with the Reds.

In those days, being called "Dummy" was not intended to reflect low intelligence or poor ball playing skills. Rather, the nickname "Dummy" was referring to being deaf and unable to speak. It should be noted that neither man was insulted by the nickname; they were both proud and inspired by their team-given names.

Horace Fogel, the Giants manager at the time, named Taylor to start the game. There was only one umpire, Joe "Pongo Joe" Cantillon, who would make all the calls on the field and at home plate. Before the game started, Dummy Taylor threw warm-up pitches from the mound. Meanwhile, Dummy Hoy did his preparation activities in the batter's circle. He then strode up to the plate, looked at Dummy Taylor on the pitcher's mound, and said in sign language, "I'm glad to see you" before stepping up to bat. Hoy led off with a hit to center field.

Hoy played a great game, as he was the only Red to collect two hits. Luther Taylor performed well, pitching eight innings and allowing no earned runs. However, a shortstop error allowed three Reds, including Hoy, to cross home plate in the eighth to give Cincinnati a 3-0 lead.

Dummy Taylor settled down and made sure that Hoy did not steal any bases during the game. It looked like Taylor's performance might be sacrificed, as he was pulled and replaced by a pinch-hitter for the Giants' last at-bat in the ninth inning. New York rallied to score five runs and took a 5-3 lead. Hoy was able to get one run, one walk, and two hits off Taylor and did not strike out. Ultimately the Reds failed to score in the bottom of the ninth inning. The Giants won the game 5-3. Taylor was credited for the victory as he struck out four and walked only two.

This game was the only time in major league history when two deaf players faced each other. It also ended up being the only time that Hoy and Taylor would face off against each other in their major league careers. While New York and Cincinnati met several times that season, Hoy and Taylor's playing time did not coincide. Taylor

James Goodwin and Randy Fisher are members of the "Dummy" Hoy Committee, which is attempting to put Hoy into the National Baseball Hall of Fame.

pitched in relief against the Reds twice, but Hoy was replaced in the center field by a young player named Cy Seymour.

Dummy Hoy started his professional career late at the age of 26. Despite the late start, Hoy managed to finish his career with 2,042 hits, 594 stolen bases (reaching the 500 mark at age 40), 1,424 runs, and a career batting average of .288. Dummy Taylor went on to pitch with the Giants for eight more years, compiling a 116-106 record, a respectable 2.75 ERA, and 21 shutouts. Taylor spent eight more years in the minor leagues before retiring.

Interestingly, later in the season, Taylor helped to initiate John McGraw's reputation as an accomplished manager during the July 23, 1902 game between the Brooklyn Superbas (Dodgers) and the New York Giants. Taylor beat the Superbas 4-1, handing John McGraw the first of his 2,763 regular-season managerial wins.

On September 6, 1942, Dummy Hoy and Dummy Taylor returned to the baseball diamond in Toledo, Ohio, in celebration of the 40th anniversary of their Palace of the Fans encounter. They performed as battery mates to open the Ohio State Deaf Softball Tournament, where Toledo played the Akron "Rubber City Silents" at Willys Park Field.

Luther Hayden Taylor passed away on August 22, 1958, at the age of 82, eleven days after suffering a heart attack. William Ellsworth Hoy threw the first ball of the 1961 World Series, played by the New York Yankees and the Cincinnati Reds. Hoy passed away six weeks later on December 15, 1961, at 99 years of age.

CINCINNATI	AB	R	1B	PO	A	E
Hoy, cf	4	1	2	1	0	0
Dubbs, lf	4	1	1	6	0	0
Beckley, 1b	4	0	1	7	1	0
Crawford, rf	4	0	0	1	0	0
Magoon, 2b	3	1	1	4	5	1
Corcoran, ss	4	0	1	1	0	2
Peltz, c	3	0	1	5	1	0
Hahn	3	0	0	0	0	0
Beck	1	0	0	0	0	0
TOTALS	**33**	**3**	**7**	**27**	**9**	**4**

NEW YORK	AB	R	1B	PO	A	E
Van Haltren, c	4	0	0	4	0	0
Smith, 2b	5	0	0	2	1	0
Lauder, 3b	4	1	2	3	3	1
Jones, rf	4	1	1	2	0	0
Doyle, 1b	3	1	0	7	0	0
Bean, ss	4	0	2	2	1	1
Jackson, lf	4	1	1	3	0	0
Bowerman, c	4	1	2	4	2	0
Taylor, p	3	0	0	0	2	1
Yeager	1	0	1	0	0	0
Sparks, p	0	0	0	0	0	0
TOTALS	**36**	**5**	**9**	**27**	**9**	**3**

	1 2 3	4 5 6	7 8 9		
Cincinnati	0 0 0	0 0 0	0 3 0	–	3
New York	0 0 0	0 0 0	0 0 5	–	5

2B: Lauder, Bowerman. 3B: Bowerman. SAC: Cincinnati, 1. SB: Smith, Doyle. LOB: Cincinnati, 8; New York, 6. DP: Lauder and Doyle; Steinfeldt and Beckley; Magoon, Corcoran; Beckley and Peltz. K: Hahn, 3; Taylor, 4. BB: Taylor, 2; Hahn, 2. HBP: Taylor, 1. WP: Taylor. H: Taylor, 6; Sparks, 1. Time: 2:03 Umpire: Joe Cantillon.

Cincinnati Times-Star, May 17, 1902, p. 6.

Hoy and Taylor in 1942 at the Ohio State deaf softball tournament. The two acted as battery mates and each threw the opening and closing pitches of the tourney. This photo, taken on the 40th anniversary of their major league game against each other, is the only one showing the two posed together. Photo courtesy of Ralph Lin Weber.

Rogers Hornsby in 1932

by Duane Winn

Rogers Hornsby's will to excellence and his combativeness on the field won him a loyal following in the stands. Sportswriters, too, admired Hornsby because he answered questions in the same straightforward manner he took on a Walter Johnson fastball.

However, his irascibility didn't endear him with major league owners and front-office men. When one adds his propensity for gambling and controversy, it's little wonder the Chicago Cubs cast him adrift in the summer of 1932, although the Cubs were in third place and still entertained hopes of a pennant.

Given all these shortcomings, Hornsby didn't attract much attention on the free market. The Pirates, though, were one team that was very much interested in obtaining Hornsby's services for a stretch drive of their own.

Not the Pittsburgh Pirates, but the Hampton, Iowa, Pirates, a crack semi-professional team that was enjoying its most successful season since coming into existence in 1923.

John Clinton Marschall had organized the team in the summer of that year when he returned home from classes at the University of Iowa. Nicknamed "Smoke" for his pitching arm, Marschall was unable to break into the Hawkeyes' starting lineup. A friend of his suggested that he take up track and field.

Duane Winn is the editor of the Brooklyn (Iowa) Chronicle. *He also is pursuing a master's degree in journalism and mass communications at Drake University in Des Moines.*

Marschall did, and he soon became an accomplished javelin thrower.

Yet he couldn't long ignore baseball's siren call. He played center field for the Pirates and surrounded himself with athletes of similar educational background. High school classmates and accomplished area amateurs supplemented the lineup.

For the first few years the Pirates played teams within a 50-mile radius. They also played host to barnstorming teams such as the House of David, Kansas City Monarchs, and Gilkerson's United Giants.

Convinced that baseball would retain its popularity even in the midst of a nationwide slump, Marschall in 1931 refurbished the old bleachers at the fairgrounds and added a 135,000-watt lighting system to enable the Pirates to play night baseball.

The gamble worked.

The Pirates were soon attracting as many as 6,000 fans to games with top-notch opponents. The attendance figures were buoyed by promotions such as ladies night, deep discounts on season tickets, and a carnival-like atmosphere, with circus entertainers, motorcycle exhibitions, and boxing matches scheduled on the same day as baseball games.

Marschall and the Pirates slowly began to expand their circle, scheduling games all over Iowa, not to mention South Dakota and Nebraska.

The Pirates also were making the transition to a strictly professional team. In place of amateurs, Marschall was able to attract players from the

American Association and Three I League. He had also secured the services of two Iowa natives, Art Reinhart and Wattie Holm, who helped the Cardinals to a world championship in 1926.

Reinhart, a native of nearby Ackley, pitched one game for the Cardinals in 1919. The lanky left hander kicked around in the minors for five years before returning to the Cardinals in 1925. In his first full year Reinhart strung together an 11-5 record and a 3.05 earned run average, which placed him among the league leaders in that category.

During the Cardinals' stretch run in 1926, Reinhart picked up a victory in a crucial doubleheader against the Pittsburgh Pirates in September at Sportsman's Park. Reinhart disappointed in the World Series. He was loser to the Yankees in the fourth game, walking four and surrendering four runs in the fifth inning without getting an out.

Reinhart was denied a chance to redeem himself. He was one of the pitchers warming up in the bullpen in the late innings of the decisive seventh game. Hornsby opted for the veteran Pete Alexander, who finished the game out to earn the underdog Cardinals the world championship.

Holm, a native of Peterson, also attended the University of Iowa. He was promptly signed by the Cardinals and was sent down to Syracuse. An outfielder, he played from 1924 to 1928 with the Cardinals. A career .278 batting average, he was a good contact hitter who struck out only 86 times in 1,500 at-bats. Holm, too, contributed to the Cardinals' title with a Series home run.

Both players might have been able to find major league employment had times been flush, but the Depression had forced teams to tighten their belts. Attendance was sagging and teams were forced to cut salaries and ax players.

Marschall also inked Bud Knox, the former Pittsburgh Pirates catcher, and Lynn King, a Drake University alum who would step up to the major leagues a few years later.

Even those who took note of Marschall's ability to sign major league-level talent, however, raised an eyebrow when the *Mason City Globe-Gazette* on August 24, 1932, announced that Hornsby and the Hampton Pirates were nearing agreement on a contract.

The *Globe-Gazette* had picked up the story from the United Press International. The story came their way by a Carroll daily newspaper reporter who prefaced his report with the following proviso: "It may be just another one of those things."

ACKLEY HERITAGE CENTER

Art Reinhart honed his skills on the sandlots of small-town Ackley in Iowa. He helped the Cardinals to a World Series title under manager Rogers Hornsby.

Nonetheless, the rumor spread as quickly as a prairie fire in Hornsby's native state. When Hornsby was contacted by the press, he disavowed any such arrangement. Marschall was not with the club in Carroll when the story broke. His whereabouts were unknown, but he was expected to rejoin the club at Sioux Falls, South Dakota, the following day.

When a reporter hooked up with him the following day, Marschall expressed optimism that a deal could be struck.

"Reinhart and Hornsby used to be buddies on the St. Louis Cardinals," he told the *Globe-Gazette*. "Reinhart has been in negotiations with Hornsby to play with us. I am not prepared, however, to make an announcement yet."

The prospect of a player of Hornsby's stature toiling for a semi-professional team might sound ludicrous. However, there were incentives.

Hornsby was deep in debt. According to one biographer, Charles Alexander, Hornsby was embroiled in a dispute with the Internal Revenue Service concerning a tax deduction. If disallowed, Hornsby and his wife would owe the federal government several thousand dollars.

Hornsby, always a profligate spender, also owed baseball acquaintances several hundred dollars when his horseracing selections finished up the track.

The top prize in the Council Bluffs tournament was $1,600. A piece of the purse, coupled with the $300 to $400 per game that Marschall pledged to pay, would have alleviated Hornsby's financial suffering.

When weighed against a month or two of inactivity, the opportunity to play with the Pirates didn't seem to be a bad scenario. He would be reunited with two World Series pals and play against top-notch competition, just a step below the major leagues.

Remember it was Hornsby who said, "It don't make no difference where I go or what happens, so long as I can play the full nine." On another occasion he stated, "Baseball is my life. It's the only thing I know and care about."

The score books, in the possession of Marschall's son, John, don't contain an entry for Hornsby. There was no incentive for Marschall to keep the matter secret. The news that Hornsby would play in the tournament would have swelled attendance figures.

The *Council Bluffs Daily Nonpariel*, which covered the tournament, would have certainly recognized Hornsby. But there is no mention of him in a newspaper box score.

There are other factors that conspired to make the deal fall through. The Pirates had two African Americans in their starting lineup. Hilton, who reportedly played for the Monarchs, played second base. Simms, one time a member of the Gilkerson's United Giants, patrolled center field.

Hornsby, according to Alexander, was a member of the Ku Klux Klan, although it was doubtful he was active in the organization. Still, the presence of two African Americans on the same field, on the same team, may have led Hornsby to reconsider.

Swede Risberg was a member of the Sioux City Stockyards, who were entered in the tournament. Since his banishment from baseball for his role in the Black Sox scandal, Risberg had traveled from town to town, finding employment with semi-professional teams when he could. He had applied for reinstatement several times, but his pleas were turned down by Commissioner Landis.

Landis, if he caught wind of Hornsby's participation in a tournament with Risberg, would likely have severely reprimanded Hornsby. It's likely, said Alexander, that Landis would have prevented Hornsby from ever playing major league baseball again. It's a pity the deal was never consummated.

Hampton was considered a dark horse, but upset the Cuban Giants en route to a title game with the House of David. In a delicious bit of irony, Grover Cleveland Alexander reprised his role in the World Series five years earlier. After his team scored the go-ahead run in extra innings, Alexander closed out the Pirates to secure a title for the House of David.

Hornsby's experience with the Pirates provided him with a template for his baseball days after his major league career was over. He found out that a washed-up major leaguer could still make another large payday when he helped a Denver semi-professional team to a tournament title in 1937.

GENUINE VETERAN BALLPLAYERS *Catcher Hank Gowdy was the first player to enlist in WWI, joining up after his last game on June 26, 1917. He returned to play in 1919. When WW2 broke out, Gowdy was a coach for the Cincinnati Reds. At the age of 53, he enlisted in 1942 as an army captain, and he was assigned to Fort Benning, Georgia, whose baseball field was named after him years before. He is the lone major leaguer to serve in both world wars.*

Only the Marines called up WW2 veterans for the Korean War, and so 33-year-old Ted Williams was called up to serve in Korea. He flew 39 missions. Ted was the only major league player in both wars. — JIM CHARLTON

John Carden

by Bill Hickman

Harry Agganis, Ken Hubbs, Lyman Bostock . . .

Some men's lives are tragically brief. Yet when they are over, we often find that these men have made their mark in the world. Former New York Giant John Bruton "Smokey" Carden was one such man.

Carden was born in Killeen, Texas, on May 19, 1921. He was one of 12 children (three died in infancy) born to parents who owned a 460-acre farm nine miles outside Killeen on land that is now Fort Hood. For as long as his sister Ila can remember, John played baseball as a youngster.

The pitching talent of this right hander became evident at Texas A&M University in College Station. Creating family continuity with his older brother Weldon (Red), who was an Aggie catcher on the 1941 and 1943 varsity teams, John starred for the same team in 1942 and 1943. John was known alternately by his initials, J.B., and by "Smokey" in college. It's easy to deduce the derivation of his nickname. A 1942 Aggie newspaper mentioned that John "has been smoking that fastball of his by many would-be hitters." Former Aggie teammate Ira Glass, who later played in the White Sox organization, remembers him as a "big ol' boy who could throw that aspirin."

In 1942, Smokey's team won the Southwest Conference with a 13-2 league record and finished 19-3 overall. He won five of those league games, and no

Bill Hickman is a retired federal manager with a long-time interest in baseball cards and photos. He chairs SABR's Pictorial History Committee. His work has been published in Sports Collectors Digest.

reports have been found to indicate a loss on his part. That team also contained another future major leaguer, Les Peden, who played third base behind John. Les moved to the position of catcher in the minor leagues, and appeared with the Washington Senators for nine games in 1953. Les remembers the Carden brothers as really good guys who were inseparable. Cullen Rogers, the team's left fielder, recalls Smokey as a "great guy and great winner."

The Aggie team captain and catcher, J. D. Scoggins, was also a terrific ballplayer, but lost his life in combat in the Pacific during World War II. According to John Scoggins, his cousin J. D. was slated for the New York Yankees organization and had an excellent chance to become a major leaguer. Les Peden indicated that J. D. was the best athlete he saw at Texas A&M.

In 1943 with the Cardens as battery mates, the Aggies tied for the conference title with a 6-2 record. Smokey was the ace hurler of the staff, with fine performances like his season-opening, 13-strikeout win over Rice. Weldon picked off at least 10 runners that year, and contributed punch to the lineup. There were only three teams playing in the conference in 1943 due to World War II. Texas A&M was a military school, and its students were all considered to be in the military. As soon as the conference season was over, the team broke up and went off to active military duty.

Smokey moved on to the Marines, where he served

for two and a half years. He joined the Quantico, Virginia, baseball team in June 1944. He would become friends with Jerome Holtzman, a fellow Marine who is now the official historian for Major League Baseball. The Quantico team included infielder Cal Ermer, who went on to play one game for the Washington Senators in 1947 and then to manage the Minnesota Twins in 1967 and 1968. By mid-August, Smokey had a 5-2 record. Included in these wins was a 6-1 beating of the Heurich Brewers, the defending champions of the Washington Industrial League. On August 19, he faced the Norfolk Tars Navy team, which was loaded with former and future major leaguers. He struck out seven, but lost the game 11-5. According to the *Quantico Sentry*, the Marine base's newspaper, his teammates committed six errors which "produced a mess of unearned runs." On August 30, he got revenge on that same Tars team. Facing a lineup which included Eddie Robinson, Glen McQuillen, Clyde McCullough, and Hank Schenz, Smokey bested them with a 2-1 win on a six-hitter. He struck out six. On September 3, he struck out nine batters from the Navy Aeronautics Bureau in just five innings. With Quantico ahead 13-0, the Leathernecks' manager pulled Smokey.

As the 1945 campaign began for Quantico, the *Quantico Sentry* was making statements such as: "Heading the returning veterans is Pfc. John (Smokey) Carden, sensational righthander, who breezed through opponents last year with his fiery fastball" and "In Carden, he [Quantico's manager] has one of the finest righthanders in the services today." During that season, the Quantico team would play three major league teams. As the staff ace, Smokey was called to be the starting pitcher in all three games. If not for two critical fielding errors on the part of his teammates, he would have won two of those three games.

The first contest against major leaguers came on opening day of Quantico's season, April 2, 1945. Smokey began well by striking out the first two Boston Braves to face him. But things began to unravel in the second inning, as a single, an infield error, a hit batsman, followed by two more hits, led to Boston's first two runs. The Braves scored three more runs in the third, and Carden was through for the day, as Quantico lost 7-0.

The May 7 game against the Philadelphia Athletics was one that should have been a victory for Smokey. He held them scoreless for eight innings on only five hits. He struck out eight and walked only one.

Quantico carried a 2-0 lead into the ninth. The A's half of the ninth began with a single by Bill McGhee. An out moved him to second. Joe Cicero then singled in McGhee to make the score 2-1. Bobby Wilkins then hit a double-play ball to third base, but Cal Ermer dropped it, and everyone was safe. The A's pitcher was up next, and he produced a sacrifice bunt which moved the runners to second and third. Ed Busch next hit "a hard smash" to short, which the Marine infielder Taylor booted away, and the game was tied. Charlie Metro's double followed, and that ended the scoring with a 4-2 win for the A's. It was a heartbreaking game for Smokey, but it set the stage for his most important game against major leaguers.

On August 3, 1945, Quantico played the New York Giants before 5,000 spectators at the Post Diamond. Smokey handcuffed the Giants on two singles over the first seven innings. Future Hall of Famers Mel Ott and Ernie Lombardi combined for an 0-for-5 day at the plate against him. This was an accomplishment against Ott, who had smashed his 500th home run in his last game. Ott hit two additional homers against the Phillies once he left Quantico.

So Smokey and the Marines carried away a 4-2 victory that day. He struck out three, and had two hits himself in his three at-bats. Though Carden tired in the eighth and had to be relieved, he had left a lasting impression on the Giants. Former New York Giants 21-game winner Bill Voiselle, probably referring to this game, more than 50 years later recalled: "I do remember him pitching, and he pitched a good game. He may have beaten the Giants that day." Voiselle is correct.

After the exhibition game against the Giants, Smokey went on to post an 18-7 record for the 1945 Quantico season, with an ERA of 2.55. In the last few weeks of the season, the Marine squad was carrying only two pitchers, so he was truly a workhorse. On one occasion, he played a doubleheader by relieving in the first game and pitching the entire second game, winning both. He also proved to be adept with a bat, leading the team with a .389 batting average and 35 hits, including two homers.

As his military career drew to a close, Carden signed with the Giants in May 1946 for a $2,000 bonus and reported directly to them without the benefit of any minor league experience.

He pitched in his sole major league game on May 18, 1946, in the Polo Grounds against the Chicago Cubs. On a cold and drizzly day when the reigning National League champions has already scored 12

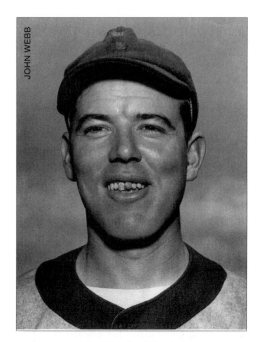

JOHN WEBB

John "Smokey" Carden,
ace pitcher for Texas A&M.

runs against the Giants before he entered the game, he was given the chore of handling the Cubs in the eighth and ninth innings. Displaying the control problems of a big fastballer, he gave up four walks and four hits in two innings, leaving the game with an ERA of 22.50.

Smokey finished the year at Richmond. He debuted against the Roanoke Rosox with a two-inning no-hit relief job. In his best game, which transpired on August 4, he shut down the Norfolk Tars 3-0 and yielded only three singles in his complete game. He outdueled Tex Hoyle, who would later on have major league experience with the Athletics. In another game, he bested future Cub Turk Lown with a 2-1 victory over the Newport News Dodgers. Altogether, he won six and lost eight for the Richmond Colts, but chalked up an impressive ERA of 2.84. After the season, he married Mary Ellen Focke ("Ellen") on September 30, 1946.

Smokey started 1947 at Sioux City, but struggled with arm trouble. He missed three weeks of play in August due to elbow surgery following his stint with the Sioux City Soos. He moved on to Trenton. Once again he was with a team that was going to enjoy success. The Trenton Giants, managed by Tommy Heath, moved from last place to first that year, winning 52 of its final 62 games and electrifying the entire community. John made his first start with Trenton on July 29 and beat Hagerstown 3-1 by hurling a three-hitter. On

September 1, with 6,531 fans crammed into Dunn Field—capacity 3,500—John pitched a four-hitter to beat future major leaguer Curt Simmons and his Wilmington teammates by a score of 2-1. According to Trenton teammate and future New York Giant Bobby Hofman, Carden "was a great guy to have around if there was a fight." Apparently, Smokey's size and Marine status commanded plenty of respect in those situations. He stood 6-foot-5 and weighed 210 pounds.

Although Smokey's arm surgery had helped him improve his pitching during the last part of the 1947 season, his arm still had not felt entirely comfortable. Some dental problems had infected his entire body and were indirectly causing difficulty for his right arm. In the fall of 1947, he had these problems taken care of, and he entered 1948 prepared for a stronger season.

John began 1948 on the New York Giants spring training roster, but the parent club did not retain him going into the season. Instead, he had a fine 11-5 record with the Knoxville Smokies in 1948. His Knoxville skipper was Dave Garcia, who would manage the California Angels and Cleveland Indians years later. Former Knoxville teammate and subsequent New York Giants pitcher George Spencer remembers John as a good friend and fastball pitcher with an exceptionally high leg kick. Neal Watlington, who was John's battery mate at Knoxville, was destined to catch for the Philadelphia Athletics in 1953. Neal describes John as having been "a real nice guy, very competitive, and as a pitcher, he had real good stuff." John's 1948 performance with Knoxville exceeded that of his teammate, Hoyt Wilhelm, a future Hall of Famer. John posted an 11-5 record with a 3.47 ERA. Hoyt's record was 13-9 with a 3.62 ERA.

A *Sporting News* account of Carden's career listed him at Sioux City and Minneapolis as well in 1948. He was optioned to Minneapolis April 2 that year, but then outrighted to Sioux City April 13 without seeing any action for the Millers. Carden's wife, Ellen, confirmed he was indeed at Knoxville all year.

Smokey was slated to play for Minneapolis team in 1949. He spent the off-season working on his father-in-law's farm near his home in Mexia. On February 8, 1949, he was making final preparations to leave Mexia and report to spring training. Not wanting to leave his wife and her parents without telephone service, he ascended a power and telephone pole on the farm in order to fix a broken telephone line. In those days, it was standard practice for the owners of rural telephone hookups to be responsible for repairing

Military and Organized Baseball Record

Year	Team	League	G	IP	H	ER	SO	BB	W	L	ERA
1944	Quantico	Military	n/a	n/a	n/a	n/a	n/a	n/a	8	4	n/a
1945	Quantico	Military	34	207⅔	179	59	160	51	18	7	2.55
1946	New York	National	1	2	4	5	1	4	0	0	22.50
1946	Richmond	Piedmont	16	111	105	35	50	37	6	8	2.84
1947	Sioux City	Western	12	47	65	34	43	29	1	4	6.51
1947	Trenton	Interstate	7	31	n/a	13	17	9	3	1	3.77
1948	Knoxville	Tri-State	21	140	130	54	100	39	11	5	3.47
MINOR LEAGUE TOTALS			56	329	n/a	136	210	114	21	18	3.72
MAJOR LEAGUE TOTALS			1	2	4	5	1	4	0	0	22.50

their own lines. He had made such repairs before, but this time he accidentally touched a 2,300-volt rural electric power line, and was electrocuted.

In visiting the mourning family, Mel Ott and two other Giants conveyed their confidence that Smokey was a player who had possessed the talent to make it back to the big leagues. The *Mexia Daily News* opined, "Carden was one of those rare individuals who seemed to like everyone, and in turn, was appreciated and admired by all who knew him."

Cal Ermer, in a letter to this writer, gave a similar perspective, but in different words. Cal described Smokey as a "great guy, with a warm heart." Cal went on to say, "I used to have people asking me about Harmon Killebrew and Brooks Robinson, and I would answer this way: 'They were better people than they were ballplayers' and Smokey belongs in that class." Cal also had great respect for Smokey's pitching ability and described him as a "gentle giant with a Nolan Ryan fastball and a good curveball."

When John Carden died, his wife Ellen was pregnant with a son who would be born in June 1949. She subsequently married a man named Sam Webb, and John's son is named John Wallace Webb. John Wallace in turn produced a son of his own, Brad Webb, who became a pretty fair pitcher at the University of Pittsburgh. No doubt, Smokey would have been very proud.

Sources:

This information on John Carden comes with my gratitude to the many people who supplied it to me. Ellen Webb graciously shared recollections of her late husband's life and baseball career. Ila Bretzius, J.B.'s sister, provided background on his life on the family farm, as well as his baseball experiences. Bill Carden, John's nephew, clarified many aspects of his family life and opened the doors to conversations with others in J.B.'s family. John Wallace Webb has also been an enthusiastic supporter of the research.

Pat Doyle, who heads a service firm called Old Time Data, supplied most of the minor league statistical information. The major league statistics come from *Total Baseball* VII. David Barker, a baseball researcher with substantial experience in tracing Texas college baseball records, supplied most of the information on Carden's Aggie career. Todd Walters of Texas A&M's Cushing Library provided some articles from the school paper, *The Battalion*, which gave accounts of 1942 Aggies games when Carden pitched.

Gene Sherman, former broadcaster for the Sioux City Soos, and Jerome Holtzman, *Chicago Tribune* sportswriter and president of the Baseball Writers Association of America, shared their recollections of friendships with Carden at Quantico. In fact, Gene Sherman drove John to the Polo Grounds when he first reported to the Giants. Greg Beston, who was working on a book on one-game major leaguers, supplied the date of Carden's sole major league game. Randy Linthurst, a SABR member from Florida and former sportswriter, saw Carden pitch for Trenton in 1947 and supplied John's history for that year, as well as the quote from the late Bobby Hofman.

Ira Glass, Les Peden, and Cullen Rogers all shared their perspectives as John's former Aggie teammates. George Spencer and Neal Watlington reflected on the 1948 season as Knoxville teammates. Bill Voiselle, who pitched full seasons for the Giants starting in 1944 and moved to the Boston Braves about a third of the way into the 1947 season, recalled John's hurling against the Giants.

Cal Ermer considered Smokey to be his best friend while they were teammates during the 1945 season at Quantico. The two visited New York together the first time Smokey was invited to meet with the Giants. Cal's background as a major league manager lends additional support to the points he made about Smokey.

My other sources of information were: John Carden's obituaries as they appeared in *The Sporting News* of February 16, 1949, and in undated clippings from the *Mexia Daily News*; the 1942 and 1943 Texas A&M yearbooks; the box score from his sole major league game; the *New York Times* of May 14 and 19, 1946; the April 1948 edition of *Baseball Digest*; several 1946 issues of the *Richmond Times-Dispatch*; the *Richmond News Leader* of September 9, 1947; and many 1944 and 1945 issues of *The Quantico Sentry*.

Big Problems and Simple Answers

An Explanation of the Negro Leagues

by Sammy J. Miller

I think that no players in the majors today could conceive of going through what Negro Leaguers did for a chance at a baseball career. At the same time however, most of the veterans of baseball's black leagues will say that, if given the chance, they would do it all over again.

A statement like that says a lot about the players in the Negro Leagues. It certainly carries more weight than it would coming from a former white big leaguer. The differences between the white and black leagues were great, but not in the way that most people think. The most common mistake that people make in their perception of the two leagues is the level of talent in each. Too many people tend to go to the extreme in their view of the Negro Leagues. They either think that the level of play was grossly inferior to the majors, or far superior. Both of these assumptions are incorrect. Truth be told, the level of talent in both the leagues were comparable. Any established star in the Negro Leagues would have been able to play on any major league team and continue to perform at his usual level. Chances are, the Negro League player, for a time, would do better in the white majors than he did in the Negro Leagues, just as his white counterpart's performance would most likely fall off for a time in the Negro Leagues. The reason for the changes, however, has nothing to do with talent, but

rather that the business of the game differed so greatly in the two leagues.

In the white majors, teams had a safe haven in their home fields. At the beginning of each year they knew that they would be at that stadium for seventy-seven games, and play eleven games in each of seven stadiums during the season. They would, at the very most, play two games in the same day only once every few weeks. White major leaguers traveled in comfort and were secure in the knowledge that once they reached a city, they would play there for two or three days before hitting the road again. The traveling done by major leagues was planned so that it would be easy on the players. And that's exactly what it was. Some former major league players may deny that and claim that the traveling was tough on them, but in comparison to the schedules of the major Negro League teams, traveling in the white majors was a cakewalk.

There was no preset number of games that a Negro League team would play each year. On the other hand, in major league baseball, the number of games played in an official season was set in stone—154. In comparison, official league games in the Negro Leagues never totaled more than 99. That was the high-water mark reached by the Detroit Stars of the Negro National League in 1927; several other teams played nearly as many league games during the 1920s seasons.

By the 1930s, however, the number of league games had dropped. In the Negro National League,

Sammy J. Miller has co-authored four books on the Negro Leagues and is currently the editor of The Negro Leagues Courier, the newsletter of SABR's Negro Leagues Committee.

the Pittsburgh Crawfords of 1935, considered by some to be one of the greatest teams ever, played only 72 games in a split-season schedule. The drop in the number of league games for Negro National League (NNL) teams continued at such a pace that by 1945, the NNL pennant-winning Homestead Grays played just 45 league games, while the pennant-winning Cleveland Buckeyes of the Negro American League played 69 league games.

These numbers refer only to league games, not the total number of games played. It was rare if a major Negro League team played less than two hundred games in a single season. The reason that such a small percentage were leagues games is simple. In order for black baseball to be able to operate at anything close to a break-even level, the teams had to make all of America their home field. At any time during the era of the black baseball leagues, the population of those of African American descent was approximately 9% of the United States. In 1940, to pick a random year, the population of the United States was 131 million people, making the total black population in the area of 12 million people spread across the country. Fans of the Negro Leagues were overwhelmingly black, and black baseball had a much smaller consumer base from which to draw.

In the Northeast, Newark was one of the cities with largest percentages of blacks. In 1940, the overall population was around 430,000 people, with blacks making up nearly 11% of the city. It was the home of the Negro National League Newark Eagles. If the Eagles could pull every black living in Newark to a game, as well as entice 1% of the white population of the city to also attend, it would result in a crowd of less than 50,000 people. Needless to say, no Negro league team was ever able to attract every person of African American descent in their city to a game. On Opening Day in 1942, at Ruppert Stadium in Newark, the Eagles did draw a crowd of around 13,000 fans, or just under 29% of the city's black population. And that was in the 1940s, the heyday of black baseball.

During the years of World War II, the Negro Leagues rivaled the major leagues as a business. In 1942 and 1943 attendance declined at major league games, while it steadily increased at Negro League contests. The reasons behind this are simple.

The United States' need for men for the armed forces and to produce war materiel resulted in the country facing a shortage of manpower. In order to fill this gap, the job market was suddenly opened to individuals previously excluded. One of these groups

that benefited was African Americans.

As a result, the second great migration of African Americans took place, with hundreds of thousands of blacks leaving the South. Of this number, roughly half of them moved to the Midwest and East Coast, areas which were the traditional homes of the major Negro League franchises.

By 1944, nearly 8% of the jobs in war industries were held by African Americans. These workers' salaries would rank them among the highest-paid African Americans in the United States, making, on average, the same as a white female worker, another group used to fill wartime industry positions.

Before the war, the average African American worker had an annual income of about $457 a year, while the average white worker made $1,064 per annum. By 1944, the average African American defense worker was making $1,976 annually. Workers in urban areas had more money but faced the same situation that all Americans faced; due to wartime restrictions, there was less on which to spend their money. While African Americans had wages that had quadrupled during the war years, production of consumer goods had dropped drastically.

For example, there were no civilian cars produced, bicycles were rationed, no civilian production of toasters, percolators, or other such household appliances. Rationing of leather resulted in women's shoes available in six colors only, full skirts and knife pleats were banned, lace was limited, and there was a general shortage of men's clothes. In addition cigarettes, coffee, tea, butter, eggs, meat, and other foodstuffs, as well as gasoline, was rationed and restrictions were placed on travel by everyone, including major league teams.

More money in the pockets of its fan base was not the only advantage the Negro Leagues had during the war years. While stars like Ted Williams, Joe DiMaggio, Bob Feller, and countless other major league drawing cards were off serving Uncle Sam, the major Negro Leagues stars of the day, Satchel Paige, Cool Papa Bell, Josh Gibson, Jud Wilson, and a plethora of others were still to be found plying their trade at the local ball yards. This was not because African American ballplayers did not help in the war effort. Scores of Negro League players' careers. including future Hall of Famers Monte Irvin and Leon Day, were interrupted by the war, There were other reasons that the Negro Leagues' biggest drawing cards were not called up for military service. While still a dazzling pitcher, Paige was too old to serve. Gibson, who was still knocking mammoth home runs, was declared medically unfit for military service due to bad knees. Various other reasons kept other top Negro League players from trading in their baseball flannels for Army khakis.

The old adage that all good things must come to an end proved true in the case of Negro League baseball. With the end of the war, Negro League baseball once again fell on hard times. Not, as some people believe, solely as a result of the Brooklyn Dodgers' signing of Jackie Robinson. The signing of Robinson of course played a big role in the ultimate demise of the Negro Leagues, but so did something else which ended when the fighting in Europe and the Pacific did: wartime jobs. A prime example of this was the shipbuilding industry, which flourished on the East Coast during the war and employed 200,000 African Americans during the war. But in 1946 it employed only 10,000 African Americans. Even the boom in the construction field that followed the end of the war did not increase the job market of blacks all that much. While there were countless new jobs available there were also countless new people in need of jobs returning to the country. In addition, individuals who had made their living in the lumber and oil towns that underwent a financial boom during the war now needed jobs, since that boom had ended. African Americans, for the most part, were returning to the financial straits they were in before the war.

The Negro Leagues could not continue as they had during the war years. In addition to less money in the pockets of its fan base, much of that would be spent on tickets to major league games to see Jackie Robinson play. Just a year or two away from selling out Yankee Stadium or Ebbets Field for Negro Leagues games, it was back to the prewar style of operation.

In 1939, according to James Overmyer in *Queen of the Negro Leagues: Effa Manley and the Newark Eagles*, the Eagles averaged 3,480 paid attendance on Sundays and 2,176 paid attendance on other dates at their home field of Ruppert Stadium, where they played 22 games on 15 different dates.

The Eagles did not get to keep all of the money that was made at these games. The stadium owners, the booking agent, and the visiting team each got a percentage of the gate, the amount made by ticket sales. Therefore, by taking into account the smaller crowds plus the division of the profits among three or four different entities, one can see that Negro League baseball home games were far from a cash cow. As a result Negro league teams owners had to find ways to

make money and at the same time keep it in the coffers of black American and out of the pockets of the white stadium owners and white booking agents. A few owners took the next logical step.

Encased in the pages of Negro League history, hidden among the names of over 400 different ballparks that Negro League games were played in, there are only a handful that shared a common trait. These six parks were not grand or majestic. But these parks were special. They were the only home fields of major league–level teams that were owned by African Americans. Hilldale Park in Philadelphia, Martin Park in Memphis, Wilson Park in Nashville, Greenlee Field in Pittsburgh, Tate Park in Cleveland, and Dyckman Oval in New York City are names that mean little to most people today. But at one time they were traces of equality in a landscape of bigotry.

By playing in a black-owned ballpark, the team owners automatically cut down on the number of hands reaching for a piece of the gate. Also, public opinion could be swayed to the favor of the owner by allowing the park to be used by civic organizations when his team was out of town. The Martin Brothers, owners of Martin Park in Memphis, Tennessee, and the Memphis Red Sox, did just this. Twice every year the park was turned over to local musicians for the Starlite Review, a concert used to raise money to send black handicapped children to school. Such endeavors apparently helped the Red Sox and their standing in the city. Despite the fact that the only title the team ever won was the first-half Negro American League title in 1938, the team always had a solid fan base. It was one of the most stable franchises in the Negro Leagues, lasting from 1923 to 1960. But even with such solid fan backing and a rent-free park, the Red Sox proved an already well-known point, that league games alone did not generate the profits necessary to maintain a team in the Negro Leagues. Besides league games, Negro League teams had to find another way to supplement their income. This was done by barnstorming.

Barnstorming was the practice of traveling across the country, playing all comers, for either a guarantee or a percentage of the gate. A guarantee was an agreed-upon figure that would be paid by the sponsor of the game to a team. It has been stated by several former players that the best way to sure make a Negro League team got the highest amount available was to take the opposite of what was offered. The teams reasoned that if a sponsor offered a guarantee, then that person was sure that a large crowd would come to the game and so he would make back the guarantee plus a hefty profit. In such cases teams would reportedly demand a percentage of the gate. At the same time, if a sponsor offered a percentage of the gate, the team owners would figure the sponsor was unsure how many fans would show up, and so they would demand a guarantee. If the game was to be played between two Negro Leagues teams rather than a local team, the gate was usually split into a winner's and loser's share, with as much as 60% going to the winner.

Negro League teams met outside their home parks for league games on a somewhat regular basis. The Yankees in the 1940s were making a reported $100,000 a year off Negro League games from renting out the team's minor league stadiums and Yankee Stadium. Other teams, like the Washington Senators, depended on the rental fees to make ends meet. League games were also played in such out-of-the-way places as Springfield, Ohio's Municipal Stadium or Oklahoma City, Oklahoma's Holland Park. But the majority of the games played on tours were against local, semi-pro, or minor league teams.

Practically all of the traveling done by Negro League teams was by car or bus, not by train. The reasons were financial. Games that were played on these tours were no more lucrative than league games, and in a lot of cases less so. Therefore, the only hope of showing a profit was to play as many games as you could in as many towns as possible. An example of this is a 1939 tour made by the Newark Eagles in which the team, in 16 days, traveled to 17 cities and played 17 games. The tour, however, did not take place during any of the big summer holidays. If it had, the team might have played up to four games in three or four different cities in a single day. This was not an uncommon occurrence on the Fourth of July for some teams.

These teams managed to keep such demanding schedules by spending most of their time on the bus. It was a Negro League player's home. Once a game was over, the team might not even take time to change clothes. If the next game was going to be played later in the day the players might just walk off

Left to right: Pittsburgh Crawford players Oscar Charleston, Josh Gibson, Ted Page, and Judy Johnson circa 1935.

the field and on to the bus and go on their way. If the players were given the time to change, then the uniforms, wet with perspiration would be hung in the back of the bus or out the bus windows to dry.

Where the players ate on the road depended on where they were and how much time they had. If they were in one of the league cities, then there were black-owned restaurants that over the years gained popularity with the ballplayers. Two were the Crawford Grill in Pittsburgh and the Sky Rocket Grill in Homestead, Pennsylvania. If the team was on the road, however, getting food could be a problem.

While the South was better known for its segregation, stores and restaurants that would not serve blacks could be found all over the country. The annals of black baseball, as told by the men that played in them, are filled with stories of places that refused them service or would serve them only through a window in the back of the store or restaurant. When it came to places that the teams knew would just flat-out refuse them service, there were two options. The first was the one that was practiced by most teams, and that was to keep driving until they found a place that would sell them, for example, some bologna and crackers, and maybe some sodas. That was dinner.

The second approach to food on the road worked if the team had a light-skinned player. The team would send him into an establishment to buy food for the entire team. This exercise proved successful, unless something happened to make the owner of the restaurant or store suspicious. If the rest of the team stayed out of sight, however, it usually worked well.

When it came to staying overnight, many of the same problems teams faced when looking for a restaurant came back to haunt them. Once again, league cities did not cause a problem. In every major city in the United States there were actually two cities, one black and one white, with each offering everything the other did, from hotels to nightclubs. If a Negro League team was spending the night in a league city, everyone was happy. That night promised a real bed and a meal in a fine restaurant. Once you left the big cities, however, that all changed.

The chances of finding a place that would put up an entire baseball at the time was difficult enough, but if the team was made up of all black players, then the chances declined even further. In some towns where the teams appeared regularly, there were black boardinghouses that would take them in, or the team might divide up among the local black families. Most of the time, though, when away from the major cities,

Negro Leaguers spent their nights on the bus.

Traveling for weeks at a time, sleeping, eating, basically living in a car or on a bus, and being able to play at least one game every day and do it at a major league level seems incredible. It is remarkable that despite the hardships of traveling that the level of their play didn't suffer to any great extent.

While it could be argued that traveling continuously and playing seven to ten games a week would take a toll on a player, there are countless examples from the black baseball leagues that prove this argument wrong. The first to come to mind is Satchel Paige, who at times would pitch every day for a month. Catcher Larry Brown would also go a long way to dispel such an argument. Brown spent 30 years behind the plate in the Negro Leagues, including 1930 when he caught 234 games but could only muster a lifetime .260 batting average. Baseball has seen many that were the equal of him as a defensive catcher but probably none were better.

There were costs to be paid with that lifestyle, sometimes the ultimate price. Three Negro League players paid that while traveling with their respective teams, two in a car accident and one as the result of mechanical problems with a bus.

Catcher Ulysses "Buster" Brown and pitcher Raymond "Smokey" Owens, both with the Cincinnati Buckeyes, were traveling in a car with three other members of the team and team owner Wilbur Hayes on September 7, 1942. They were heading home from a series of games against the New York Black Yankees when one of the car's tires went flat. The men stopped and changed the tire outside Geneva, Ohio. At around 3:00 A.M. as Owens, who was driving, pulled back onto the road, the car was struck from behind by another car. Both Brown and Owens were killed instantly. Two pitchers, Eugene Bremmer and Herman "Lefty" Watts, had to be hospitalized because of their injuries. Hayes and pitcher Alonzo Boone received only minor injuries.

In the summer of 1944, while the Memphis Red Sox were traveling home from a tour of the eastern states, the team's bus developed mechanical problems and left the team stranded in the northern part of the state. It was a Friday night and the team had to be in back Memphis for a doubleheader on the following Sunday. The team left the bus and boarded a train. Reports vary as to what happened next, but the end result was that an intoxicated man, angered by some occurrence—some say over a dice game—drew a gun and fired one shot. The shot struck Memphis pitcher

Porter Moss, an innocent bystander, just below the heart. The doctor at the next station refused to treat Moss, and so the injured man continued on the train for another hour to Jackson, Tennessee. There he underwent an operation, but died the next day. The shooter was later caught and sentenced to ten years.

While these were the only three deaths that occurred while teams were on the road, there were a great number of accidents. In the 1930s, the Newark Eagles bus crashed due to brake failure; the Philadelphia Stars' team bus collided with an automobile; and the pair of cars in which the Homestead Grays was traveling both wound up in the ditch.

September 1944 saw five players from the Birmingham Black Barons injured after the team bus collided with a car and then flipped over.

In the 1950s, after some clothing caught fire on the Monarchs team bus, the players stood and watched while the bus burned on the side of a Florida highway. Police radio reports, according to Buck O'Neil, were "Don't worry, it's just some niggers broke down."

Problems faced by traveling teams were not restricted to traffic accidents or racism on the road. Name any major league ballpark of the era and chances are, Negro League games were played there. The same can be said for most minor league parks as well. At times, however, the diamonds on which Negro League teams played while on the road left much to be desired. It was not uncommon for local fields to have rocks in the infield or the occasional tree stump in the outfield. There were even times when there was no actual ball field at all, and a large farm field or open area was marked off and used for the game. That was just part of barnstorming, as were biased local umpires, threats on what would happen if the visitors beat a local team, and black teams being run out of town for winning.

The reason was that's the way things were in the country at that time. Segregation was the reason for nearly every major problem associated with Negro League baseball.

One question regarding the Negro Leagues would be: Why did the players put up with hard schedules, the terrible traveling conditions, the dangers, and the racism? According to the Negro Leaguers themselves, they did it for the sheer love of the game.

DÉJÀ VU? *In the heat of Gulf War II, as the U.S.A. was abandoned by a number of allies, most notably France, it became popular to rename all food items prefaced with "French" by "Liberty." Thus we now have Liberty toast and Liberty fries on some menus.*

Students of the Deadball Era know that there was a similar rejection of all things German as the Great War of 1914 consumed the world. A week after the U.S. entered the war on April 6, 1917, the Committee of Public Information (CPI) was formed to disseminate propaganda at home. Headed by the muckraking journalist George Creel, the CPI helped demonize the enemy with real and imagined stories of atrocities that helped fuel a wave of anti-German sentiment.

The names of everyday items were modified to eliminate any Germanic connotation. In a jingoistic fervor, sauerkraut was replaced by Liberty Cabbage, and German shepherd dogs became known as Belgium shepherds. City College of New York reduced by one credit every course in German. Dachshunds were renamed Liberty Dogs. Even German measles became Liberty measles.

A popular veteran ballplayer of the day, Herman Schaefer, was affectionately nicknamed "Germany," despite the fact that he was a native of Chicago. Sometime after his move from the Federal League to the New York Yankees in February 1916, Schaefer denounced his ethnic nickname, demanding that henceforth he would be known as "Liberty" Schaefer.

— ROBERT H. SCHAEFER *(not a known relation of Herman)*

George Sisler and the End of the National Commission

by Sam Bernstein

What was George Sisler thinking when he signed a contract to play professional baseball in Akron, Ohio, in January 1911 at the tender age of 17? After all, he had not consulted with his family or any other adult except for Jesse Goehler, who, acting as a representative of the Akron club, signed the future Hall of Famer to play after his high school graduation from Akron. Yet Sisler's action, the action of impetuous youth, contributed mightily to the eventual downfall of the ruling triumvirate of organized baseball, the National Commission.

This saga includes as dramatis personae a few of the most powerful men of professional baseball at the time. We will see how the lives of George Sisler are intertwined with those of Branch Rickey, Barney Dreyfuss, August "Garry" Herrmann, and ultimately, although indirectly, Judge Kennesaw Landis.

The story begins in 1911 as Sisler was completing his senior year in high school. "Peerless George" was born March 3, 1893, in Nimisilia, Ohio, south of Akron. "Many baseball books show that Sisler was born at Manchester, a few miles east of Clinton. But Nimisilia is the correct place, if you can find it—or pronounce it."[1]

By the time Sisler was in high school, he was making a name for himself as a left-handed pitcher. Sisler

remembers, "I got a lot of publicity in my last year in high school, and when I was still a student I signed up one day to play with Akron."[2]

Ernest J. Lanigan, a former executive at the Baseball Hall of Fame in Cooperstown, NY, wrote an undated notation to George Sisler's file at the Hall of Fame Library:

> Three years before Fohl [Lee Alexander Fohl] was in charge of the Akron club, which was owned by Columbus, and one night he phoned Bob Quinn, Columbus business manager, that there was a youth at Akron High School that looked like the prospect of the century and suggested signing him.
>
> "Sign him," said Quinn, "at $100 a month, even if you have to release somebody."
>
> "I can't sign him," said Fohl, "but I know someone who can."
>
> And the Someone Who Could—Umpire Jesse Goehler—signed Sisler, then 17, to an Akron contract for $100 a month. He reported to the club one day, but there was no uniform to fit him, so he didn't play. And he never showed up again. Akron transferred his contract later to Columbus and Columbus sold him to Pittsburgh, but Garry Herrmann of the National Commission ruled that Akron had no right to the player, that Columbus hadn't and that Pittsburgh hadn't. Rickey signed him for the Browns, and that was the start of a lifelong feud between Herrmann and Barney Dreyfuss that led eventually to Judge Landis getting into the baseball picture.[3]

Sam Bernstein, MSW, is a school social worker in Elizabeth, NJ. When not rooting for the Mets, his main research interest is the life of Barney Dreyfuss.

Sisler later contended, "I was only 17 years old when I wrote my name on the slip of paper that made me property of Akron. . . . After I signed it I got scared and I didn't even tell my dad or anybody 'cause I knew folks wanted me to go on to college and I figured they'd be sore if they knew I wanted to be a ballplayer."[4] Sisler also maintained that he never reported to Akron or any professional club until after he graduated from the University of Michigan, dismantling the myth that there was no uniform to fit him.

Eventually Sisler did confess to his father that he had signed a contract with Akron. "In a way that's what saved me, I guess. For by not telling my dad he never had a chance to Okay my signature and in that way the contract didn't hold." After graduation from Akron Central High School, Sisler was told to report to Akron on March 17, 1912, for spring training with the Columbus club. When he did not report to either team, Columbus sold his contract in 1912 to Barney Dreyfuss, owner of the Pittsburgh Pirates for $5,000.

George Sisler enrolled at the University of Michigan in Ann Arbor for the fall term in 1911. However, his Akron contract was duly "promulgated in April of that year by Secretary Farrell, of the National Association." *The Sporting News* later reported, "The Agreement for the transfer of the player by Columbus to Pittsburg was filed with the National Commission and as it was in proper form was approved and promulgated by the Commission."[5]

The first volley in the battle to emancipate George Sisler from his Akron contract came from Sisler himself (with assistance from Branch Rickey[6] and George B. Codd, a Michigan circuit court judge) when he wrote to Garry Herrmann, chairman of the National Commission. Sisler wanted his amateur status reinstated so he could play varsity baseball that spring for Michigan. Dated August 27, 1912, Sisler wrote, "Two years ago this winter while I was attending high school, I signed the baseball contract given me by an umpire who watched me pitch the summer before. The proposition came very suddenly and unexpectedly, and I was an easy mark as I now look back upon it. At that time, being only 17 years old, I thought it would be a great thing to sign a league contract and supposed that I would be a sort of a hero among my fellow students and the people around Akron in general."[7]

When Sisler requested that the National Commission sustain his amateur status, he was recognized as an up-and-coming athletic star at Michigan under the watchful eye of Branch Rickey.

Rickey revolutionized baseball by creating an extensive farm system when he was an executive with the St. Louis Cardinals. In 1947, as general manager of the Brooklyn Dodgers, Rickey signed Jackie Robinson to a major league baseball contract. Sisler first met "the Mahatma" in the spring of 1912.

Rickey had attended the University of Michigan Law School, and he coached the Michigan varsity baseball team to make ends meet. In September 1911, he and two law school classmates opened up a legal practice in Boise, Idaho. In January 1912 he wired the Michigan athletic director, "am starving. Will be back without delay."[8] Baseball was, until 1913, only a way for Rickey to get what he wanted, a law degree. When he realized that the law business was not succeeding and that he was placing his health in jeopardy, he decided to devote himself to baseball full-time.[9]

Rickey had some experience as a judge of baseball talent. He had worked at Allegheny College as coach and athletic director. In 1904 he signed to play for the Cincinnati Reds under the ownership of Garry Herrmann, who had taken a liking to Rickey and his honest virtues. Rickey had refused to play on Sundays as a promise to his mother, so the Reds manager Joe Kelley fired the rookie catcher before he appeared in a regular season game. Herrmann reversed the decision and allowed Rickey to remain on the team. After thinking about it, Rickey decided to leave the Reds anyway, with Herrmann's blessing.[10] He later was a catcher and outfielder with the Cardinals and Yankees, appearing in 120 games.

Branch Rickey returned from Boise in the spring of 1912. "Candidates for several varsity baseball teams were reporting," Rickey said in describing a pivotal moment in his life, "for registration, assignment and tryout. Here before me stood a handsome boy of eighteen, with dark brown hair, serious gray eyes and posture. He was about five feet eight or nine, well built but not heavy, and he wore a somewhat battered finger glove on his right hand. He said he had pitched on a high school team in Akron, Ohio, and that he was George Sisler, engineering student in the freshman class.

"'Oh, a freshman,' I said. 'Well, this part of the program is only for the varsity. You can't play this year.' He showed extreme disappointment. I said, 'You can't play this year, but you can work out with the varsity today.'

"The workout was unforgettable. He pitched batting practice and, for the next twenty minutes, created no end of varsity embarrassment. His speed and con-

Sisler graduated from the University of Michigan in 1915 with a degree in mechanical engineering.

December 28, 1912, Garry Herrmann wrote to Judge Codd with a response on behalf of the National Commission, of which he was chairman. Although the commission would not rule on the amateur status of Sisler, his contract was made "dormant," he stated, "The player's status is and will be wholly dependent on his own acts regardless of formal claims by the Pittsburg club, or any other National Agreement Club, of the right or property in contracting with him."[13] Rather than declare Sisler an amateur, the National Commission sidestepped the issue by saying that Sisler was not a professional—yet. Sisler was now eligible to play for the Michigan varsity under Rickey.

J. G. Taylor Spink reported that many clubs were following Sisler's brilliant performance and were interested in signing him when he graduated.[14] "By the time he graduated college," noted historian Donald Honig, "Sisler's baseball abilities were known to every big league club. Mysteriously, however, only the Pirates seemed interested. By dint of Gentleman's Agreement among all the owners, the old voided contract Sisler had signed was being honored by Major-League baseball. Rather than commit the slightest offense against their hallowed reserve clause, the owners were recognizing a contract that their own ruling body had voided."[15] All teams that is, except the St. Louis Browns, where Branch Rickey, Sisler's baseball mentor, began his managerial and executive career in 1913.

Judge Codd pressured the National Commission to declare Sisler a free agent. "Through the influence of powerful friends Sisler was eventually declared a free agent by the National Commission, not, however, until the threat to carry the matter into the courts had been resorted to. The commission, in declaring him a free agent, however, recommended that he give Pittsburg the preference, which was only fair."[16]

Barney Dreyfuss was furious. He was one of the most innovative magnates and considered an outstanding judge of baseball talent. Branch Rickey told Lee Allen, historian at the Baseball Hall of Fame, "Dreyfuss was the best judge of players he had ever seen."[17] Dreyfuss was successful in baseball because he understood the business of baseball and its rules. He appealed to the National Commission for a review, especially after National League President John Tener wrote in May 1914 that while the Pittsburgh club had conformed with the "laws and regulations" of organized baseball and that it might have a moral right to the player, he concluded that "The Pittsburg Club's claims and contentions are all

trol made him almost unhittable. All of his moves were guided by perfection of reflexes, which made him quick, graceful, accurate—the foundation of athletic greatness. It was all there.'"[11]

Sisler had played football, basketball and baseball in high school, and he was offered scholarships at the University of Pennsylvania and Western Reserve but he chose Michigan because of Russ Baer, his high school catcher. "Russ today [1953] is a banker in Akron. At that time he wanted to study law and decided to enroll at Michigan. I thought I would have a better chance in baseball as a pitcher if I had Baer as my catcher, so I followed him."[12]

George Codd pushed hard on Sisler's behalf. On

based on the assumption that the signing of an Akron Club contract by Sisler was perfectly legal, valid, reasonable and binding."[18] Tener offered, and it was adopted by the National Commission, that Dreyfuss and the Pirates be given an unimpeded first chance to sign Sisler. The mistake that Dreyfuss may have made was the assumption that he had a clear and easy path to the player when in fact Branch Rickey held the upper hand. Dreyfuss received a letter from Sisler dated June 2, 1915, asking for "your very best offer."[19] When Dreyfuss learned on June 18 that Sisler had signed with St. Louis, he immediately asked the National Commission to review his charges of interference and tampering by Rickey and the St. Louis Browns. The commission asked Dreyfuss for evidence to prove the allegations, which he couldn't provide.

The case for Sisler had really come down to contract terms, notwithstanding his previous association with Rickey. "Branch Rickey, however, refused to enter into this collusion [the Gentleman's Agreement]. Always the maverick, Rickey saw to it that the Browns signed Sisler. The draconic machinery of Baseball's jurisprudence went so far as to suspend Sisler while the question was being investigated. Rickey, determined not to lose his prize, made some not-so-veiled threats about civil law versus baseball law, and the National Commission finally ruled on behalf of the Browns."[20] The St. Louis club offered Sisler $7,400 as opposed to $5,200 from Pittsburgh.[21] By June 18, Sisler was on the Browns team for good and appeared in 81 games.

The Browns eventually moved Sisler to first base to take advantage of his hitting. "He was in fact generally acclaimed the greatest of all first basemen until nudged aside by the power hitting of Lou Gehrig."[22] In 1922, his greatest season, Sisler earned the first American League MVP award after hitting .420. George Sisler was elected to the Hall of Fame in 1939, the 10th player so honored.

Barney Dreyfuss refused to let go of his grievance against the National Commission. Dreyfuss "never forgave Herrmann for voting with [American League President Ban] Johnson in awarding the crack first baseman to the Browns. Barney was an implacable enemy, and cried for vengeance."[23] Barney wanted Herrmann out as chairman, feeling that he had a conflict of interest as owner of the Cincinnati Reds. Dreyfuss had supported Herrmann in the past especially after Herrmann's role in negotiating peace between the American and National Leagues in 1903. Dreyfuss felt that Herrmann had a history with and

Between 1920-22, Sisler hit an amazing .407, .371, and .420.

was too close to Ban Johnson. It was Johnson, in fact, who had nominated Herrmann as chairman.[24] The business of baseball was evolving and a different kind of leadership was needed, and Dreyfuss pushed hard for a "neutral" chairman of the commission.

According to Spink, Dreyfuss's first attempt to overthrow Herrmann was "a one man campaign" when he introduced his resolution to the National League meeting in December 1916.[25] Harold Seymour notes that while Dreyfuss's initial resolution failed, "his was never an entirely lone voice against Herrmann in National League councils."[26] The National Commission was struggling with other demanding problems, externally and within baseball. Organized baseball was dealing with the impact of war in Europe, anti-trust suits from the Federal League, player disputes, and allegations that Herrmann was "under Ban Johnson's thumb"[27] or unfavorable to American League clubs because of his conflict of interest.

Two years after the Sisler case was over, another major dispute erupted involving a pitcher, Scott Perry of the Philadelphia Athletics. He had pitched briefly for the NL's Boston Braves but left the team after 17 days. Perry played for some independent and minor league teams before signing to pitch for Connie Mack's A's.[28] Perry, who won a few games for Philadelphia, was ordered to report to the Braves but Philadelphia obtained an injunction keeping him an Athletic. National League owners were upset and Dreyfuss cried foul, stating, "Herrmann decides against us we have to take it; he decides for us, and the American League goes to court."[29]

Dreyfuss's movement to make significant changes

began to gather momentum during the postwar era. NL President John Heydler was unhappy by the way the commission handled a threatened players' strike at the 1918 World Series. Spink wrote, "The entire incident left a nasty taste in everyone's mouth. I have always felt that mercenary–minded players on those 1918 championship teams [Red Sox and Cubs] were mostly to blame; their judgment in pulling a strike at such a time was more than deplorable—it was downright stupid. Yet, the old Commission, especially Johnson and Herrmann, took a lot of abuse, and their conduct in dealing with the strikers was termed undignified. It was felt by many that it showed that the game needed a strong one man head."[30] Later, two owners, including Red Sox magnate Harry Frazee approached William Howard Taft about replacing Herrmann, but he declined.[31] NL President Heydler later conveyed to Spink that he realized the end of the three-man commission was near after the players' strike in Boston.[32]

Whether Ban Johnson was controlling Herrmann's swing vote or Herrmann was trying to avoid civil litigation, the National Commission received more criticism in Johnson's handling of pitcher Carl Mays' defection from the Red Sox in 1920. Johnson suspended Mays, but the Red Sox traded him to the New York Yankees, claiming that they had not suspended him and defied Johnson's power. The Yankees secured an injunction against the American League allowing Mays to pitch for them. This action caused alienation between Johnson and several AL clubs.[33]

As the power of the National Commission began to crumble, Barney Dreyfuss could only feel like he had accomplished what he set out to do in 1916. Several initiatives were under way to reform the leadership of the game. The final blow came in September 1920 when "the officialdom of Organized Baseball, ostensibly represented by a two-man National Commission, was in chaos." That's when the Black Sox scandal broke and accelerated the movement toward a radical change in baseball and the hiring of Judge Landis.

The case of George Sisler pointed out, "Baseball and law have the same affinity that oil and water possess—they don't mix, that's all."[34] The National Commission, always mindful of welfare of the game, tried to avoid legal confrontations and in doing so created animosity among the magnates. Certainly Sisler had no idea when he signed that contract in 1911, he would challenge the structure of the game.

The result of his action had a curious and interesting result: the game would be run by a Landis, a federal judge, and uniquely influenced by Rickey, a lawyer.

Notes

1. Allen, Lee and Tom Meany. *Kings of the Diamond*. New York: Putnam, 1965, p. 104.
2. Smith, Lyall, "George Sisler as Told to Lyall Smith", *My Greatest Day in Baseball as Told to John P. Carmichael and Other Sportswriters*. Lincoln, NE: University of Nebraska Press, 1996, p. 158.
3. Lanigan, Ernest J. Baseball Hall of Fame Library player file on George Sisler.
4. Smith, p. 158.
5. *The Sporting News*, June 15, 1916.
6. Mann, Arthur. *Branch Rickey: American in Action*. Boston, MA: Houghton Mifflin, 1957, p 82.
7. *The Sporting News*, June 15, 1916.
8. Mann, p. 60.
9. Lipman, David. *Mr. Baseball: The Story of Branch Rickey*, New York: Putnam, 1966, p. 39.
10. Lipman, p. 53.
11. Mann, pp. 60-61.
12. Biederman, Les. "Gorgeous George H. Sisler," *The Sporting News*, February 25, 1953.
13. *The Sporting News*, June 15, 1916.
14. Spink, J. G. Taylor. *Judge Landis and Twenty-Five Years of Baseball*. New York: Thomas Crowell, 1947, p. 41.
15. Honig, Donald. *The Greatest First Basemen of All Time*. New York: Crown, 1988, p. 23.
16. Ward, John J. "The Famous Sisler Case," *Baseball Magazine*, October 1916, p. 35.
17. Allen, Lee. *Cooperstown Corner*. Cleveland: SABR, p. 164.
18. *The Sporting News*, June 15, 1916.
19. *The Sporting News*, June 15, 1916.
20. Honig, p. 23.
21. "Dreyfuss vs. Herrmann," *Baseball Magazine*, October 1916, p. 22.
22. Honig, p. 21.
23. Spink, p. 43. In 1945 Sisler stated to Lyall Smith (p. 158), "I didn't know at the time I signed that contract I was stepping into a rumpus that went on and on until it finally involved the National Baseball Commission, the owners of two big league clubs and Judge Landis."
24. Bruce, John E. "The Chief Justice of Baseball's Supreme Court," *Baseball Magazine*, February 1912, p. 54.
25. Spink, p. 43.
26. Seymour, Harold. *Baseball: The Golden Age*. New York: Oxford University Press, 1971, p. 261.
27. ——. Ibid, p. 261.
28. ——. Ibid, p. 262.
29. ——. Ibid, p. 43.
30. ——. Ibid, p. 45.
31. Seymour, p. 263.
32. Spink, p. 45.
33. White, G. Edward. *Creating the National Pastime*. Princeton, NJ: Princeton University Press, 1996, p. 107.
34. Ward, p. 33.

The Statistical Impact of World War II on Position Players

by Steve Bullock

In December 1941, the outbreak of the Second World War elicited drastic changes throughout nearly all sectors of American society while the nation struggled in an unprecedented mobilization toward global conflict. This was particularly true in the realm of major league baseball, where over 90% of all active players at the outset of the war eventually served in the armed forces. This subsequently placed teams in the awkward position of having to employ players with little talent, men who were past their athletic primes and, in two cases, even athletes with fewer than four limbs.

The majority of major league players who did serve in the American military lost between one and four years of their baseball careers, which often proved devastating for their professional lives. Although a small number of players suffered debilitating injuries or illnesses, the primary impact of the war on players of the World War II era entailed interruptions in and the curtailment of their careers. In most professional occupations, a hiatus of up to several years is relatively insignificant. However, the brevity of a typical professional baseball player's tenure magnifies this type of absence, if only from a statistical standpoint. Inevitably, the years missed by players due to the war have led to unending specula-

tion about what might have transpired on the field if not for the war. Each major league player who served in the military had precious years of their careers stripped away, and hundreds of minor leaguers had their careers derailed before they even began.

The most obvious examples of this phenomenon involved several of the most dominant offensive players of the era. Although it is impossible to precisely project career statistics for players who spent substantial time in the armed forces, the years spent away from the game obviously affected their final numbers. Joe DiMaggio and Hank Greenberg, for example, both probably would have exceeded the 500 home run plateau and 2,000 RBI mark if not for their time spent in the military. DiMaggio's situation is quite fascinating due primarily to the fact that there was such a disparity between his pre- and postwar offensive numbers. In his seven seasons before his induction DiMaggio never accumulated less than 114 RBI in any single campaign. Following his return, the Yankee center fielder drove in more than 100 runs only twice in the six seasons leading up to his retirement. Also, whereas virtually every one of his prewar seasons was truly dominant, only DiMaggio's 1948 year can be compared favorably to any of his seasons completed before the war.

Despite this relatively precipitous decline following his military service, most students of the game nevertheless recognize Joe DiMaggio as one of the greatest players in history. In contrast, DiMaggio's

Steve Bullock is an Assistant Professor of History at the University of Nebraska at Omaha and specializes in sport history. His book, Playing for their Nation: Baseball and the American Military during World War II, *was awarded the Malloy prize by SABR and the University of Nebraska Press and will be available in early 2004.*

contemporary and annual rival for batting superiority in the American League, Detroit Tigers first baseman Hank Greenberg, has traditionally been denied such accolades. Greenberg was arguably the most dominant offensive player in the game and certainly among the five best hitters in baseball during the four years before he began his stint in the Army. The Tiger star then spent nearly five complete seasons away from the diamond at a time when his offensive numbers were still at their apex. With an average no lower than .312 during the four years before his military service, Greenberg led the league in home runs twice, RBI twice, and slugging percentage once. In those same four years he also won the American League's Most Valuable Player award once and finished third on two other occasions. Once Greenberg returned from his nearly five-year absence, he never regained his prewar brilliance and was out of professional baseball by 1947.

Another of the great players of the era, Stan Musial, also lost time due to his military service. Although he was absent only for one season, some of his final statistics fell just short of important milestones. By missing the 1945 campaign, Musial narrowly missed the magical number of 500 home runs—a total reached by only 16 other individuals in the history of the game. Less obvious to the casual observer are his career hits and RBI marks, which fell just shy of noteworthy plateaus. If Musial had not been absent in 1945, he almost certainly would have been only the second player to eclipse 2,000 career RBI. Regarding his hit total, although his career tally places him fourth all-time today, at the time of his retirement Musial had accumulated the second highest number of safeties in baseball history, behind only Ty Cobb. With a typical season in 1945 added to his career statistics, Musial would have been within about 350 hits of the great Tigers outfielder. In such a circumstance, it is not inconceivable that Musial would have attempted to prolong his career an extra couple of seasons in an attempt to reach Cobb's seemingly unattainable record.

Of the elite players of the World War II era, Ted Williams' career was arguably affected the most by his military service. With nearly five years during the heart of his baseball career spent in the military—three of which he served during the Second World War—Williams narrowly missed shattering some of baseball's most hallowed records. Although Williams returned from his military stint during World War II and displayed his usual brilliance at the plate despite his three-year absence, he seemed poised to reach even greater heights. When Williams began his military obligation before the 1943 season, he was coming off of the two finest back-to-back seasons of his career, 1941 and 1942, during which he hit .406 in 1941 and led the league in home runs, batting average, and RBI in 1942. The Triple Crown in 1942 was not his last—he won another in 1947—yet Williams never exhibited quite the offensive skill in consecutive seasons as he did in his last two seasons before entering the Navy. Since he was reaching the prime of his career at that time, it is impossible to determine exactly how impressive his career statistics might have been without the three-year interruption for military service. However, the Red Sox slugger almost certainly would have approached, if not exceeded, Babe Ruth's career home run record of 714—the record at the time of Williams' retirement. With less than 500 RBI separating Williams from the most prolific run producer in history, Hank Aaron, the Red Sox star also would probably still claim the career RBI record.

For players such as DiMaggio, Greenberg, and Williams it is therefore abundantly clear that the Second World War had a significant impact on their professional careers. For the players who fell just short of this elite status, however, their careers were arguably affected to an even greater extent. Whereas virtually all of the premier players of the 1930s, '40s and '50s have been enshrined in the Hall of Fame, several talented professionals sacrificed prime years of their careers to the war effort and fell just short in their bid for enshrinement in Cooperstown. Probably the most glaring example of this is Yankees and Indians second baseman Joe Gordon, a nine-time all-star who played in the post-season six times during his stellar career. Gordon's statistics compare favorably to fellow second baseman and Hall of Famer, Bobby Doerr, who was a close contemporary and also a veteran of the Second World War. Doerr has the slight edge over Gordon in career RBI, although the two campaigns lost by Gordon to only one sacrificed by Doerr explains most of that disparity. Doerr also holds an advantage in career batting average by twenty points, although this might be somewhat deceiving. Doerr played his entire career in Fenway Park, notorious for its cozy left field dimensions, while Gordon played during his prime in the more spacious Yankee Stadium. This almost certainly kept his batting average lower than it could have been in more offensive-friendly confines. Despite the deeper outfield dimensions of Yankee Stadium, however, Gordon struck 30

*Frankie Frisch and Honus Wagner appear
at spring training at Penn Naval Base, 1943.*

Great Lakes manager Mickey Cochrane.

more home runs than did Doerr during their respective careers. Although Doerr does hold a minimal edge in career fielding percentage, Gordon was by no means a defensive liability with a .970 career fielding average. The one area where Gordon has a tremendous advantage is in the six championship teams of which he was a major contributor. Gordon was a catalyst for the great Yankee teams of the late '30s and '40s and also won a World Series title late in his career with the Cleveland Indians. In contrast, Doerr played in only the 1946 World Series with Boston, and although he hit a sparkling .409 during the seven-game set, he never played in the World Series again.

Comparing Gordon to another Hall of Fame second baseman, Tony Lazzeri, whom Gordon replaced in the Yankees lineup in 1938, an even stronger case can be made for Gordon's inclusion in the Hall of Fame. When analyzing career statistics for both players, Gordon leads or has nearly identical numbers in almost every category. The only two notable exceptions are Lazzeri's advantages in career batting average and RBI, 24 points and 216, respectively. Again, the disparity in RBI can be dismissed due to Gordon's two-year hiatus for military service, while the difference in batting average can be partly offset by Gordon's superior power numbers—Gordon's 253 home runs compared to Lazzeri's 178. In balancing team championships, Lazerri's impressive five World Series titles fall short the six won by Gordon.

For every elite star like Ted Williams or near-great player like Joe Gordon, there were many other lesser-known position players who also had their careers interrupted or ended by the outbreak of hos-

tilities. Most of these individuals not only had years of their careers stripped away because of their military service, but the hiatus inflicted irreparable harm to their baseball abilities, often causing a premature close to their chosen vocation. Philadelphia Athletic second baseman Benny McCoy, for example, enjoyed a promising three-year career before the war and seemed destined for stardom with skills that included exceptional speed and occasional power. McCoy, however, was one of the first major league players to enter the military, and he never again played in the big leagues after the war. First baseman Buddy Hassett, a solid player for three teams, also saw his big league career come to a screeching halt with the outbreak of the Second World War. A .292 career hitter, Hassett's career spanned the seven years leading up to the war and ended when he entered the armed forces.

Unlike McCoy and Hassett, Washington Senator shortstop Cecil Travis did return to the major leagues following a stint in the military but without much success. Travis had been an exceptional hitter in the eight years prior to his entry into the Army, batting lower than .300 only once before the war while exhibiting occasional home run power and a low strikeout ratio. He was also a three-time all-star participant and led the American League in hits with 218 during the 1941 season, his last before joining the Army. The Senators star, however, suffered severe frostbite to his lower extremities during the Battle of the Bulge and never regained the mobility needed to perform at the major league level. Upon his return, the Senators moved Travis to third base to accommodate his limited range hoping that he might regain his potent prewar batting stroke. Travis spent a dismal three years following the war battling American League pitching and managed to hit only .252 in his best postwar season. By 1947 he had retired from baseball, and a promising career had been derailed for reasons beyond his control.

One of Travis's teammates, outfielder Buddy Lewis, was another of the lesser-known players affected by their military commitment. In the six years before Lewis entered the Army Air Force, Lewis, a below-average defensive player but an exceptional hitter, never hit below .291 and three times batted over .300. While exhibiting occasional power and an ability to steal bases, the Senators outfielder went to the 1938 All-Star game and also led the league in triples in 1939. Upon his return to the major leagues following a three-year absence beginning in 1942, Lewis never again hit .300. Although he did again represent the Senators in the All-Star Game (1947), his statistics that year did not compare favorably to any of his prewar campaigns.

From an individual perspective, therefore, it is abundantly clear that the war affected numerous professional players to a greater or lesser extent. The list of anecdotal stories and statistical information regarding individual professional players returning from the war with diminished skills are quite plentiful. However, the question then arises whether the interruptions in players' careers, when taken as a group, caused substantial declines in their abilities and statistics or if the trials and tribulations of a few have skewed the perception of those athletes that participated in the war.

First of all, in comparing groups of players who served during the war and those who did not, one can identify startling differences both between and within these groups and decipher some of the changes initiated in major league baseball by World War II. The first striking disparity between the players who served in the armed forces and those who remained in civilian life are the average ages of the two groups. During 1942, the first full year of the war, the mean age of the players who served in the American military was significantly lower (26.9 years old) than those who did not serve (29.4 years old). The logical explanation for this is simply that draft boards and armed forces recruiters preferred younger individuals for induction, while older players were also more likely to have chronic, age-related conditions that might disqualify them from military service. Also, the percentage of older players who were married, and subsequently less desirable for military service than single men, was

most likely higher than in younger players.

Another interesting characteristic of major league players during World War II is that players who occupied certain positions were disproportionately represented within the armed forces. The revelation that first basemen (46.7%) and catchers (31.8%) had the highest and third highest percentages, respectively, of players who did not serve is not exceptionally surprising considering that those position players also had the highest average ages at the outset of the war. In addition, many teams relocated exceptional offensive players to first base from other more athletically demanding positions, such as the outfield, once they had passed their athletic prime or if they had sustained an injury that hampered their efficiency elsewhere. Either scenario would suggest lower numbers of first baseman who were prime candidates for induction into the armed forces. Regarding catchers, many at this time had debilitating hand and finger injuries because of the catching style of the day (two-handed as opposed to the modern one-handed style) along with chronic knee and leg problems common among some due to years of donning the "tools of ignorance." These factors, along with their elevated mean age, would have excluded many of them from military service.

	1942 Age	
Position	Mean	N
2	28.38095	21
3	29.38462	13
4	26.86667	15
5	27.42857	7
6	27.46667	15
7	27.34286	35

Also not surprising, second basemen (4) maintained the highest percentage (94.7%) of military service among all position players. Second basemen predictably were the youngest and, one can assume, healthiest of the position players and thus prime candidates for military service. What is startling is that the percentage of shortstops (6) that did not serve (41.2%) was extremely high despite the fact that their mean age was virtually identical to those of third basemen (5) and outfielders (7), who maintained predictable rates of service in the armed forces. Because it is virtually impossible to compete as a shortstop on the major league level with any kind of physical malady that might disqualify one from military service, the low number of shortstops who served is baffling.

At first glance, the offensive skill of both players who did and did not serve is very comparable, with nearly equal career batting averages for the two groups (.272 vs. .274) and similar batting average statistics for the final prewar campaign of 1941 (.272 vs. .271). A closer examination of offensive statistics, however, shows slight deviations between players who did and did not serve, particularly in the power categories. In 1941, players who did not serve tended to hit more home runs (9.1) and compile more RBI (59.3) than their contemporaries who lost time due to the war (7.9 home runs and 54.7 RBI). This is most likely due partly to the fact that most teams relied on first basemen to be sluggers and run producers, and a disproportionate number of first basemen did not serve in the armed forces. Interestingly, the slugging percentages of those who did and did not serve is virtually identical (.397 vs. .395), which reveals that players who served were more apt to hit doubles and triples than their civilian counterparts.

One might expect that since players who did not serve were more apt to be sluggers, they then would be more likely to be free swingers and therefore exhibit higher numbers of strikeouts, which was true only to a slight extent. What is somewhat surprising is that players who did not serve had higher mean numbers of stolen bases, at-bats, and walks during the 1941 season, although their on-base percentages were virtually the same. Those numbers clearly suggest that players who did not serve were more often utilized as starters and batted higher in the order in 1941 than those who did serve. The higher number of at-bats and walks is logical considering that teams usually tended to rely on more experienced and thus older players. Regarding stolen bases, however, the disparities are confounding when one considers that the group that did serve had higher percentages of second basemen and outfielders, positions that normally account for the majority of stolen bases. The only apparent explanation is that players that did not serve, because they accumulated approximately 10% more at-bats (438 vs. 400), were on base more often and thus had more opportunities to steal bases.

Possibly a more equitable test in balancing the offensive production of these two groups would be to compare their statistics at similar stages in their careers. When comparing statistics for the years 1937 and 1940, when the mean ages of those who did not serve and those who served, respectively, was approximately 25.5, there are several interesting revelations. First of all, the offensive production of those who served surpassed that of those who did not serve in several vital areas. While mean home runs, slugging percentage, and stolen bases were virtually identical, the mean batting average (.282) and on-base percentage (.350) of those who served was significantly higher than their counterparts at comparable ages (.277 batting average and .338 OBP). The nearly 12-point disparity in the on-base percentages in favor of those who did serve is particularly noteworthy, for teams and players especially prize that statistic as demonstrating a player's value to his team.

Comparing both groups' on-base percentages in those years to the league averages further evidences the offensive superiority of those who served. In 1937, the group that did not serve maintained an on-base percentage of .338, approximately six points below the league average, while in 1940 the group that did serve compiled an on-base percentage of .350, about 16 points above the league average. Therefore, the resulting differential is a very significant plus 23 in favor of the group that served. Also telling is the fact that those players who did serve surpassed those who did not serve in RBI production (57.4 vs. 54.7) and, most important, in Total Player Rating (.667 vs. .205). The elevated TPR of the players that did serve suggests that they were more valuable and more productive than their civilian counterparts. One can conclude that at similar points in their careers, those players that did serve were more efficient offensive players.

Furthermore, besides their careers being interrupted, for the players that served, their absence apparently also statistically affected them to varying degrees. The first striking statistical disparity within the group of players that served is the nine-point decrease in batting average (.272 to .263) from the final season before the outbreak of the war, 1941, to the first full season following the war's conclusion, 1946—the year in which virtually all of the players in this study who served were again active. The first logical question that then arises is whether the decline in average was caused by a deterioration of skill because of years spent in the service or simply an age-related decline typical in the latter portions of a player's career. In 1941, players that did serve had a mean age of slightly over 26 and in 1946 that number rose to slightly over 30. In comparing the statistics of 1939 and 1943 for those who did not serve—the seasons during which those players maintained approximately the same mean ages—a determination can be made regarding the possibility of an age-related decline in production. From a superficial point of view, when comparing the two groups at similar ages it seems that the theory suggesting an age-related decline is the most logical conclusion to the decrease in averages—both groups witnessed a substantial decline in their averages at the age of 30 compared to their marks at the age of 26. However, looking closer at the data undermines that conclusion to some extent. In 1941, the players who served hit 11 points over the major league average of .262 while in 1946 they dipped to nine points over the major league norm of .256. Conversely, in 1939 the players that did not serve managed to compile a mean average which exceeded the major league average of .275 by six points, while in 1943 they managed to exceed the major league mark of .253 by 15 points. Thus, the differences between 1941 and 1946 in the group that served was minus two while between 1939 and 1943 in the group that did not serve was plus nine. Subsequently, this results in a disparity of 11 points between the two groups at similar ages. Therefore, even though the group that did not serve aged to a degree that one might expect a decrease in batting average, they actually increased their mean average when compared to the major league norm. In contrast, those that did serve witnessed a decline in their relative postwar batting averages, indicating a factor not associated with an age-related decline in productivity.

In dismissing age as a factor in leading to a dip in batting average between 1941 and 1946, another logical explanation might be then that players who spent one to four years in the military lost some of their skills because of inactivity. This would not be completely surprising considering the reflexes and reaction times that are necessary to compete on the major league level. However, the statistics indicate several interesting anomalies within the group that served. The revelation that those who spent only one year in the service improved on their 1941 averages by about six points is not extremely surprising, given the fact that many professional players may have retained their skills during such a brief absence by competing on military baseball teams during the war, albeit usually not against major league competition on a consistent basis. The improvement in the one-year group is even more impressive when considered in relation to the league averages of those years. In 1941, players who served one year batted just a shade under the league norm of .262, yet in 1946 they hit 13 points above the league average. Thus, it appears that forfeiting one season due to the war greatly assisted some players in compiling high averages.

More predictably, those who spent two and three years in the service witnessed a substantial decline, 9 and 23 points respectively, in their 1941 and 1946 batting averages. Part of this decline should be viewed as a general trend—the league averaged dropped seven points in 1946 compared to the 1941 season. Thus, for those who spent two years away, their nine-point dip is relatively insignificant and suggests that their absence impacted their batting skills only negligibly. In contrast, those who lost three years of their careers due to military service seem to have been affected the most by their time spent away from the diamond. As a group, they compiled a very impressive .289 average in 1941, 27 points better than the league standard and 18 points better than any of the other groups that served, before a precipitous postwar slip. In 1946 they dropped dramatically to just 11 points over the league average, and maintained only the second highest average among those who served.

Amazingly, those players who sacrificed four years of their careers to WWII actually enjoyed an increase of five points between their 1941 and 1946 batting averages. This finding is tempered somewhat by the fact that their prewar average was nine points lower than any other group's 1941 average and subsequently 11 points below the league average. Also, their 1941 mean age was much lower than the other players who served, indicating inexperience at the major league level and thus less offensive expertise. In addition, even after their five-point increase, the group that missed four years still had the second lowest postwar batting average of those that served.

When an analysis of the two final prewar years is undertaken in relationship to the first postwar season in order to negate any one-season anomalies and obtain a more comprehensive view of the effects of the wartime absence on those who served, several interesting facts become increasingly clear. First of all, for those who spent one year in the service, their dramatic increases in batting average following their absence does not seem so startling. In combining the 1940 and 1941 averages of the players who missed one year and comparing those to the league standards, the one-year group hit six points above the league norm during those two seasons. In comparison to the 1946 numbers in which those who served one year batted 12 points over the league average, this difference of six points is substantially less than the nearly 13 point differential which is evident if considering the last prewar year alone. The numbers, however, still suggest that those who missed one year actually benefited statistically from their absence.

For the group that served two years, very little difference is evident when considering the two final prewar years compared to only one. The numbers simply reinforce the conclusion that their wartime absence had little effect on their batting averages. In contrast, among the group that missed three years, utilizing the two final prewar years strengthens the determination that their hiatus did affect their batting statistics significantly. An average of the variations from the league norms for their 1940 and 1941 batting averages results in the figure of plus 28. During the first postwar year that figure dropped dramatically to plus 11, thus again suggesting that the absence affected the group negatively to a great extent.

League Averages: 1940, .267; 1941, .262; 1946, .255

Years Missed	1940 BA	1941 BA	1942 BA
0	.275	.271	.255
1	.280	.261	.267
2	.261	.265	.256
3	.295	.289	.266
4	.277	.252	.257

Interestingly, among the group that served four years one can see the most dramatic reinterpretation of the statistics once the two final prewar years are included. When only variations from the 1941 and 1946 league batting averages were considered, the resulting conclusion was that the group that was inactive for four years witnessed an increase of 12 points relative to the league average upon their return. However, when the 1940 season is also included, their prewar numbers and postwar numbers are virtually identical, blunting the seemingly remarkable gains they made after the war.

Utilizing similar methods regarding the impact of the war on the power statistics of players who served, no discernible patterns emerge from the general data. Among both players who served and those who did not, home run totals dipped at least slightly in 1946 compared to 1941. However, this is not particularly revealing, since the overall number of home runs tended to decline after 1941 and remained low through 1946. In 1941, major league hitters struck a total of 1,331 home runs, with the numbers steadily declining from that point until in 1946, when a modest offensive power surge transpired. It was not until the following year, however, when batters smacked 1,565 home runs, that the number of round-trippers

surpassed prewar totals. Therefore, it is not surprising that the statistics for the groups of players who both served and did not serve followed this general trend.

When one looks closer at the statistics, however, it seems obvious that the extended absences endured by those players that served in the military also negatively affected their home run totals in the years following their return. Again utilizing comparable data from the 1939 and 1943 seasons—the years when the ages of players who did not serve were almost identical to the 1941 and 1946 ages of those that served—notable differences are clearly evident. In comparing the years 1939 and 1943 for those players who did not serve, totals decreased an average of approximately one per person, or 13%, while the major league home run totals between those two years decreased a drastic 38%. Therefore, in relation to the rest of the league, the players who did not serve actually witnessed an increase in their power statistics when comparing their statistics at the age of 30 in relation to their numbers at 26. Despite earlier revelations that those players who spent one or two years away from the diamond due to military service increased their offensive productivity, their power statistics seem to have been affected by their absence. In 1946, the number of home runs in the major leagues was about 9% lower than in the last prewar war year of 1941. When comparing the home run totals during those same two years for players who missed one year of action, a decline of 12% is observed (9.2 home runs to 8.1) while those who missed two years witnessed a steeper decline of 26% (4.8 home runs to 3.6). The disparity for the one-year group in relation to the league average decline, therefore, was a mild 3% while those players who missed two years endured a drop of 17% below the league norm. The three- and four-year groups also had drastic declines in their home run production, even when considering the 9% decline by the league as a whole between 1941 and 1946. The players who missed three years dipped 18% (10.3 home runs to 8.4), while the players with four years of military service sank 50% in their home run numbers (3.2 home runs to 1.6).

Other power statistics observed in 1941 and 1946 also reveal several more interesting variations. Whereas one would expect the slugging percentages of players who served to be detrimentally affected by their absence due to the fact that home runs play such an instrumental part in the calculation of that statistic, it seems to be only marginally true. In comparing 1941 slugging percentages of those who served with their 1946 numbers, only the group who missed three years showed any substantial decline beyond the aforementioned league-wide offensive dip with a drop of 52 points. Furthermore, when considering the slugging statistics for those who did not serve in the years 1939 and 1943, little, if any, inference can be made from the statistics. The slugging percentage of this group declined by about 51 points, which was virtually identical to the league average decline. The difference between the groups that served and did not serve was minimal at best.

However, when considering the RBI production for both groups at similar points in their careers, large disparities are clear, and it is evident that extended absences by players who served detrimentally affected their offensive output. For those players who served at least one year, a decrease in RBI output is plainly evident with those who were inactive longer suffering the most. Each subgroup of those who served endured a substantial decline in their run production when their 1941 seasons are compared to the first postwar campaign. However, this again was partly due to the overall trend in professional baseball, for during the 1946 season major league teams scored just over 1,215 fewer runs than in 1941, thus leading to lower RBI totals across the board. This 11% decrease partly but not completely explains the drop in RBI production by every group that served. As has been the pattern previously, the players who missed only one year of action were affected least by their absence, knocking in only 12% fewer runs in 1946 (51.3) than in the last prewar season (58.1)—a negligible 1% disparity from the league decline. Those who spent two years in military service seemed to have been affected to a greater degree, dropping their run production 19% (43.4 RBI to 35)—8% lower than the rest of the league. Continuing the descent, the players who missed three years sagged 23% from 1941 to 1946 (64.3 RBI to 49.6), while those who missed four years dipped precipitously by driving in 32% fewer runs

Left to right: Cmdr. J. Russell Cook, Lt. Cmdr. Mickey Cochrane, Steve O'Neill, and Commodore Emmett.

between those seasons (39.8 RBI to 27.4). These dips in production, 12 and 21% below the league average decline, respectively, indicates that players returning from military obligations did not retain their prewar abilities in hitting with men in scoring position.

In comparing the numbers of those who did not lose seasons due to the war to those who did miss substantial playing time, the decline in RBI production by the group that served becomes more revealing. Weighing the years of 1939 and 1943 for the group that did not serve, those players witnessed a rather unexpected increase in RBI output (49.7 RBI to 56.3). This is somewhat surprising because in comparison to the 1939 season, the numbers of runs scored in the major leagues dropped dramatically by 2,182 or 18%. When combined with the modest increase in RBI of 12% by those who did not serve during those years, they boosted their production by 30% in relation to the league average. When compared to the decline among those that served, this is particularly impressive and suggests that military service did in fact affect RBI productivity.

In analyzing the vitally important statistic of on-base percentage in the same manner, players who missed seasons due to military service seemed to have been affected negligibly. The overall on-base percentage in major league baseball declined about four points in 1946 compared to 1941. However, only the players that missed three years actually saw a dip in their on-base percentages during the first postwar campaign (.369 OBP to .339). The remaining groups witnessed modest increases in their 1946 on base percentages of approximately nine, one, and 24 points in the one-year, two-year, and four-years-served groups, respectively. These numbers, however, are very comparable to the disparities in the on-base percentages of players who did not serve in the years of 1939 and 1943. The average league on base percentage declined 20 points within those two years, or about 6%, while the players who did not serve saw their on-base percentages decline by approximately 10 points or 3%. Thus, no direct correlation between this statistic and wartime absence can be proven to a high degree of certainty.

However, when using *Total Baseball*'s statistic, Total Player Rating, in players who did and did not serve, once again evidence of the negative impact of military service becomes clear. Of the players who missed at least one season, the TPR's of those players varied greatly both before and after the war. According to the TPR statistic, those players who missed three years were the most valuable group to their teams before the war while their numbers following the war sank dramatically. This confirms earlier analyses, which suggest the wartime absence for that group had a sizable impact on their postwar production. One baffling anomaly is that the group who missed two years showed a remarkable improvement in their 1946 TPR ratings when compared to their 1941 numbers. This can be somewhat explained by their low 1941 TPR rank, which was the second lowest of the four groups. However, the other groups who served had either very modest gains in their TPR or, more predictably, a decline in those numbers.

When compared to the average increase in the TPR statistic for those players who did not serve for the years 1939 and 1943, the results of the group that served again decreased in relation. The group who avoided military service enjoyed a .530 increase in their TPR between 1939 and 1943 (.176 TPR to .706), while the players who served exhibited a relative decline in their on-field performance (.528 TPR to .255). Most notably, the group who served three years endured a startling decline in their TPR (1.264 to .382) from 1941 to 1946. Also, despite earlier revelations that the group who missed one year actually witnessed moderate to substantial improvement in their production, their slight increase of .14 in their TPR statistic (.431 to .445) reveals that improvement may have been overstated.

Therefore, while the majority of major league players lost at least one season due to military service, it should come as no surprise that extended absences negatively affected the careers of the athletes involved. This is evident not only in individual cases where some lost as many as four years of their prime to the war, but also collectively for the group of players who served. For some, serving in the armed forces proved detrimental in reaching statistical milestones and for others prevented them from possibly reaching the Hall of Fame. Clearly military service initiated a general offensive decline among position players, the repercussions of which were felt years after the conclusion of the war both by the individual players and major league baseball as a whole.

Notes:

1. Although Greenberg's postwar statistics do not rival his prewar numbers, he was instrumental in Detroit's 1945 World Series victory upon his release from the Army and playing in the final weeks of the season. Also, the Tiger star did lead the American League in home runs and RBI in his first full season back but had a batting average much below his norm. Following the war, Greenberg never again hit over .300 and retired within two years of his return to the major leagues.

2. At the time of Musial's retirement, only Babe Ruth had surpassed that total. Hank Aaron eventually accomplished the feat several years after Musial's departure from the game.

3. Doerr also spent time in the military during the war, though only one year compared to Gordon's two-season absence.

4. For the purpose of this study, players who played at least one season before and after their military service with at least 50 at-bats in each of those seasons will be considered for the group that served. For a control group, players who played at least the 1941-1946 seasons with no time missed due to military service will be considered.

5. Total Player Rating is a statistic devised by *Total Baseball* researchers which determines a player's worth by comparing his statistics to players throughout his league at his position during a particular season. The higher the TPR rating, theoretically the more valuable a player is to his team. For an in-depth description as to exactly how a player's TPR is calculated, see John Thorn, et al., eds., *Total Baseball* (New York: Total Sports, 1999), p. 655.

Ted Williams in 1941

by Paul Warburton

Baseball's last .400 hitter was probably the sport's best pure hitter ever. Over 60 years have passed since 1941, and no one has duplicated "Teddy Ballgame's" feat of hitting .406. Great hitters such as Rod Carew, George Brett, Tony Gwynn, and Todd Helton have carried .400-plus averages far into the season but died in the home stretch.

In 1941, Williams knocked out 185 hits in 456 at-bats, including 33 doubles, 3 triples, and a league-leading 37 homers. He also walked 147 times, giving him an incredible .553 on-base percentage. Up until Barry Bonds' 2002 campaign, this was the highest on-base percentage ever recorded in one season. Williams also led baseball in slugging percentage with a .735 mark and struck out only 27 times, a career low.

Ted led the AL with 135 runs scored and finished second to Joe DiMaggio in RBI with 120. DiMaggio hit .357 with 125 RBI and set an all-time record by hitting in 56 consecutive games. During the summer of 1941, America's last summer before its entrance into the Second World War, Williams and DiMaggio took turns grabbing the headlines in the sports pages of newspapers across the nation. Their names have been forever linked together in baseball lore since 1941, and countless comparisons have been made between the two giants of the sport.

Paul Warburton is a former baseball player, captain of the hockey team and sports editor at Moses Brown Prep in Providence. He lives in Wakefield, RI.

Under today's rules and the rules common to most of baseball history, Williams would actually have been credited with a .412 batting average in 1941. At that time a fly ball that drove in a runner from third base counted as a time at bat and not as a sacrifice fly. Williams was charged with a time at bat for six such fly balls in 1941 that would have been scored sacrifice flies today.

It is not surprising that Ted was baseball's last .400 hitter. His career batting average of .344 is sixth all-time and the highest since Rogers Hornsby retired in 1937 at .358. Williams also holds the highest career on-base percentage at .483. Babe Ruth is second at .474. Williams' career .634 slugging percentage is second only to Ruth's .690. Probably the best statistical measure of a player's offensive value is total average. This is derived by dividing a player's bases made (total bases + stolen bases + walks + times hit by pitches - number of times caught stealing) by his outs made (at-bats - hits + times caught stealing + times grounded into double play). Williams owns the second-highest all-time total average at 1.320. Ruth is first at 1.399.

Williams knocked out these fabulous stats despite losing more time to military service than any other player in baseball history. He missed all of the 1943, 1944, and 1945 seasons, when he served his country as a Marine fighter pilot in World War II. He then missed all but 43 games to the Korean War in 1952 and 1953 for the same reason. All totaled, he missed

727 games during his peak years due to wars. Consider the number of games he missed, plus the difficulty of hitting major league pitching at so high a level after returning from such long periods of absence, and the magnitude of Williams' statistical greatness becomes staggering.

By the time he reached the Red Sox in 1939, Ted's 6'4" frame had filled out to 175 pounds, and he was hitting many balls over 400 feet. He gave the Fenway Park faithful an inkling of things to come when he batted .327 with 31 homers and led the league in RBI with 145, stilll a rookie record. At age 20, he also began to be known for his boyish cockiness. In one game in Detroit he blasted a homer off Bob Harris that landed on top of the right-field pavillion at Briggs Stadium. As he crossed home plate, he told Tiger catcher Birdie Tebbetts, "I hope that guy is still pitching the next time I come up. I'll knock it clear over the roof." This is exactly what Ted did.

Sometimes he practiced his swing while standing in the outfield. He did not fare well playing right field, the sun field, at Fenway Park. The next season he would be shifted to left field, where he would eventually become a good if somewhat underrated fly chaser. There were times that he sulked after tapping an easy ground ball and did not run hard to first base. If he had a bad day at the plate, it might noticeably affect his fielding adversely. The Boston writers, led by Dave Egan of the *Boston Daily Record*, often magnified his mistakes. In 1939, Ted's father and mother separated, and he decided not to go home during that winter. He sent money to his mother, but home was not a happy place for him.

In 1940, Ted's relationship with the writers worsened. The first time Williams did something to displease sports reporter Harold Kaese, he wrote, "Well, what do you expect from a guy who won't even go see his mother in the off season." It was comments like this that turned Williams against the writers. He explained in his autobiography, "Before this, I was willing to believe a writer was my friend until he proved otherwise. Now my guard's up all the time, always watching for critical stuff. If I saw something, I'd read it twenty times, and I'd burn without knowing how to fight it. How could I fight it?"

In 1940, Ted's batting average improved to .344, but his power numbers fell off to 23 homers and 113 RBI. Only seven of his homers came at Fenway. Some of Fenway's fans started to boo him. After being booed one day after striking out and following it up with an error in left field, Williams vowed never to tip

his cap again. He never did tip it during his playing days, even after hitting a home run in his final at-bat in Fenway in 1960.

The 1941 season, however, was probably Ted's most enjoyable. Even his most zealous critics could find little fault with him that magical summer. It was the hitting perfectionist's perfect season. The so-called kid with the swelled head proved to the baseball world just how remarkable a talent he was. He showed that he was the equal of anyone playing the game and won many fans over. From then until the end of his career all the potshots that the press took at him could not deny his true greatness. It may be that no one will ever hit .400 again.

The 1941 season did not start out promising for Williams, however. In the second exhibition game he caught his spikes sliding into second base and chipped a bone in his right ankle. He came out of the exhibition season still limping and relegated to pinch-hitting duties only. On April 15, a sparse opening day crowd of 15,000 at Fenway Park saw the Red Sox rally for three runs in the ninth inning to top Washington, 7-6. Ted delivered a key pinch-hit single in the rally.

Strangely enough, Ted's teammate Bobby Doerr believed that Williams' ankle injury might have actually helped Ted hit .406. Doerr explained his theory; "I remember him going into the trainer's room every day to get his ankle taped up. In batting practice you could see him kind of favoring it. I kind of wondered then, and I kind of got to thinking as the season went on, that it was sensitive enough to make him stay back for as long as possible to keep the pressure off his front foot."

Williams agreed that he was able to hold back a little longer in 1941. Ted said, however, "But I never thought it was because of my ankle. I never thought that. From 1941 on, I was getting stronger and stronger and stronger. I was late to mature, and I think I was the strongest between the ages of 22 and 32. As a result, I was able to hold back and hold back, getting quicker and stronger than at any time."

Boston won five of its first six games without Ted in the lineup. He tried to play left field at Griffith Stadium during a 12-5 loss to Washington on April 22. He whacked a single and a double in four at-bats but wound up aggravating the injury further. In the next four games he appeared only once, pinch-hitting unsuccessfully during a 6-3 loss in New York. Ted never was a good cold weather hitter. Fenway almost always had chilling adverse winds during the first couple of weeks of the season. Not being in the lineup every day then probably helped Ted's batting average in 1941.

Ted was back in left field on April 29 in Detroit. He bashed a long double and a 440-foot home run off Johnny Gorsica, but Gorsica outpitched Lefty Grove to win, 5-3. Ted always considered Detroit as his best park to hit in with its short right field porch. In 585 career at-bats there he homered 55 times and knocked in 162 runs.

On May 7 in Chicago, Ted walloped a 500-foot two-run homer into the upper right-field stands at Comiskey Park off Johnny Rigney in the third inning. Rigney liked to challenge hitters with high, hard fastballs, and the book on Ted was that he murdered the high fastball. Ted came to bat against Rigney again in the eleventh inning with the score tied at 3-3. Rigney tried to surprise Williams with a slow curve. Ted drove it over the roof of the second tier in the deepest part of right center and sent it bouncing into a parking lot estimated at some 600 feet from home plate. Only Ruth and Gehrig had hit balls over that roof before.

The Yankees arrived in Boston for the first time of the season on May 11, and the Red Sox routed them, 13-5, before an overflow crowd of 34,500. Ted singled twice and doubled in six at-bats while Joe DiMaggio singled three times in five at-bats. Joe was off to a slow start barely hitting .300, when he began his historic 56-game hitting streak on May 15. Ted singled once in three at-bats that day during a 6-4 loss to the first-place Indians. That single, however, started him on a 23-game hitting streak of his own.

Over the course of those 23 games, Ted would hit .487 (43 for 88) while DiMaggio hit .368 (32 for 87). On May 21, Ted went 4-for-5 with a double off the Browns' Bob Harris as the Red Sox won, 8-6. Williams was always a terror against the Browns. In 1941, he hit .426 with nine homers and 26 RBI in 61 at-bats against them. From 1939 to 1953 he feasted on Brownie pitching, batting .393 with 60 homers and 223 RBI in 754 at-bats.

The Red Sox played three games at Yankee Stadium from May 23 to May 25. The first game was called because of darkness after nine innings with the score tied, 9-9. The Yanks won the second game, 7-6, as DiMaggio's two-run single in the seventh inning proved to be the decider. Boston won the final game, 10-3, as Williams singled three times and doubled. His average was now at .404.

During a four-game series against the A's from May 27 to May 29, Ted ripped eight hits in 15 at-bats, including a double and two homers, to bring his aver-age up to .421. On Memorial Day in Boston, the Yanks and Red Sox divided a doubleheader. New York won the opener, 4-3, and Boston took the second game with a 13-0 rout. Ted was 3-for-5 on the day with a double and scored four times. DiMaggio had two singles in five at-bats but experienced the worst day of his career on defense, making four errors. Ted ended May at .429. He had hit .436 for the month.

The Sporting News opined: "Unless all people who know anything are 100 percent wrong, Williams is due to firmly establish himself this year as one of the truly great left-handed batsmen. There isn't anything particularly new about this estimate of his ability, either. In 1939, his first complete season in the major leagues, Williams did things with a bat and ball that made all wonder where his limits were. He hit homers in many parks that went so far as to be almost unbelievable. He didn't hit them off young or unskilled pitchers altogether either."

As June opened, an announcement was made that all servicemen would be admitted free of charge for the remainder of the season at all major league parks. Ted began June in Detroit with four hits in nine at-bats including his eighth homer as the Red Sox swept a doubleheader, 7-6 and 6-5. Lou Gehrig died on June 2, and flags were at half-staff in all major league parks for the day of his funeral on June 4. Cleveland was leading the league on June 2 at 30-19. Another baseball star who would distinguish himself in military service during World War II, Bob Feller, had won 11 of the Indians' games, including three shutouts. Chicago was 1½ games out. The Yanks were three games back and Boston was four out with a 22-19 record.

The Red Sox teed off on Cleveland pitching on June 5, socking 16 hits in a 14-1 win. Williams singled twice, homered, drove in three runs, and scored four times. The next day his average reached its high-water mark for the season at .438 as he doubled and clouted a two-run homer off Rigney in a 6-3 win in Chicago.

Around this time Carl Felker characterized Williams in *The Sporting News*. Felker wrote, "Ted Williams rolled up a newspaper, gritted his teeth, faced the mirror in a hotel room in St. Louis and took a cut at an imaginary ball. 'Hitting is the biggest thing in my life,' he exclaimed. 'I love it. And the thing I like next best is to hunt ducks in Minnesota.' But right now, duck hunting doesn't occupy any part of Ted's thoughts. He is concentrating on the job of trying to top the .400 mark in hitting for the 1941 season. And he believes he has a good chance to reach his goal—

perhaps even to smash the all-time figure at .438 set way back in 1894 by Hugh Duffy, now a coach with the Red Sox. 'If you don't have confidence in yourself, who will?' asks the Boston kid."

Felker continued: "Every chance he gets, Williams practices hitting. 'I've always done that,' he declared. 'It's my pet theory—practice your swing all the time, from morning to night. Strengthen those muscles you're going to use. I go out to the ball park in the morning for batting drill. Even when I'm in the outfield, I take my imaginary cuts at the ball. I'm always taking swings in my room. It all helps.'"

Concerning Ted's ability to hit left handers well, Felker added, "Williams doesn't believe southpaws are any tougher for him to hit than right-handers. 'At Minneapolis, where I played in 1938, we had a short right field fence (actually only 278 feet) and the other clubs would save their left-handers to send against us there,' Ted related. 'As a result I was fortunate in getting to look at a lot of southpaw pitching.'"

Williams' 23-game hitting streak was stopped in the first game of a doubleheader in Chicago on June 8 by Ted Lyons. Lyons walked him three times, including once with the bases loaded. The Red Sox won, 5-3, behind Grove. On June 12 in St. Louis, Ted's two-run homer off knuckleballer Johnny Niggeling was the difference in a 3-2 win. Back in Boston on June 15, Ted whacked four hits in six at-bats including another double and homer as the Yawkeyites swept the White Sox, 8-6 and 6-4, before 34,000-plus.

On Bunker Hill Day in Boston, the Red Sox took the opener of a doubleheader from Detroit, 14-6, but dropped the second game, 8-5, before 23,000. Ted drilled a two-run homer and doubled in five at-bats. In New York, the Yanks completed a three-game sweep of Cleveland before a combined crowd of 100,675 for the series as "Joltin' Joe" ran his streak to 29 games.

On June 23, Cleveland still led the league at 40-25 when they entered Boston for a three-game set. The Yanks were two games back, and Boston was four games off the pace. The Red Sox won the opener routing Mel Harder and his successors with 18 hits, 13-2. The next day Williams cracked a two-run homer in the fourth inning to tie the score at 2-2, and Boston went on to win, 7-2. The loss knocked the Indians out of first place as New York took over the top by besting St. Louis, 7-5. "Joltin' Joe" homered to bring his streak to 37 games. In the final game Cleveland rebounded to win, 11-8. Feller, showing signs of overwork, was hit hard but still recorded his 16th win.

Williams went 5-for-10 in the series, scoring six runs and knocking in three. He was now at .412 with 53 RBI and a league-leading 63 runs scored. DiMaggio was at .349 with 62 runs scored and a league-leading 57 RBI.

The Red Sox invaded Yankee Stadium for a big doubleheader on July 1, trailing the Bronx Bombers by five games. It was the Red Sox 's last real chance to get into the pennant race and they failed miserably. A crowd of 52,832 saw the Yanks win, 7-2 and 9-2. DiMaggio laced three singles, tying Wee Willie Keeler's 1896 mark by hitting in consecutive game number 44. He broke Keeler's mark the next day with a three-run homer that went over Ted's head and sailed into the left-field stands. The Yanks won again, 8-4, to open up an eight-game lead over Boston. Ted managed just three singles in nine at-bats in the important series without an RBI.

On the last day before the All-Star break, Ted went 4-for-8 with two doubles as the Bosox bested the Senators twice, 6-2 and 6-3, at Fenway. Ted was getting second billing during DiMaggio's streak but he was still drawing a lot of attention with his .405 average at the break.

The All-Star game was considered as big an event as the World Series in those days, as both leagues played for keeps to get bragging rights. With the American League trailing 5-4, Ted came to bat with two on and two out in the bottom of the ninth against Claude Passeau. He fouled off the first pitch, took two balls, and then lifted a fly ball toward the foul line in right. He described his historic homer in his autobiography: "I had pulled it to right field, no doubt about that, but I was afraid I hadn't got enough of the bat on the ball. But gee, it just kept going, up, up way up into the right field stands in Detroit—halfway down to first, seeing that ball going out, I stopped running and started leaping and jumping and clapping my hands, and I was so happy I laughed out loud. I've never been so happy, and I've never seen so many happy guys. They carried me off the field, DiMaggio and Bob Feller, who had pitched early in the game and was already in street clothes, and Eddie Collins leaped out of the box seats and was there to greet me." Ted called the home run "the biggest thrill" of his career.

The Red Sox stayed in Detroit for a four-game series after the All-Star game. On July 12, Ted received a base on balls, then took a big lead off first base. The Tigers pitched out and catcher Birdie Tebbetts fired down to Rudy York, trying to pick

Williams off. Ted slid back to first hard, and when he did his foot hit the corner of the bag and twisted. It was the same foot that he had injured in the spring. He limped around a few more innings before retiring to the clubhouse. The ankle swelled up like a balloon. He had received three walks in the game before fouling out in his last at-bat. On the previous day he had been collared in four at-bats by Bobo Newsom. His average had now dipped to .397, and the dream of a .400 season seemed in serious jeopardy.

Meanwhile Joe DiMaggio ran his streak to 56 games before being stopped on July 17 before 67,468 in a night game in Cleveland. From the time he broke Keeler's record until the end of his streak he had been on fire, whacking 24 hits in 44 at-bats. He now led the league in RBI with 76 and home runs with 20. During one span in the streak the Yankees won 30 of 35 games to run away from the pack into a solid lead in the standings. On July 21, they led Cleveland by 7 games and Boston by 14. Joe's average was up to .375, and he told reporters that he hadn't given up on catching Ted for the batting title. During the streak he had hit .408. During the same 56 games, Ted hit .412.

Ted spent the next 12 games on the bench while his foot healed. He pinch-hit four times in those 12 games. He walked once, hit an RBI fly ball, popped out, and cranked a three-run homer. He returned to left field in Fenway on July 22 and tagged Chicago's Rigney yet again for a gigantic homer into the right-center bleachers in the second inning. Stan Spence replaced him in the field later in the game, but Ted was back for the full nine innings the next day, socking a single and a double in five at-bats. In his first 12 games back from the injury Ted collected 19 hits in 35 at-bats to bring his average back up to .412.

After DiMaggio's streak was stopped in Cleveland, he ran off another 16-game streak, hitting safely in an unbelievable 72 out of 73 games. He went almost two months without striking out. Yet Ted was pulling away again in the batting race. His three singles on July 26 helped deny Feller his 20th win. His two-run homer on July 29 was the key blow in a 3-2 win over St. Louis. He smashed a grand slam against the Browns the next day. He ended July at .409 to "Joltin' Joe's" .377. On August 1 he went fishing on an off day and caught a record-breaking 374-pound tuna.

In two consecutive doubleheaders in St. Louis on August 19 and August 20, Ted went 8-for-14 with five homers, seven runs scored, and eight RBI. DiMaggio cooled off and dipped to .356. Joe then sprained his ankle on August 19. He would miss three weeks.

DiMaggio's injury now gave Ted a good chance at the Triple Crown, if the pitchers did not walk him so much. He was in the midst of a 21-game road trip that visited all seven cities. During the road trip he was walked 32 times in 96 plate appearances. He had 26 hits. He hit .406 on the trip with a .623 on-base percentage. On August 30 he celebrated his 23rd birthday with a single and a home run during a 12-3 win over the A's at friendly Fenway.

The Sporting News reported, "The orders the pitchers get now when Ted comes to bat, particularly with men on base is to walk him. They start walking him as early as the first inning. If he isn't walked intentionally with the catcher moving off to one side, they might as well put on the act, because they pitch so wide to Ted it would be silly for him to swing on any of the pitches. . . . It is the exception when Ted is pitched a ball not down near his left knee or so far on the outside as to be almost a wild pitch. Therefore his chances of hitting are kept way down. Ted has one of the best eyes for pitches of any batter in baseball." Later while in the Marines, Ted's eyesight would be tested at 20/10, and he would set the student gunnery record at Jacksonville.

On Labor Day in Boston, Ted smashed three tremendous home runs in a doubleheader sweep of the Senators. This gave him 34 homers on the season, passing New York's Charlie Keller for the league lead. He was also walked four more times. One of the homers came off Bill Zuber, the pitcher who had come close to ending Ted's career with a beaning at Minneapolis in 1938. The writers said it was the longest homer Ted had hit at Fenway all season.

The Yanks clinched the pennant with a 6-3 win at Fenway on September 4. Atley Donald, a pitcher noted for his control, walked Ted four straight times before he managed a single in his final time at bat. They were the only free passes that Donald gave up all afternoon. The same frustrating experience had happened to Ted three weeks earlier at Yankee Stadium. After a first-inning RBI single, he was walked four straight times to a chorus of boos from New York fans, who had paid their money to see Ted hit. Yankee pitchers were well aware of Williams' competition with Keller and DiMaggio for the league's home run and RBI crowns.

The four walks to Ted in the game on September 4 were unfortunate for another reason. A 14-year-old boy named Billy Kane started out on a 250-mile hitch-hiking trip from his home in South Brewer, Maine, on September 1 to see his hero, Williams, at Fenway

Park. He arrived in town on September 2, which was an off-day for the Red Sox. He walked through Boston to Fenway and fell asleep under the bleachers. When the police found him there, he told them his story. He was taken to the station house and the desk sergeant phoned Williams in his hotel. Ted had already gone to bed, but when he heard the kid's story he dressed quickly and took the kid out for a good meal. He then put Billy up for the night at his hotel. The next day the youngster was permitted to sit in the Red Sox dugout during the game. After four walks, Ted whacked a single. The kid supposedly said to Williams after, "Dog-gone, Ted! Gee, pal, but I was pulling for the home run."

On September 7 at Yankee Stadium, Ted hit a single and a pair of doubles off Lefty Gomez in an 8-5 loss to the Yanks. Yankee Stadium was the only park that Williams did not hit a home run in that magical summer. In the fifth inning, however, he crushed a 450-foot double off the top of the center-field wall, missing a round-tripper by mere inches. The next inning Gomez walked him on four pitches with the bases loaded, giving Ted his only RBI of the day.

On September 15, Ted belted his 35th homer of the season, a three-run shot off Chicago's Johnny Rigney (his sixth off Rigney in 1941) in a 6-1 win at Fenway. His three RBI that day tied him with DiMaggio at 116. The Yanks' Keller was leading the league at 122, but he had twisted his ankle on September 7 and was lost for the remainder of the season. It was likely that both Ted and Joe would pass him in RBI.

When the Yanks came to Fenway on September 20, Joe and Ted were still tied in RBI at 116. Ted had two-thirds of the Triple Crown locked up and was battling Joe for the RBI crown. The Yanks won the first game, 8-1. Joe singled, doubled, and drove in two runs to take the lead again at 118. The next day Boston clinched second by winning, 4-1. In the sixth inning, Ted launched a two-run homer off Ernie "Tiny" Bonham to tie Joe for the RBI lead once more.

Ted was now hitting .406 with six games left to play—three in Washington and three in Philadelphia. He was quoted saying: "Lots of times I could belt the ball into the stands if I wanted to take a chance, but I have to think about my average this season. Next year, everybody will be talking about my 1941 mark. Then I'll be swinging from my heels and giving the home run record a whirl. I'll go after 'em all, one at a time. I'll beat Gehrig's mark for runs batted in, Hornsby's and Cobb's batting records, and Ruth in homers. I'm

the boy to do it, too."

The Sporting News remarked: "From the rock-bound coast of Maine to the sun-kissed shores of California, the real fans are rooting almost to a man for Ted to continue above the .400 mark . . . . Williams has a grip on the fans of this country that is remarkable. He is only a youngster, having become 23 on August 30. It may be that his great ability as a batter for one so young has appealed to the fans. There is a boyishness about Ted that gets everybody. A string bean in build, with a frame so shy of the usual sinew and muscle which great hitters of other days have had, he does not appear to have the power to do what he does and yet he does it."

On September 23 and 24, the Red Sox played three games in Washington, and Ted managed just two singles in ten at-bats. His average dropped to .402. Meanwhile in New York, the "Jolter" smashed two home runs and drove in three runs to take the RBI lead for keeps. On September 27, Ted got just one hit in four at-bats, a double to deep right center, against A's rookie knuckleballer Roger Wolff during a 5-1 Red Sox win in Philadelphia. His average had now dipped to .39955 with a season-ending doubleheader scheduled for the next day at Shibe Park.

Ted described the evening before the big doubleheader in his book: "That night before the game Cronin offered to take me out of the lineup to preserve the .400 (.39955 rounds off to .400). I told Cronin I didn't want that. If I couldn't hit .400 all the way I didn't deserve it. It sure as hell meant something to me then, and Johnny Orlando, the clubhouse boy, always a guy who was there when I needed him, must have walked ten miles with me the night before, talking it over and just walking around. Johnny really didn't like to walk as much as I did, so I'd wait outside while he ducked into the bar for a quick one to keep his strength up. The way he tells it, he made two stops for scotch and I made two stops for ice cream walking the streets of Philadelphia."

On the last day of the season a sparse crowd of 10,000 showed up at a cold and miserable Shibe Park. Ted recalled, "As I came to bat for the first time that day, the Philadelphia catcher, Frankie Hayes, said: 'Ted, Mr. Mack told us if we let up on you he'll run us out of baseball. I wish you all the luck in the world, but we're not giving you a damn thing.'"

Williams started off the first game with a line single between first and second off Dick Fowler. The next time up he homered. Then he hit two singles off a left hander he had never seen before, Porter Vaughn. In the second game he hit a ground single to right, then doubled off a loudspeaker horn in right center (Boston writers said it was the hardest ball he had hit all year). Mack had to have the horn replaced in the winter, so badly was it dented. Ted was already 6-for-8 on the day, when the second game was called on account of darkness after 8 innings. As it happens, Ted was scheduled to leadoff the top of the 9th and they probably would have pitched to him.

Suppose he'd gotten up one more time? With one more at bat, assuming the Athletics didn't have the good sense to give him an intentional walk, he may have gone 7 for 9—which would have given him a .407 average. If he'd made an out, it would have reduced him to .405.

But darkness descended, with Philadelphia ahead, 7–1, so Ted never had that final at bat. For the day Williams wound up with six hits in eight at-bats to finish at .406. He added to his legendary story, "I don't remember celebrating that night, but I probably went out and had a chocolate milk shake."

The final day of the 1941 season would not be the last time Ted rose to the occasion. On opening day in 1946, in his first game back after three years in the military, Ted blasted a 400-foot home run in Washington. In 1952, in his last game before leaving for military duty in the Korean War, Ted broke up a 3-3 tie with Detroit by creaming a home run off Dizzy Trout. Ted flew 39 combat missions over Korea. When hit by small-arms fire during one mission, he crash landed his damaged jet and escaped from the flaming wreckage fortunate to be alive. In his first Fenway appearance back from the cockpit near the end of the 1953 season, he homered off Mike Garcia and went onto bat an incredible .407 in 37 games.

In 1957, at age 39, Ted topped the league with an amazing .388 batting average and slammed 38 homers, coming within five leg hits of hitting .400 again. He batted .453 during the second half of 1957. Off the field, his concern for charitable causes in Boston and his efforts on behalf of the Jimmy Fund were numerous, often unpublicized and made genuinely from his heart. Today he is most remembered for hitting .406 in 1941, but Ted Williams' whole career—both on and off the field—was nothing short of colossal. He was a true American hero. The greatest pure hitter ever? I'd say so.

Is There a Home Field Advantage in the World Series?

by Alan I. Abramowitz

This year, for the first time in the history of Major League Baseball, the home field advantage in the World Series will be based on the outcome of the midseason All-Star Game. In an effort to make the All-Star Game more meaningful and overcome the negative fallout from last season's tie game, Baseball Commissioner Bud Selig decided that starting this year, the representative of the league that wins the All-Star Game will get to play games one and two and, if necessary, games six and seven of the World Series in its home stadium, giving it a presumed advantage.

This new policy has stirred considerable debate among baseball commentators, fans, and players. In most other professional sports, the team with the better regular season record is awarded home-field advantage in the post-season. Since the advent of divisional play in 1969, baseball too has followed this practice during the American and National League playoffs. However, home field advantage in the World Series has continued to alternate each year between the National League representative and the American League representative.

Some critics of the new policy feel that it is inappropriate to give one of the World Series teams an advantage based on the outcome of what is essentially an exhibition game. But before considering the appropriateness of deciding the home field advantage based on the results of the All-Star Game, a prior question must be addressed: Is there really a home field advantage in the World Series? Does the team that plays games one and two and, if necessary, games six and seven on its home field really have an advantage over its opponent?

The answer to this question is not obvious. After all, the team that opens the Series at home only plays more games on its home field if the Series goes the full seven games. In a four or six game series, the two teams play an equal number of games on their home field. In a five game series, the team that begins play on the road actually ends up playing more home games than the team that begins play at home.

A total of 76 World Series have been played under the current 2-3-2 home-away-home format that was adopted in 1924. (Because of travel restrictions during World War II, the 2-3-2 format was not used for the 1943 or 1945 Series and no World Series was played in 1994.) Of the 445 games played in these Series, the home team has won 254, or 57%. However, of these 76 Series, 14 went only four games, 14 went five games, and 17 went six games. Only 31 Series went the full seven games. As a result, teams playing games one and two at home have played only 52% of all games on their home field.

Despite playing only slightly more than half of all games on their home field, however, teams playing the first two games at home have won 44 of the 76 World Series played under the 2-3-2 format, or 58%. So there does seem to be a significant advantage to starting the World Series at home. But why is this?

Alan I. Abramowitz is the Alben W. Barkley Professor of Political Science at Emory University He received his B.A. from the University of Rochester in 1969 and his Ph.D. from Stanford University in 1976.

Among both critics and supporters of Selig's decision, it has generally been assumed that the home field advantage in the World Series is based mainly on the fact that if the Series goes the full seven games, the team starting the series on its home field also gets to play game seven on its home field. Surprisingly, however, playing game seven at home is not a significant advantage in the World Series. Of the 31 Series that have gone the full seven games, the home team has won only 16 while losing 15 (52%). We have to look elsewhere in order to explain why teams that begin the World Series at home have won the Series 58% of the time.

It appears that the home field advantage in the World Series is due almost entirely to the momentum gained by playing the first two games of the Series at home. Teams beginning the World Series at home have won game one 47 of 76 times (62%) and game two 44 of 76 times (58%). Even after losing game one, the home team has come back to win 17 of 29 times (59%) in game two.

Altogether, the home team has swept the first two games 27 times, split the first two games 37 times, and been swept at home only 12 times. Not surprisingly, when the home team won the first two games, they went on to win the Series 20 out of 27 times (76%). Also not surprisingly, when the home team lost the first two games, they went on to lose the Series 9 out of 12 times (75%).

Even when the home team split the first two games, they went on to win the World Series 21 out of 37 times (57%). However, when a split occurred, it made a difference which game the home team won. Home teams that won game one but lost game two went on to win only 9 out of 20 Series (45%). In contrast, home teams that lost game one but won game two went on to win 12 out of 17 Series (71%). In fact, these teams were almost as successful as those that swept the first two games at home.

The conclusion that emerges from this analysis is that in the World Series, momentum matters. Winning the first two games at home, or even losing game one but winning game two, usually provides the home team with enough momentum to carry it to victory in the Series. So there is a significant advantage to beginning the World Series on your home field. Whether the All-Star game is an appropriate means of determining which team enjoys that advantage is another question.

Ducky and The Lip in Italy

by Tom Barthel

At the end of the 1940 baseball season, all of the baseball men knew they would soon be facing the war's demands. Shortly after the last game of the 1940 World Series, the order went out from Washington that all men ages 21-35 had to register with their local draft boards. Some men probably would not be called immediately: Joe Medwick, for instance, was married and had two children of whom he was the sole support; Pitcher Red Ruffing was missing toes.

Nevertheless, on October 29, 1940, capsules were drawn from a fishbowl to determine draft order. Those men whose numbers were picked first were about to be asked for twelve months' service, though men over 28 could be released after 180 days of service. Hank Greenberg, 29-year-old Detroit outfielder, for instance, had one of the low—that is, sure to be called—numbers.

Now that men were called to duty in large numbers, President Roosevelt asked six organizations to band together to handle the recreation needs for the armed forces. The six—the YMCA, YWCA, National Catholic Community Service, National Jewish Welfare Board, Traveler's Aid, and the Salvation Army—were confederated as the United Services Organization—USO—on February 4, 1941, in New York. Soon after incorporation, according to the

Tom Barthel is the author of The Fierce Fun of Ducky Medwick (Scarecrow), and a forthcoming biography of Pepper Martin, to be published by McFarland. He is currently working on books on barnstorming, the Bushwicks, and the 1941 Dodgers.

USO, "entertainment industry professionals helped the USO to begin 'Camp Shows' with the entertainers waiving pay and working conditions to bring live entertainment to the troops at bases within the United States."

This is one of the stories of one of six groups of men, all baseball men, who were willing to put themselves in the kind of danger that soldiers had to endure. These baseballers sailed on the Bering Sea, rode half-tracks across the Sahara, sat on coral in the jungles of New Guinea; they traveled into the Battle of the Bulge, climbed the mountains of Burma, and bounced through the ruts of the frozen mud of Italy.

Most of them were not scheduled to serve in the Army for many different reasons, age, for most of them, being the primary reason. They did their USO work quietly, they did it bravely, they did it unselfishly. They did not have to do it, but they did anyway.

Pirates manager Frankie Frisch, after his return from the first USO tour, a 1943 trip to the Aleutians, was called to the office of the commissioner, and the Pirates manager suggested more trips by baseball men. Frisch believed the trips were very effective in raising the morale of servicemen. Landis agreed.

So in early summer of 1944, Commissioner Landis's office in Chicago again asked for volunteers from baseball to travel overseas after the World Series, this time under the aegis of the USO.

As Frank Coffey's book points out, in World War II there were four USO circuits. The first was called

---

the Victory Circuit, which comprised the big stars of movie and radio who appeared far from the front and performed in front of larger audiences who came to see the show. The second circuit was labeled Blue for vaudevillians and other lesser-known performers who performed in smaller shows closer to the front. The third was called the Hospital Circuit. The kind of USO tour the baseball men had signed on for was known as the Foxhole Circuit, the battlefront circuit.

The trips would not be leaving until the 1944 season was over, and meanwhile Frick's office worked on rounding up volunteers. Umpires, sportswriters and managers were approached and soon a total of 23 men agreed to go, with a departure date penciled in for about a month after the 1944 World Series.

Typical of some ballplayers during war time, Joe Medwick, from his suburban St. Louis home, was "employed as personnel counselor at the Curtiss-Wright St. Louis plant on the one to 8 A.M. shift."

Receiving orders on October 25 to gather in New York, Medwick was told in the Army's papers to go to the TWA office in St. Louis to pick up tickets reserved by the Army Office of Special Services. Medwick was ordered to fly to New York City for processing and assignment. The New York Giants left fielder in 1944, Medwick, at .337, finished the 1944 season as the best right-handed hitter in baseball, 20 points lower than old teammate Dixie Walker and 10 points behind future teammate Stan Musial.

Once landed in New York, Medwick was instructed to check into the Hotel New Yorker, and there he palled around with the 22 other baseball men. There were two umpires, six managers, six writers, one part-time player, Paul Waner, and seven full-time players. Besides Medwick, there were three young men—Nick Etten, Johnny Lindell, and Tuck Stainback—and three older players—Dixie Walker, Bucky Walters, Dutch Leonard. These 23 would be put into five traveling groups, going to different parts of the world.

The five groups were processed, getting inoculations for smallpox, cholera, yellow fever, typhus, and tetanus, and then the men were told to make out emergency wills and send them to their homes. (USO work resulted in 28 deaths during World War II.) Next, each man was given an identification card, and the back of each card said that in case a man was captured, he was to be given the same privileges as a captain in the Army of the United States. Then the 23 were measured for officers' uniforms at one of Manhattan's toniest stores.

They were not told their itinerary. They were told that when they arrived, they would be assigned a special services officer who would plan their trips.

Once the majority of the processing in Manhattan was finished, from their hotel on 55th Street the men were put on a bus for Fort Totten, located at the confluence of the East River and Long Island Sound in Queens. At Totten more processing was completed and more equipment was handed out. Then the 23 were told to wait. Their travel did not have priority.

As the five groups waited for air transport, Special Services suggested some rehearsing in this country, and so Medwick and some others practiced their shows at Fort Totten and at nearby camps while getting used to Army food. Some men went home while waiting. Frisch, for example had a home in New Rochelle, and all of Medwick's family still lived in Cartaret, New Jersey.

The different units were now organized, but their assignments, as was usual, were kept vague so as to be kept, in effect, secret. For many days, as departure became more likely, every morning at a ten o'clock formation some groups were alerted to the possibility of leaving soon and were confined to the barracks area. But the odds were that the troupes would stand down at the five o'clock gathering in the afternoon. The groups, going different places, were all leaving at different times on different transport.

The days of waiting passed well into November. The only way, the group of 23 decided, to handle being on and off alert so many times was to make a joke, or in this case, a song about it, the song being a new version of "Shuffle Off to Buffalo." In his best Flatbush/Alabama tenor, Dixie Walker took the lead on the song with the rest joining in and contributing various verses.

Singing was heard on the birthday of umpire Bill Summers on November 10 and on Joe Medwick's 33rd birthday, celebrated in the barracks on November 11. After three weeks of waiting, the volunteers were ready to get on any plane any time.

The last group to leave, the Medwick group bound for Italy, finally got their alert when a sergeant came upstairs and called the four names very early on Thanksgiving Day. The group dressed in their uniforms and excitedly finished packing their bags.

Driven to headquarters, their bags were weighed and Giants outfielder Joe Medwick, manager Leo Durocher, Yankee first baseman Nick Etten, and *PM* writer Tom Meany were shown to the bus that took the unit the seven miles to LaGuardia Airport. Once they passed through customs there, they moved quickly to a final briefing room for lectures on water landings, the use of Mae West inflatable life vests, and the use of a raft and a signal generator. A giant plane awaited them on the LaGuardia runway.

The plane often used for these sorts of trips was a Skymaster. This DC-4 passenger plane in wartime became a Douglas C-54/R5D Skymaster just as the DC-3 became a C-47 Skytrain. The plane held around thirty passengers and a crew of six. With cruising speed of 239 mph at a ceiling of 20,000 feet, the big plane had a range of 3,900 miles.

Getting into the plane, Medwick's troupe checked to have aboard with them 200 dozen autographed baseballs and the 22-minute movie of the 1944 World Series. The USO unit called "Here's the Pitch" was airborne. St. Louis writer J. Roy Stockton's column later said, "Flying the ocean in years to come may be a commonplace weekend lark. It was a thrill to us."

Once out over the ocean, they ate their Thanksgiving meal—baloney sandwiches—in the noisy, chilly compartment of the plane. The aircraft probably landed once in Bermuda to refuel. For the most part, the plane ride was spent napping, going to the cockpit for a smoke, signing the "short snorters," the taped-together collection of currency from countries visited, sort of autograph pads that air crews favored so much. Out over the Atlantic, the men must have realized that their uniforms that looked so good in Manhattan might not be all that comfortable, or that serviceable, or that warm. They were clearly worried, as Tom Meany wrote, "how able-bodied men such as themselves would be welcomed—or vice versa—by a bunch of guys fighting for their lives," particularly since both Etten and Medwick were under 35.

Joe told no one, though his former manager and friend Durocher knew, about his punctured eardrum, a puncture that probably happened when he was beaned in June 1940. That punctured eardrum had led to his 4-F classification, lower than the 2-B he had been classified for a while, a slot for men over 30 and with two children.

Roy Stockton remembered the particular frustration of the newspapermen: "We were told we couldn't keep diaries or any record showing places we had visited, army units or individuals. We couldn't carry cameras. We couldn't carry written messages." (This prohibition, combined with sensitivity to military secrets, led to the kind of disjointed narratives that appeared in newspapers when the men returned.)

But these men were doing what they considered to be their patriotic duty and accepted the hardships as they knew all the service men and women must accept their hardships.

As the plane droned through the November skies, Medwick's thoughts might have drifted back to the family war map, pinned up in the home. It was a practice among many Americans to keep track of the war on the maps as the news arrived.

In this way Medwick would have known of the invasion at Salerno, with 9,000 Allied casualties, in September 1943, and known about the fall of Naples to the Allies a month later. He would have known about the successive defensive lines the Germans had set up: the Winter Line and Gustav Line. He would have been horrified to read about the five-month stalemate that developed on the beaches at Anzio in murderous trench warfare. Equally terrible was the unrelenting fire the British and Americans and their Allies took from the Germans, who seemed to be dug in on every mountaintop and hill surrounding the many Italian valleys. By the end of 1943, the American Fifth Army in Italy had 40,000 casualties and 50,000 sick.

Yet Rome fell on June 4, 1944, and from that point on, the landings in France received most of the attention and most of the manpower, including most of the veteran troops in Italy.

As the veteran units were withdrawn, the British Lady Astor, stupidly even for her, called the British Eighth Army, carrying much of the burden in the Italian campaign, "D-Day Dodgers." It was unlikely the American Fifth Army in Italy liked her label either. The fighting had been muddy and murderous, with the Nazis often having the high ground. Whatever successes were gained in Italy were due largely to the individual soldiers' valor, resilience, and determination.

This determination and valor prevented the Nazis from sending units to France, and even though fighting on the Gothic line north of Florence had caused 29,000 Allied casualties between September 10 and October 26 of 1944, still that terrible sacrifice was undervalued, it seemed. Losses were so heavy that Churchill requested that the United States send at least two additional divisions to the Italian front, but he was turned down.

The U.S. Army preferred to send new U.S. combat units to France rather than to Italy for "an increasingly bloody and stalemated campaign in a secondary theater."

A secondary theater described much of Medwick's career. Though Joe, in Ted Williams' phrase, "owned the National League for five years," yet he was not in the American League, the clouting league, the league of the World Series winners. Unlike DiMaggio, Medwick had played on but two pennant winners since 1932. Now he was a soldier in greasepaint.

Nick Etten, the American League leader in both homers and walks in 1944, was the 31-year-old first baseman for the Yankees. Leo Durocher was the smooth-fielding shortstop for the Gas House Gang Cardinals and current Dodger manager.

At the end of a 24-hour flight, the group landed, probably in Naples.

Once they were greeted by their Special Services officer and off the runway, the mud on their dress shoes made Joe and the rest find out quickly about field shoes and canvas leggings, items they quickly purchased at a post exchange. After that shopping, their Special Services officer introduced them to their driver, who showed them to their vehicle, a converted weapons carrier towing a trailer, to carry their supplies. They were reminded yet again about wearing their steel helmets.

Soon they learned how exhausting this trip would be, and they learned that they would pretty much live in the clothes that they had on. Too, they began to learn the new slang, chiefly the phrase "sweating it out." Italy, since D-Day called the Forgotten Front, still meant "Jerry was always looking down your throat" whether it was at Monte Cassino or Luxembourg. Another phrase of the time to describe talking baseball to GIs was to call the chats Walkie-Talkie Fanning Bees. The servicemen had been alerted only that some players might come to Europe, but as was usual the various papers—*Yank*, *Army Talks* as well as local unit papers and the daily *Stars and Stripes*—kept silent about exactly where the shows would be. (Twice in December in the Naples edition of *Stars and Stripes* there were interviews with Durocher. But the questions were very general.)

For the USO troupe traveling first around the Amalfi coast area, the show really started as soon as the weapons carrier pulled into the unit area. Soldiers swarmed around the truck, tossing questions at each of the group. Manager Durocher was the most well-known, having been on radio shows and having some dialogue in the movie *Whistling in Brooklyn*.

For Medwick's group, the rehearsals proved that the shows ought to work like this: writer Tom Meany served as the master of ceremonies, first introducing the ballplayers. Next, the World Series film of 22 minutes was shown, and then each player would talk a bit and answer questions. Sometimes the audiences would be unusual for the movie. British soldiers, for example, hearing that an American movie was about to be shown, would arrive, and then quickly groan and leave, finding out the movie was not cowboys and Indians. A ten-minute quiz program would be the end of the show. Ten or twelve GIs would be asked up to the front of the building (often a tent or barn), and Meany would ask true-or-false questions until there were three winners left, all of whom would be given autographed baseballs.

That would have been the end of the show for Medwick and the others except afterward, many soldiers, hungry for baseball news, hungry for life back home, would come up to the stage and ask for autographs and ask about their favorite players and how their favorite teams might do in 1945. They might ask about a favorite bar in Brooklyn, too. In this way the group might do four shows a day, traveling some distances over rough terrain between shows, terrain strewn with destroyed German armor.

The shows, Tom Meany wrote later in his New York City newspaper *PM*, were "most unusual. Any time four guys with a 25-minute film can hold a soldier audience for two hours just by talking . . . it was a defiance of all theatrical theories and the law of gravity. Neither Etten, Medwick nor I hold any illusion about our talent . . . but the stories of Medwick and Etten always were well-received and in the bull sessions afterward they were quite as well received as Leo" who often spoke for 45 minutes of the 120.

Traveling north from Naples, they performed, for one, in the Aldorado Playhouse in Caserta, and the troupe acted in a radio show, with Medwick taking the role of an umpire. By Christmas they "entertained on a hill north of Rome and fell to, with all the others, on a real turkey dinner with all the trimmings." The troupe also filled the Red Cross theater in Rome, the Barbarini, which no other entertaining group had been able to do.

As the troupe traveled to perform at yet another unit, the group certainly saw enough of blown-out buildings, wrecked railroad yards, bomb craters. They learned there were three signs you needed to pay close attention to: "Road and ditches cleared of mines." Then "Road *to* ditches cleared of mines." Last, "This road *not* swept for mines." They learned to remember and give passwords, and they did not hesitate to show their dog tags to sentries. They

From left: Officer, Leo Durocher, Joe Medwick, two soldiers, Nick Etten, Tom Meany.

learned to eat and like powdered eggs and grapefruit juice, a GI staple, as well as lots of Spam and canned chocolate pudding. The troupe members all learned to live by candlelight, and learned, too, not to break down at the sight of terribly wounded soldiers in hospitals but to try to cheer them up. As the draft regulations changed as the war was winding down, Medwick learned to talk to GIs interested in the proposed work-or-fight policy.

The days of their shows frequently lasted from 5 A.M. to 11 P.M. Performing more than those four shows a day and often to small groups, the majority of their shows were so close to the front lines that their audiences were limited to small groups, the officers not wanting to risk larger units within range of enemy artillery.

Once they set up for a show, but the scheduled audience was mud-bound and there was no show, not with a crowd of zero. At the end of the day's work, "Here's the Pitch" was billeted with some unit and was expected to talk to all hours there as well. They were glad to do so, seeing how happy all the GIs were to see them. Before television, few fans had ever seen the players this close, and Joe's group had players and managers with experiences with the Giants, Phillies, Yankees, Pirates, Cardinals, and Dodgers.

Tom Meany told the story of being asked by one soldier, "How's Smitty," referring to a fanatical Brooklyn fan, an undertaker who closed down his shop so he could travel on the Dodger road trips. Joe had solved one other question he and Durocher knew would be asked. Tom Meany wrote about it this way: "One of the questions invariably asked of Joe Medwick was why he was traded from Brooklyn to the Giants. It was really an attempt to embarrass Leo Durocher. Joe finally came up with an answer that pleased everybody, 'Rickey came and I went.'"

Their worry about how they as healthy men not in service might be treated was dispelled early in their tour. During a show at the Fifth Army Rest Center, Durocher spotted 41-year-old Mule Haas, the former Cubs outfielder, now a $60 a month corporal. Haas told Meany, "Morale was an overworked word. Every civilian enterprise from manufacturers to night clubs professes to be maintained for the purpose of the serviceman's morale [but] I know that the kids tonight got a kick out of the show. They were talking about it for days in advance.' I asked Haas how he felt about ball players who were not in the Army. 'Being in the Army or being in baseball was a matter of luck. There was nothing more democratic than the draft. When your number was called you go.'"

While the Third Army of Patton rapidly advanced through southern Europe, the Fifth Army in Italy was still slowly slugging it out and frequently under attack. But, as Meany pointed out, war doesn't have to be spectacular to be dangerous. So "Here's the Pitch" was greatly appreciated simply because the soldiers in the Mediterranean Theater of Operations knew what they were doing wasn't glamorous.

One of those soldiers, a soon-to-be-named Congressional Medal of Honor winner, Red Shea, so selected because of his capture of three German machine gun emplacements in one battle, rode in the weapons carrier with the troupe. The hero asked Meany "if I could spare one of the autographed baseballs signed by Durocher, Etten and Medwick. When I gave him the ball, Red thanked me profusely and said, 'This is the biggest thrill I ever had—getting a baseball and riding in the same vehicle with Durocher, Etten and Medwick.' There was nothing for us to do but look out the window and pretend we hadn't heard." Meany claimed, "Shea's reactions were like those of practically all the soldiers. The war went out the window when they had a chance to talk about home life. It wasn't just baseball, although that was the principal medium in our case. It was anything about home."

One thing about home and baseball was the bright colors. Here the colors were either white or brown. Brown was the mud everyone in Italy dealt with—mud on the lines before the mess tents and barracks; mud in waves as you traveled or mud frozen into hard ruts and waves; mud caught up in the wheels of trucks and the treads of tanks; mud to have to yank each foot out of. Brown too was the color of everyone's clothing. Medwick, like the others in "Here's the Pitch," wore a brown top thigh coat over a brown vest over a brown shirt and light brown tie, the whole uniform being splattered and caked over with brown mud. White in some of the hospitals; white too of the snow that winter in Italy as the troupe moved up the Italian peninsula.

In the cold there, Durocher talked to *Yank* magazine about Beans Reardon, the umpire on tour in the Pacific. "My only regret," he told GIs, "was that I can't see how Beans Reardon, the umpire, was taking it on his trip . . . . No self-respecting foxhole would take him."

Once the troupe was told there would be no film because the Germans had recently captured the Special Services projector and the generator. Once they did a show for 9,500 at a Naples racetrack. Along the way they met Herman Besse, Phils pitcher, among the wounded in Italy and Shirley Cobb, daughter of Ty Cobb, now a nurse in Italy. They kept moving north toward the Gothic Line, where the Allied offensive had stalled due to the rain and even more mud. That German defensive line proved to be a killer.

By New Year's Day 1945, after being in Italy a month, the troupe moved south again, and from Naples, Medwick's unit flew north to Peretola airfield in Florence and then were billeted on the Arno River in the Hotel Excelsior, liberated four months earlier. "The Excelsior has been taken over by the British but it was also used by war correspondents, visiting USO Camp Shows units and ENSA troupes . . . the British equivalent of USO. The resulting welter of uniforms in the lobby gives it the appearance of a cafeteria on an MGM lot during the filming of a war picture— Scotsmen in plaids and kilts, British officers with swagger sticks and monocles, turbaned and bearded Sikhs from India and Americans." The claim was that there were 26 nations fighting in Italy.

Nick Etten, making history he said, lobbed a baseball from the fourth balcony to a military policeman below. Medwick ate in the opulent dining room, part of the 25-lira-a-day charge. While a string ensemble played, cups of consommé were served on fine linen, the hot broth sipped with fine silver. The main course was served on a covered dish, and after the cover was removed with flourishes by one of the many waiters, what Medwick saw on his plate was Spam.

Up in his room, Joe listened to Armed Forces Radio as well as Berlin Sally. In Florence, the unit played the Apollo and watched the Spaghetti Bowl, a football game in the Stadio Communale between teams from the 5th Army and the 12th Air Force, before 25,000 along with WAC cheerleaders and seven generals.

Meany reported, "We were up and down [Route 65] every day . . . and in the general direction of Bologna but not quite to Bologna because there was a guy named Von Kesserling and some of his associates between us and Bologna," as they visited soldiers in Empoli and Sesto. It was in Sesto that someone not only slept but also snored through Medwick's talk. "Backstage, Joe complained about the visitor's manners" till he was told that the snorer was "an Eyetie who was supposed to be working for Capt. Tracy." Many of the troupe's performances were, in fact, north of Florence, in places very close to the Gothic Line. They were now doing many of the shows in tents, in the cold rains of January. Even when "Here's the Pitch" played to combat units, as in Fano to the east or in Via Reggio to the west, everyone in the audience carried his rifle, since Nazi soldiers from the Russian Front were reinforcing the German side of the Gothic Line. In Gagliano and Monghidora and Loiano, all north of the Hotel Excelsior, everyone was well armed. Medwick's USO unit went to Porretta, inside the province of Bologna, where they were told that they were "within 700 yards of the front."

As in many other places, a question heard there

was repeated: "Was it true about the cigarette shortage at home?" When the answer was yes, "the boys seemed pleased."

At another site, too close to combat to show the movie, the troupe found itself performing in a tent's semidarkness. They could see, however, that the entire audience wore their steel helmets and carried their weapons. "All we had," said Meany, "were those funny looking USO caps." As Durocher was telling yet another umpire Magerkurth story, he was about to imitate the umpire's boisterous "Yer out!" but as he did, he heard "CRR-UMP" as a giant artillery shell landed, then shook the canvas tent and showered it with dirt.

Durocher looked at the officer in charge, whose holster was unbuckled.

"Go right ahead," said the officer. "You don't have to worry about a thing until you see the boys running out on you. Then you better follow 'em."

"Follow 'em, hell," said Leo. "I'll be right behind the first guy that goes out the door."

That show ended in the darkness with the players signing autographs, many times on baseballs, and the darkness was so profound that even faces weren't distinct. On their way back to their sleeping quarters, Nick Etten said, "You know, Leo, I'm not sure but I think the last guy I handed out a ball to was Field Marshal Kesserling."

One of the last places where they did a show was Pistoia, at an evacuation hospital 22 miles northwest of Florence. There the troupe could see the armed partisans, including the gun-laden women, bandoleers hung around their necks.

After 42 days in the Mediterranean, after playing to 70,000 men, after 20,000 miles, Joe and the rest of the troupe arrived back in the United States on January 15.

When they were in Rome, Medwick and Durocher were taken in an audience to visit the Pope. The Pope blessed a rosary for Leo, which he would bring to his mother. The Pope, the story goes, asked about Medwick's prewar occupation. Joe answered, "Your Holiness, I'm Joseph Medwick. I, too, used to be a Cardinal."

YES, WE HAVE NO BALATA *With rubber needed for the WW2 war effort, and supplies from the Dutch East Indies cut off, the Spalding company turned to substitutes in the manufacture of baseballs. Pre-war baseballs were used in 1942, but in March 1943 Commissioner Landis, AL president Will Harridge, and Reds GM Warren Giles approved the use of the so-called "balata ball." Replacing the high-grade cork in the center of the ball was a combination of ground cork bound with balata, a non-strategic material obtained from the milky juice of tropical trees.*

It was a disaster. Giles felt that he had been misled and fumed after watching the Indians and Reds total one extra-base hit in 21 innings of spring training. He surmised that Spalding used "ground up bologna instead of balata and cork." Not until the twelfth game played did Joe Gordon hit the majors' first home run. Only nine homers were hit in the first 72 AL games. Spalding reluctantly admitted its mistake and promised new and improved balls. Not wanting to wait with the AL, the NL immediately switched to pre-balata balls, and hitting improved. The next year cork and rubber were again available.

— JIM CHARLTON

Philadelphia Baseball's Unappreciated Founders: Al Reach and Ben Shibe

by Jerrold Casway

Two of America's most important sports figures were dissimilar men, who impacted the development of the national pastime in Philadelphia and set new standards for the emerging sporting goods industry. Al Reach was a pioneering second baseman for the original Philadelphia Athletics of the 1860's, and was possibly the game's first professional ballplayer. Later, he became a successful maker of sporting equipment and the founding president of the National League Phillies. Ben Shibe took another avenue to prominence. Never active in sports because of an injured leg, he managed the family's leather and harness company into a sports manufacturing enterprise. Shibe was most noted for his automatic baseball-winding machine. Beginning in the 1880's, Shibe and his sporting goods partner, A. J. Reach, made balls for all the major leagues. Both men were also innovative stadium builders and founders of the new Athletics of Philadelphia.

Al Reach was born in London, England on 28 May 1840, the son of Benjamin Reach, "a trading agent." His parents emmigrated to Brooklyn, New York when he was almost a year old. Raised with strong work and ethical values, the young Reach sold newspapers on Broadway, worked as a ship caulker and became an iron molder, working twelve hours a day in a foundry.

Jerrold Casway is a professor of History and the Social Sciences Division Chair at Howard Community College in Columbia Maryland. His book, on Ed Delahanty will be published this spring.

Following in his father's cricket-ball playing tradition, Reach discovered he had a talent for the popular "New York" style game of baseball. On the sandlots of Brooklyn he gained notoriety as a catcher for the Jackson Juniors of Williamsburg. His move to the famous Eckford baseball club of Brooklyn in 1861 brought him to the attention of prominent east coast teams. Impressed with the integrity and business acumen of Colonel Thomas Fitzgerald, the president of the original Philadelphia Athletics, Reach in the summer of 1864 started playing ball in the Quaker City. He was one of the first ballplayers to compete for pay. Al earned $25 a week and commuted to Brooklyn between games. At the start of the 1866 season Fitzgerald set him up with a center city cigar and tobacco store above Fourth and Chestnut Streets. The site quickly became a popular gathering spot for the city's sportsmen, and before the year was out, Reach was brokering tickets and merchandising baseball gear. After the season he married and moved to Philadelphia.

For most of the next decade, "Pops" Reach was one of the sport's most popular and respected ballplayers. Fast and sure-handed, Reach set the standard for playing second base. He was said to be the first to play his position mid-way between the bases. He also stationed himself very deep, about twenty-feet behind the infield line. Reach was known as the "Scratcher" for his ability of digging up hard-hit balls. At five-foot-six-inches and 155 pounds, Al Reach hit lefthanded with skill and power. His feats and gentlemanly behavior for the renowned Athletics were lauded by the sporting press. In 1874, Reach became the playing manager of the Athletics and led them to England on baseball's first European tour. Three years later, after the National League was formed, Reach retired to devote his attention to his expanding business ventures.

The year of the English tour, Al Reach, anticipating an increased demand for baseball and sporting equipment, established a large retail store on south Eighth Street. His commercial successes were due to his athletic reputation and his "sterling integrity ... [and] steady industry." But with the advent of the new decade, he was ready to get into the manufacturing side of sports supplies, thus his relationship with Benjamin Franklin Shibe.

Ben Shibe was born on 28 January 1838 in the Kensington section of Philadelphia known as "Fishtown." He had little formal education, but had a great interest in things mechanical. Eventually, Shibe adapted these skills to his father's small harness-making business, and with his brother John, produced leather sporting goods. By 1881, his ingenious machinery and many patents made it difficult for Reach to compete with Shibe's company. It did not take long for both men to realize it would be mutually advantageous if they merged their businesses. The result was a co-partnership. The new wholesale company was named for Reach and run by Shibe as president. They also moved to larger quarters across the street from Reach's old store site. The hottest merchandise for the expanded Reach Company was the Shibe baseball, considered to be the best on the market. The merger was perfectly timed because Reach was about to invest in a new National League franchise that was being re-located from Worcester, Massachusetts.

The Philadelphia Phillies ball club was incorporated in November 1882 with Reach heading a group of prominent investors. A critical member of this association was John Ignatius Rogers. Born in Philadelphia on 27 May 1844, Rogers got a law degree from the University of Pennsylvania, specializing in corporation and real estate law. Active in politics, Rogers served a term in the state legislature and was appointed Judge-Advocate of the state national guard, with the rank of colonel. It was these political contacts that made the would-be colonel a logical choice to help Al Reach bring a National League team back to Philadelphia.

Ownership was composed of four investors, who divided 150 shares at $100 apiece. Reach, with twenty shares, and Rogers with ten were minority partners. Nevertheless, Reach was named president, and Rogers became the club's secretary. And though both men assumed majority ownership by the end of the decade, Rogers initially deferred to his more experienced colleague when the ball club was being established. Years later, the colonel's role changed when the litigious, self-promoting attorney became the league's spokesman in baseball's burgeoning labor-management disputes.

With nothing more than a "right to franchise," Reach renovated an old, oddly shaped ballpark at 24th and Columbia Avenue (Recreation Park), and hastily assembled a team. To commemorate the inaugural season, Reach also began publishing the *Reach Official Baseball Guide*. But Al Reach was accustomed to success, and after a dismal first year, he signed the sport's leading manager, Harry Wright. The team showed immediate improvement and within a few years their little ballpark proved to be inadequate. In 1887, Reach and Rogers built a spacious state-of-the-art wooden baseball stadium at Broad and Lehigh for the unprecedented cost of $80,000.

Despite good attendance and the growth of the sporting goods market place, Al Reach was alarmed by the rising operational costs of a major league franchise. His biggest concern was the threatening troubles over players' salaries and the infamous reserve clause contracts. By 1889, the ballplayers' new union, the Brotherhood, was suggesting a strike and a rival players league. The anticipated litigation and feuding alarmed the business-conscious Al Reach.

Compounding the pending costs of a baseball war was the increased pressure from the A.G. Spalding sporting goods empire. The Reach Company could not bankroll the expansion necessary to meet the new demands, particularly the subletting contracts to produce more baseballs for Spalding. Unwilling to go into debt with a baseball strike on the horizon, Reach and Shibe in December 1889 sold all of their retail outlets to the enterprising A.G. Spalding for $100,000. Reach retained the company's name and the production side of the business. In the new corporate agreement, Reach got 600 shares of full-paid, non-assessable stock, and Shibe received half that number. The critical part of the transaction was that Reach and Shibe held on to the wholesaling business of baseballs. Under the watchful direction of Shibe and Robert Reach, Al's brother, a large factory was set up in the Frankford section of Philadelphia. They even had a training school for their workers. When the new American League was founded in 1901, Shibe's winding machines were outfitting balls under a variety of brand names. It was estimated that the Reach Company was producing 1200 dozen baseballs a day.

The Spalding transaction and Reach's sale of center-city properties helped the Phillies president survive the disruptive strike year of 1890. But the prospect of greater post-strike expenses strained his deteriorating relationship with John Rogers.

Colonel Rogers' role as a litigator allowed him to assume a greater presence in league and franchise affairs. The colonel, however, was a long-winded meddler, whose grudges and grievances were legendary. Suspicious and manipulative by nature, Rogers wanted the kind of recognition and admiration reserved for his partner. Determined to assert himself in team business, Rogers blindsided Reach.

Both men held equal shares of the Phillies restructured stock, and agreed that neither would disturb the balance by pursuing the remaining shares. Rogers did not abide by his promise, and under the guise of helping Harry Wright's widow, he purchased the old manager's stock. Rogers now became the majority owner with 53% to Reach's 43%. From this point forward, Colonel Rogers, not Al Reach, made the major decisions affecting the running of the franchise and its facilities. Reach became a figurehead president as Rogers made himself the new secretary-treasurer with a substantial raise in salary. In addition, Rogers spent large sums of money on unnecessary refurbishing and alienated ballplayers with his mean-spirited bargaining. The source of much of this discontent derived from the financial crisis of rebuilding the Phillies fire-vanquished ballpark.

When an August 1894 fire destroyed the Broad and Lehigh wooden stadium, the insurance covered only $20,000 of the $150,000 replacement costs. Before the reconstruction started, Reach and Rogers agreed that the new facility would be a model for new ballpark construction, the emphasis being on viewing and safety. Wood was covered by galvanized iron and soaked in asbestos paint. Obstructive posts were eliminated and relegated to the rear of the pavilions. In its place was an innovative cantilever construction of hanging steel platforms (roofs and double decks) from vertical gravity-bearing piers. Reach also installed a new water main pipe system that could "deluge every portion" of the grandstands. The structure was a forerunner of the steel and concrete stadiums of the next century.

But the hastily built ballpark had many serious layout faults that required constant attention. These renovations, together with Rogers's obsession of making the stadium a multi-purpose moneymaking facility, undid the relationship with his partner. By the end of the 1899 season, Reach allegedly offered Colonel Rogers around $150,000 for his shares.

The Reach-Rogers schism fully erupted when the new American League threatened the old league's status quo. This strain also exposed the instability of the Rogers-run Phillies, and brought Al Reach's sporting goods partner, Ben Shibe, directly into the fray. The underlying cause was Ban Johnson's desire to move his Western League teams into the cities abandoned by the National League. These ventures soon expanded to existing old league cities like Philadelphia. The new league's point man in the Quaker City was Connie Mack, a manager in Johnson's old organization. While looking for suitable stadium sites, Mack made inquiries about possible backers. After many closeted meetings, Mack and his investors announced that Ben Shibe would be the principal owner and president of the new Athletics ball club.

Shibe had always been interested in Philadelphia baseball. In the late 1870's he was the main stockholder in a prominent semi-pro Shibe Ball Club. He later became a minority partner in the American Association Athletics, a position he held until the franchise collapsed in the wake of the players' strike. At the end of the decade, Shibe resurrected the Athletics name for an Eastern League team. But his jump to the American League was a puzzling one, given his close ties with Phillies president A. J. Reach.

Shibe and Reach were a lot more than old business associates. Ben Shibe's only daughter, Mary in 1894 married Al Reach's only son, George. But the marriage was a product, not a factor in the families being close. It was said that the partners were like brothers and did nothing without consulting the other. They even invested money together and spent most of their social hours in each other's company. The conclusion was that Ben Shibe would not make a decision to invest in a competing league without Al Reach's input.

To understand their decision, one must take into consideration the role of Colonel John Rogers. Reach believed Rogers had violated his trust, and rather than go through another costly league war with

Rogers, he preferred to divest himself of his interest in the Phillies. Another factor was the status of the Reach-Shibe baseball. It had been the official ball of Ban Johnson's Western League and was now adopted by his new baseball association. Reach also was put off by Rogers' corrosive relationship with his players that drove Napoleon Lajoie and three starting pitchers in 1901 to the first-year Athletics. Therefore, Reach had both motive and incentives to abandon John Rogers and support Ben Shibe.

The Shibe-run Athletics played their games at 29th and Columbia Avenue. They finished fourth while the Phillies came in second with a dissent-ridden ball club. In 1902, Ed Delahanty and eight of his Phillies teammates joined other American League clubs. The Phillies decline, coupled with failing attendance, contrasted with the success of Shibe's Athletics. In March 1903, John Rogers, disgusted with the disintegration of his franchise, joined Reach and sold the team for $170,000 to a syndicate led by socialite, James Potter.

In contrast, Shibe's Athletics were very successful and in 1909 they opened the season in a new ball park, the first steel and concrete stadium, five blocks west of Reach's cantilever ball field, soon to be known as the Baker Bowl. The new ball yard, Shibe Park, retained its name until 1953 when it was renamed Connie Mack Stadium, for the man who guided the Athletics for over fifty years.

Soon after Shibe Park was erected, "Uncle Ben," with the same humility that marked his career, turned the daily management of the franchise over to Connie Mack and Shibe's two sons, Tom and John. Ben Shibe died on 14 January 1922. "Pop" Reach, the grand old man of baseball retired to Atlantic City, New Jersey, leaving the Reach Company in the hands of his son George, Ben Shibe's son-in-law. Al Reach died in 1928 on the same day as his long-time partner. Both men and their families were even interred within a few hundred yards of each other at West Laurel Hill Cemetery, just outside of Philadelphia.

Connie Mack carried on the baseball legacy begun by these two founding Philadelphia sportsmen. The city and major league baseball would forever bear the influence of these two patriarchs. Although neither man graces baseball's Hall of Fame, their mark on the national pastime is unmistakable every time a baseball is put into play.

CAL AND LOU *In recent years, baseball fans have argued whether hitting home runs was easier for Mark McGwire, Sammy Sosa, and Barry Bonds than it was for Babe Ruth, Roger Maris, and Hank Aaron.*

Similar arguments occurred in the early 1990s when Cal Ripken was chasing Lou Gehrig's record of 2,130 consecutive games played. The comparisons of the two "iron men" centered around which player had the more difficult circumstances to overcome in recording such an amazing feat of endurance. Those who argued in favor of Gehrig pointed to numerous doubleheaders, long train trips, and summers without air conditioning. Ripken's defenders countered that Gehrig never had to play on artificial turf, or at night—Cleveland and Philadelphia played the first American League night game two weeks after Gehrig's streak had ended. And, they added, shortstop Ripken was playing a much more difficult and demanding position than first baseman Gehrig.

Good arguments all, but perhaps they were missing the most important point, which are the similarities between the two men. Whatever advantages or disadvantages each had, the fact remains that in both Gehrig's era, and in Ripken's every other major league player performed under the same conditions. Yet, no one else, in any era, has come close to playing in 2,000 consecutive games. Moreover, Gehrig was among the most admired players of his time and Ripken was among the most admired of his. Deservedly so, both were quiet, decent men who preferred to let their play on the field define them. Both conducted their careers in very much the same way. They showed up every day and did their jobs—and did them very well. In the American League's first one hundred years, each was probably the best ever to play his position.

When Gehrig played in his 1,308th consecutive game, breaking Everett Scott's record, Scott said that if the record had to be broken, he was glad that it was Gehrig who had broken it. You have to think that when Ripken played in his 2,131st consecutive game, Gehrig, if he were here, would have said the same about Cal. — LYLE SPATZ

SOCIETY FOR AMERICAN BASEBALL RESEARCH

Since August 1971, when sixteen "statistorians" gathered in Cooperstown to form the Society for American Baseball Research, SABR has been committed to helping people produce and publish baseball research.

Today, SABR has nearly 7,000 members worldwide. They come from all walks of life—the one thing they all have in common? A love for the game and its history.

Members receive the latest editions of SABR's research annuals, *The Baseball Research Journal* and *The National Pastime*. Also included is a subscription to *The SABR Bulletin*, special access to online newsgroups and research forums, and other special publications.

SABR membership is open to all those interested in baseball research. Annual dues are $50 US, $60 Canada and Mexico, and $65 overseas (US funds only). Student and senior discounts are also available. For details about the benefits of SABR membership, call (800) 969-SABR or visit **www.sabr.org** today!

SOCIETY FOR AMERICAN BASEBALL RESEARCH
812 HURON ROAD, CLEVELAND, OH 44115 (800)969-SABR

SABR BACK PUBLICATIONS ORDER FORM

THE BASEBALL RESEARCH JOURNAL

THE BASEBALL RESEARCH JOURNAL, the annual publication of the society, features some of the best member research. Articles range from statistical to biographical sketches, plus nearly every other topic in baseball.

- ☐ 1985 (88pp) **$6.00**
- ☐ 1987 (88pp) **$6.00**
- ☐ 1988 (88pp) **$7.00**
- ☐ 1990 (88pp) **$8.00**
- ☐ 1991 (88pp) **$8.00**
- ☐ 1992 (88pp) **$7.95**
- ☐ 1993 (112pp) **$9.95**
- ☐ 1994 (112pp) **$9.95**
- ☐ 1995 (144pp) **$9.95**
- ☐ 1996 (154pp) **$9.95**
- ☐ 1997 (144pp) **$9.95**
- ☐ 1998 (116pp) **$9.95**
- ☐ 1999 (144pp) **$12.00**
- ☐ 2000 (144pp) **$12.00**
- ☐ 2001 (136pp) **$12.00**
- ☐ 2002 (128pp) **$24.95**

SABR BOOKS ON THE 19th CENTURY

- ☐ **NINETEENTH CENTURY STARS** Biographies of America's First Heroes, Non-Hall of Famers (1988, 144pp) **$10.00**
- ☐ **BASEBALL'S FIRST STARS** More biographies, includes Hall of Famers(1996, 183pp) **$14.95**
- ☐ **BASE BALL: HOW TO BECOME A PLAYER** 1888 reprint by John Montgomery Ward (1993, 149 pp) **$9.95**

THE NATIONAL PASTIME

THE NATIONAL PASTIME features articles by members more general in nature, although some volumes are arranged in a theme, as noted below.

- ☐ **#3, 19TH CENTURY PICTORIAL** (Spring 1984, (88 pp) **$7.00**
- ☐ **#4,** (Spring 1985, 88 pp) **$6.00**
- ☐ **#5,** (Winter 1985, 88 pp) **$6.00**
- ☐ **#7,** (Winter 1987, 88 pp) **$6.00**
- ☐ **#10,** (Fall 1990, 88 pp) **$8.00**
- ☐ **#11,** (Fall 1991, 88 pp) **$7.95**
- ☐ **#12, THE INTERNATIONAL PASTIME** (Summer 1992, 96 pp) **$7.95**
- ☐ **#13,** (Summer 1993, 96 pp) **$7.95**
- ☐ **#14,** (Summer 1994, 112 pp) **$9.95**
- ☐ **#15,** (Spring 1995, 156 pp) **$9.95**
- ☐ **#16,** (Spring 1996, 144 pp) **$9.95**
- ☐ **#17,** (Spring 1997, 144 pp) **$9.95**
- ☐ **#19,** (Summer 1999, 116 pp) **$12.00**
- ☐ **#20,** (Summer 2000, 132 pp) **$12.00**
- ☐ **#21** (Summer 2001, 124 pp) **$12.00**

SABR REVIEW OF BOOKS

- ☐ **VOLUME 1** (1986) **$6.00**
- ☐ **VOLUME 2** (1987) **$6.00**
- ☐ **VOLUME 3** (1988) **$7.00**
- ☐ **VOLUME 4** (1989) **$7.00**

- ☐ **ALL-STAR BASEBALL IN CLEVELAND** (1997 Special Publication, 64pp) **$7.95**
- ☐ **BASEBALL FOR THE FUN OF IT** A pictorial about the joy of baseball (1997, 92pp) **$14.95**
- ☐ **COOPERSTOWN CORNER** Columns from **The Sporting News** by Lee Allen (1990, 181pp) **$10.00**
- ☐ **HOME RUNS IN THE OLD BALLPARKS** Listings of top 5 HR hitters in parks no longer in use (1995) **$9.95**

BIOGRAPHIES BY SABR

- ☐ **LEFTY GROVE: AMERICAN ORIGINAL** Bio of HOF pitcher Lefty Grove written by Jim Kaplan (2000, 315pp) **$12.95**
- ☐ **UNCLE ROBBIE** Bio of HOF manager Wilbert Robinson by Jack Kavanagh and Norman Macht (1999, 200pp) **$12.95**
- ☐ **ADDIE JOSS: KING OF THE PITCHERS** Bio of HOF pitcher Addie Joss by Scott Longert (1998, 141pp) **$14.95**
- ☐ **RUN, RABBIT, RUN** Tales of Walter "Rabbit" Maranville (1991, 96pp) **$9.95**

- ☐ **BASEBALL HISTORICAL REVIEW** Best of the 1972-74 BRJ (1981) **$6.00**

THE NEGRO LEAGUES BOOK
- ☐ Hardcover (1994, 382pp) **$49.95**
- ☐ Ltd. Edition, leather-bound, slipcase, autographed (1994, 382pp) **$149.95**

MINOR LEAGUE HISTORY JOURNAL
- ☐ **VOLUME 2** (54pp) **$6.00**
- ☐ **VOLUME 3** (72pp) **$7.00**

- ☐ **BATTING** F.C. Lane reprint that shares the insights of baseball legends such as Cobb, Ruth, and Hornsby. New biographical foreword and an expanded index add much to the original work (2002, 230pp) **$14.95**
- ☐ **MEMORIES OF A BALLPLAYER: BILL WERBER AND BASEBALL IN THE 1930S** Bill Werber is the last man alive who traveled with the '27 Yankees. His colorful anecdotes recall an era long gone (2001, 250pp) **$14.95**

NAME _____

ADDRESS _____

_____

CITY, STATE, ZIP _____

DAYTIME PHONE _____

SEND YOUR ORDER TO: University of Nebraska Press, 233 North 8th Street, Lincoln, NE 68588-0255 or call 1-800-755-1105 weekdays from 8:00am to 5:00pm CST. You may also place orders online at http://nebraskapress.unl.edu

(8/2003)

BOOK TOTAL	$ _____
SHIPPING (Charges are $4.50 for the first book and 50 cents for each additional book)	$ _____
NE RESIDENTS ADD SALES TAX	$ _____
TOTAL	$ _____

MASTERCARD & VISA ACCEPTED

CARD # _____

EXP. DATE _____